Women in Indian Religions

Women in Indian Religions

Edited by

ARVIND SHARMA

OXFORD
UNIVERSITY PRESS

OXFORD
UNIVERSITY PRESS

YMCA Library Building, Jai Singh Road, New Delhi 110 001

Oxford University Press is a department of the University of Oxford. It furthers the University's objective of excellence in research, scholarship, and education by publishing worldwide in

Oxford New York

Auckland Bangkok Buenos Aires Cape Town Chennai
Dar es Salaam Delhi Hong Kong Istanbul Karachi Kolkata
Kuala Lumpur Madrid Melbourne Mexico City Mumbai Nairobi
São Paulo Shanghai Singapore Taipei Tokyo Toronto

with an associated company in Berlin

Oxford is a registered trade mark of Oxford University Press in the UK and in certain other countries

Published in India
By Oxford University Press, New Delhi

First published 2002

ISBN 019 564634 7

Printed in India at Roopak Printers, Delhi 110 032
Published by Manzar Khan, Oxford University Press
YMCA Library Building, Jai Singh Road, New Delhi 110 001

Contents

Introduction

Arvind Sharma

Feminism, as a concept, has assumed its due importance in today's world. All over the world (including India) the past few decades have witnessed a synergistic convergence of global and national trends, which have culminated in putting women's issues firmly on the national and international agenda. Even those forces which would drag their feet on this issue have been swept off by the tide of female emancipation, which has risen steadily over the past decades.

Behind these decades, however, lie the past centuries. The present is always the proverbial tip of the iceberg. What is hidden from view often underlies, and always deeply affects, what comes into view. An understanding of the past helps one to understand the present and enables one to mould it with a surer touch.

This book is an attempt to describe the historical roots of the various issues concerning women in the different religious traditions found in India, which sometimes get buried out of sight by the shifting sands of political storms. Some information on these issues is provided by contemporary journalism, but information without context is an invitation to alienation, or at least distortion. It is also an invitation to ideology to provide the context that is the domain of history. The purpose of this book is to provide that 'history'.

A word of explanation regarding the organization and nature of the book will not be out of place. The book covers the religious scene in India in nine chapters, each chapter oriented toward one tradition. The fact that a whole chapter is devoted to tribal religion in India may raise a few eyebrows. I hope they fall back to their normal position when it is clarified that the intention here is not to generate a 'new' religion but to thematize a concern for deeper exploration. One is also aware that a modern Indian sensibility feels more comfortable with treating the family resemblances of Hinduism, Buddhism, Jainism, and Sikhism (and perhaps even Zoroastrianism) as part of a larger and broader religious tradition, and argues that these distinctions rest on distinctly un-Indian positivist assumptions. These distinctions have been retained here as a bow not to any religious but to an academic tradition.

Women and Hinduism

Katherine K. Young

Given the remarkably long and rich history of Hinduism, it is obvious that women's status, worldview, and issues have changed dramatically over time. They have also changed because our scholarly lenses have recently changed, allowing for a corrective to androcentric texts and scholarship (as well as colonial interpretations). Today's 'thick' anthropological descriptions of the everyday reality (as opposed to textual norms) of Hindu women's lives have documented their differences based on region, caste/sub-caste/class identities, rural/urban orientations, stage of life, values, economic levels, and degree of secularization, westernization, or fundamentalism. They have been especially attentive to women's own religious and cultural orientations.

All this cannot, of course, be anachronistically read into the past. But understanding those many traditional pockets of contemporary Hindu society (once their obviously modern features have been bracketed out) stimulates our imagination regarding how the past might have been textured for women. To re-enter the past, which is necessary to understand the Hindu present and future, is easier said than done on account of the paucity of sources, the need to select only the most salient features of each historical period, and the increasing disarray of historical scholarship itself. The latter makes what once seemed obvious a few decades ago now topics of heated debate. At the outset it is important to acknowledge that we must use prescriptive brahmanical works when we analyze Indian history but we do not know the extent to which they actually describe reality because they are more interested in prescribing an ideal. Whenever possible, their statements must be cross-checked with other types of evidence (such as inscriptions), which, however, are not always available. It should also be borne in mind that according to most cultural historians, these texts started affecting historical reality to various degrees with the passage of time.[1]

The name Hindu is derived from *sindhu*, which means ocean or river. Even today, the largest river of the north-western part of the subcontinent is called by a derivative of this word, Indus (via the Greek version of Sindhu: Indos) as is the name of the modern nation India (even though the Indus river after Independence in 1947 has been located in Pakistan). The major religion of India today (that of about 80 per cent of the population) is also called by a derivative (via Persian): Hindu.

Hindu texts consist of two types of revelation: *śruti* and *smṛti*. The four Vedas—Ṛg, Yajur, Sāma, Atharva—and their appendages called the Brāmaṇas, Āraṇyakas and Upaniṣads comprise śruti. Beginning with the late strata of the Ṛgveda, the Vedas can be understood as a creative synthesis of the fragments of the Indus civilization and the early Ṛgvedic culture.[2] The status of the Vedas was legitimized eventually by the concept of the divine, non-human (*apauruṣeya*) origin of śruti (the most sacred category of scripture—that which is heard). The *Mahābhārata* continued the process of integration with many different traditions, as did other Sanskrit texts such as Purāṇas, Āgamas, and Tantras. These too were legitimated as divine scriptures but of a secondary status called smṛti (that which is remembered). And the vernacular texts of many regions also continued assimilation. Because integration occurred in different regions, at different times and under different conditions, creating a kaleidoscopic variety of patterns from a gradually evolving stock of symbols, values, and so on, Hinduism is best described as dynamic, assimilative, and richly diverse. Hinduism has both ethnic and universal aspects. The ethnic dimension is defined by the idea that one is born Hindu. The universal dimension is based on concepts of the *ātman* (the true self), *brahman* (the absolute) and supreme deities as inclusive of the cosmos. A corollary of the universal dimension has been proselytization in some periods and some regions (or, in the modern period, in the global context).

The Ṛgvedic Period (?1200–800 BCE[3])

This section surveys the history of women in the oldest books of the Ṛgveda. These describe a patrilineal, tribal society (ten loosely connected groups which had not yet undergone state formation) located in the north-west along the Sarasvatī river. Its economy was based largely on pastoralism with some horticulture. Raiding and warfare with horse and chariot (both among the tribes and other inhabitants of the area) were common, but there also occurred interactions and assimilations of a religious and symbolic sort.

In general, life in the Ṛgveda was viewed positively. Despite some degree of male dominance, there was considerable complementarity between men and women (true of many small-scale societies). This is represented by the fact that young women met potential husbands at festival gatherings and only subsequently sought approval for their romantic choice of spouse from their parents (though by the late strata of the Ṛgveda, their virginity seems to have been protected until marriage took place).[4] Complementarity is also represented by the term *dampati*, which signifies the 'couple', man and wife.

The presence of a 'couple' in a home was the prerequisite for the deities to receive offerings there, which were made by the couple not only to thank them for favours but also to inspire them to reciprocate with more. The family, in fact, was the centre of religious life. Progeny, prosperity, and longevity were the principal goals in this period, though heaven and immortality were occasionally mentioned.[5] Even the gods acknowledged this worldly orientation and the importance of the woman's role as wife and mother. The gods, in fact, would receive offerings only in those homes where a wife was present; she was, after all, 'half the ritual'.[6] Because the family was patrilocal and patrilineal, the husband had nominal dominance, preference being given to him as host for the guests, the gods. Nevertheless, women might have had important roles in special rituals and perhaps did the daily domestic ones themselves.[7]

The pantheon in the Ṛgveda was mostly male (which is common for pastoral societies), though there were a few goddesses (representing female roles such as mother, sister, daughter, and wife). These included Uśas, the goddess of dawn; Sarasvatī, the personification of the major river in the homeland; and Pṛthivī, mother earth who protected the dead. They also included Vāk, Aditi, Rākā, and Sinīvālī associated with eloquent speech, prosperity, and progeny.

There are important issues raised by the portrayal of women and goddesses in the Ṛgveda. This text is not only the oldest known to Sanskrit literature, it also had developed, by the classical period, the status of being the most sacred. This made the position of women in the Ṛgveda the bottom line, so to speak, against which the legitimate status of women could be tested. This was quietly ignored in conservative elite circles for many centuries but became extremely important in the early modern period. Reformers (concerned about what they perceived to be the low status and rigid norms of elite Hindu women) and scholars (excited by the Hindu renaissance) looked back to the Vedas, especially the hoary Ṛgveda, the fount of primaeval revelation, as the measure of all things worthy and sacred. This led some to view the period of time represented by this text as a Golden Age because of the freedom, education, and high status of women.

Just why reforms were considered necessary will become apparent only by examination of the history of women in subsequent periods. But first a caveat is in order. Tribal (small-scale) societies were generally more egalitarian (even patrilineal/patrilocal ones) than early states, whose very development was predicated by military force, urbanization, and the formation of hierarchy. By the time of the tenth book of the Ṛgveda, hierarchy had taken root as indicated by Ṛgveda 10:90, which describes the caste (*varṇa*) system, and Ṛgveda 10:85, the wedding hymn, which states that preference was to be given to sons, for a woman was to be the mother of males.

THE MIDDLE AND LATE VEDIC PERIODS (1200–400 BCE)

By this time, migrations had occurred toward the east. The general stresses created by the clearing of new lands for agriculture, cultural synthesizing, and eventually state formation in the Ganga valley, all had their effects on the status of elite women.[8] Vedic ritual changed dramatically from the simple household rituals of the Ṛgveda to much more complex ones, now distinguished as household (*gṛhya*) and public (*śrauta*) rituals. The massive elaboration of these over the centuries can be seen in the Yajurveda, Brāhmaṇas, Gṛhyasūtras, Śrautasūtras and Mīmāṁsā texts. Middle and late Vedic elite society of northern India became, in fact, one of the most ritualized of human history.

Ritual specialization, which became the preserve of Brahmin male priests, and the bifurcation of ritual into private and public spheres had the effect of confining upper caste women's ritual activity to the domestic sphere. Because education had expanded and was usually taught in special forest schools, it had become less accessible for girls. Families had a tendency to keep them at home (and men probably did not want them to have this secret knowledge and expertise anyhow). According to the *Taittirīya Saṃhitā* (VI:3.10.5), every brahmin man had to pay back three debts: to the sages, he must live and study with a teacher; to the gods, he must perform Vedic rituals; and to his ancestors, he must have sons. By contrast, most girls were taught only what was needed for domestic worship and the *mantras* and ritual gestures needed for their roles in the śrauta rituals. But some women, the *brahmavādinīs*, underwent the *upanayana* ritual and subsequent Vedic study (these were probably the daughters of teachers in forest schools).

At least a few women were known as intellectually inquisitive. In the Upaniṣads, for instance, Gārgī challenged Yājñavalkya in a philosophical debate at a great sacrifice (*yajña*), an indication of her learning (no technical details of her Vedic knowledge, however, are given). And some have thought that Maitreyī was also such an intellectual. She is called a brahmavādinī in Bṛhadāraṇyaka Upaniṣad 4.5.15, though an earlier version of this account (Bṛhadāraṇyaka 2.4.1) simply describes how she asks her husband Yājñavalkya, who is about to become a *saṃnyāsī* (ascetic) and is making arrangements for the care of his two wives, whether she would be immortal if this whole earth filled with wealth were hers. This gives her husband the opportunity to say 'no' and to describe the nature of the true 'self'. The *Kāśikā on Pāṇini*[9] observes that the feminine words *ācāryā* and *upādhyāyā* indicate female teachers who must be distinguished from the males. The fact that women (at least in some circles) formally studied the Vedas is confirmed by Hārīta, who describes the brahmavādinīs as those who have the rite of initiation into Vedic learing (upanayana), feed the fire, study the Veda, and obtain alms in their own house. The latter indicates that it was done symbolically to fulfil the dictate of custom and not for its real function (to teach non-possession and humility by begging). In short, marriage was becoming the sole identity marker for women. For others, the *sadyovadhūs*, only the upanayana ritual was performed, that, too, only at the time of marriage.

It is likely that a woman rarely officiated at the śrauta rituals, even though as *patnī*, the ritual partner of her husband, she had to be present and appropriately initiated. The wife had some mandatory mantras and acts (involving the preparation of foods, cleaning the ritual space, or ensuring fertility). She was seated by the householder's fire (*gārhapatya*), one of the three fires on the Vedic altar, though occasionally she was led into other ritual space. The link of the wife to the symbolism of the domestic fire and the woman's realm of home is obvious.

Even though women's ritual speech and action were minor in the public rituals, there are clues that they were viewed as extremely powerful and potentially dangerous. This was because the wife injected her power of sexuality and fertility into the ritual (through a gesture called 'taking hold of from behind' or its equivalent—contact through sight[10]) in order to provide energy for progeny, cattle, crops, and rain (the very purpose of the rituals). Without this contact with the wife, the ritual would have no life and no benefits. Moreover, it could not serve as a conduit of power from the deities. This ambiguity (both marginality of female word and gesture in the rituals, and also recognition of her essential power on which the very effectiveness of the ritual depended) was symbolized by menstruation. Because of her menstrual impurity, a wife had to be absent; but because her life-power was essential, the ritual had to be postponed until she could be present or other rituals of compensation had to be performed. As the categories of pure and impure became more important in the Brāhmaṇas, the spatial confinement and subordination of elite women increased (they could not enter the assembly, they must eat after their husbands, they could not have inheritance, they were segregated during menstruation, and so forth).[11]

The concept of wife-deity appeared in the late Vedic texts, names such as Indrāṇi, Varuṇnī, Agnāyī, and Rudrāṇī being formed from the names of prominent male gods. Goddesses received offerings mainly on new and full-moon days. The fact that they were connected as Uśas and Rātrī (or Aditi and Nirṛti) symbolizing day and night might have contributed to the later bipolar nature of some goddesses as benevolent and malevolent. Several minor goddesses were associated with wealth, children, and longevity—the *apsarās* and *yakṣīs* dwelling in trees, stars, and water who were likely related to the figure within the branches of a tree on the Indus seals.

By the late Vedic period, Śrī designated an independent female power desired by kings and contained in their cushion seat (which they could tap to provide their kingdoms with fertility, riches, health, beauty, and auspiciousness). These ideas are elaborated in the Śrīsūkta,[12] a hymn to Śrī who is said to have ten qualities—food, royal power, universal sovereignty, noble rank, holy lustre, kingdom, fortune, bounteousness, beauty, and power[13]—which made the 'old' gods jealous. (The reference to old gods might be an indication of a changing pantheon or the new textual visibility of ancient, Indus? deities).[14] Śrī was connected not only to the development of stable and just kingdoms (though she moved about to different kings) but also to agriculture and rain (on which prosperous kingdoms depended), thus her association with earth, planting, fecundity, growth, and harvest. Like the apsarās and yakṣīs, she was linked to sacred trees and, by extension, to all plant life, abundance, wealth, and good luck. Śrī was subsequently linked to Lakṣmī, the personification of wealth and prosperity. The connection of a woman's power of *tapas* (chastity), royal power, rain, and agriculture is found in many subsequent texts, such as the Tamil (Jain) epic *Cilappatikāram.*[15]

Women's rituals have been connected to the banyan tree, which symbolizes long life and fertility (via its aerial roots that hang from its branches which symbolize, in turn, the rays of the sun or the ropes that bind a woman's fertility to ensure her chastity).[16] It figures prominently in the religious lives of women and even today is connected to marriage (obtaining a husband), fertility (having a child, especially a son), and family health, well-being, and prosperity (especially long life for the husband). Women routinely worship the local banyan tree. The connection of the banyan tree with the Pole Star, and the Pole Star with constancy, fidelity, and the female stars Rohiṇī and Arundhatī give an astral, cosmic, and sacred dimension to women's lives and religious tasks.

THE CLASSICAL PERIOD (400 BCE–400 CE)

The Sanskrit texts of this period include the Sūtras (Dharmasūtras, Gṛhyasūtras, and so forth) and some Śāstras—the Epics (*Itihāsa*) or at least their redaction, and early Purāṇas. This was a period when the Vedic religion was in danger of collapsing. It was also the time when Buddhism and Jainism were flourishing, which is a related fact.

Upper-caste women's decreasing status is apparent in these texts written by men. This can be detected not only by how their role changed in the Vedic rituals, but also by how their body was described. Whereas once their womb was understood as the fertile field, now it became but a vessel for male seed. Whereas once their fertility was emphasized, now their impurity was underscored. Whereas once they were married only when mature (after puberty), now they were married before puberty (in fact, as the age of child marriage gradually decreased, the control over women to ensure their purity grew). Whereas once they had real input into the choice of marriage partner, now they were marginal to the process of arranged marriage. Whereas once both daughters and sons were viewed as important (even though there was some preference for sons on account of the patrilineal/patrilocal social organization), now sons were not only highly preferred (a man could attain heaven only if his son performed his cremation) but daughters came to be viewed as serious liabilities. This occurred largely because marriage in elite circles was *kanyādāna*—the gift of a daughter accompanied by dowry. The fact that brides accompanied by gifts were transferred to their husband's home meant that they were a poor investment.

Because of upper-caste women's lack of education, the texts began to call them *avidyā* (without knowledge). As a result, they were linked to the *śūdras* (the lowest caste). Though the Atharvaveda had allowed the śūdras to have upanayana (it was an exception in this regard), they had lost this privilege by the time of the Mauryan empire (ca. 320–186 BCE). Many had become war captives subject to corvée labour to clear the land and were controlled through an ideology of service. At the end of the period, the havoc caused by the break-up of the empire was exacerbated by foreign invasions. It was also exacerbated by the fact that many people (foreign-born kings as well as indentured servants and slaves) were turning to the heterodox (*nāstika*) religions (Buddhism and Jainism) in the west and east.

Elite men of the Vedic tradition—especially brahmins in the central area of Mathurā, Kuru, and Pañcāla—were feeling extremely threatened. Their sacrificial system based on knowledge of the Vedas on which brahmanical occupation and status depended was under assault. The stress was projected on to women and śūdras, who became linked in the process as *avaidika* (without knowledge of the Vedas). The idea that this period of time was one of decline and darkness developed at this low point of late Vedic culture. It became frozen in myth as the Kaliyuga and passed down in subsequent texts such as the Purāṇas. An anomaly was created by all this. Brahmins considered themselves the highest caste, superior by learning. And yet brahmin women were linked to śūdras and were inferior by lack of learning. To resolve this inherent contradiction, the high status of brahmin women was defined instead by their purity and chastity. That is what gave them high status when compared to other castes (though their absence of learning made them subordinate to brahmin men). But even status by purity had its problem, because their impurity at times of menstruation and childbirth made them, once again, like śūdras. The corollary of brahmin men's status (or that of any group imitating them) being defined by the purity and chastity of their womenfolk meant that men wanted to control women's sexuality (and the ideology for women's behaviour had to emphasize self-control).[17]

A serious threat to Vedic endorsed norms of family life was posed by Buddhism and Jainism because these offered women a way to bypass marriage, or even leave it if married, by joining a monastic order and becoming a nun. There are indications that asceticism was practised by Hindu women at the time. A real-life context can be deduced, for instance, from the literary portrayals of ascetic women in the *Mahābhārata*.[18] It was not asceticism per se that was the problem, but rather independent female asceticism based on choice in an age of social upheaval and growing individualism. Although Hindus' response could have been the institutionalization of Hindu asceticism to meet the challenge, they took the opposite route: reassertion of marriage for women and attacks on female asceticism.[19] This position had the effect of ending the official legitimation of widow asceticism (which even Manu allowed)[20], not to mention other forms of asceticism.

A more general fear of female independence is reflected in Manu who said that sacrifices, vows, and fasts must not be performed by women apart from their husbands.[21] Manu went further to undermine any independent streak in women in the often quoted verse that a girl, a young woman, or even an old woman was to do nothing independently, even in her own house. In childhood, they must be subject to their fathers, in youth to their husbands, and when in death to their sons. In short, women must never be independent.[22] Was not male political stress being projected on to women through fears that they would act independently, thereby further undermining the social order?

If the first half of the classical age was characterized by the decline of the status of women and śūdras (as well as their negative linkage), the second half shows an improvement. This can be traced in part to an improvement in social and material conditions. After the first century CE, the Gangetic plain experienced a better economy because of the stabilization of kingdoms, integration of foreign rulers, and international trade. Because śūdras participated in the greater prosperity of the region, they became more demanding. As a result, more concessions were given to them. And because women's status had been connected to that of śūdras, when the latter's status rose, so did the former's. *Mahābhārata* and *Bhagavad Gītā*, which were redacted about this time, contain passages with a more inclusive, though not always complementary, spirit. Gītā 9:32 for instance, proclaims '*Even* women, vaiśyas, and śūdras shall attain the supreme goal.' Nevertheless, there were debates for some centuries in brahmanical circles over whether women and śūdras could utter the sacred syllable *om*; whether they could attain the higher stages of a religious path; or whether they could attain liberation in this life.[23] Desire (*kāma*) and control (*yoga*) had become a major opposition (*dvandva*) that structured the Hindu worldview from the time of the Upaniṣads. Women (and the divine apsarās who attempted to seduce ascetics) represented the former, and men represented the latter.

The great synthesis of the late classical age was formulated as the four *puruṣārthas* (goals of the *puruṣa*): ethics (*dharma*), wealth (*artha*), pleasure (*kāma*), and liberation (*mokṣa*). It also included *varṇāśrama-dharma* or appropriate behaviour according to (1) *varṇa* or caste (brāhmaṇa, kṣatriya, vaiśya, and śūdra) and (2) *āśrama* or stage of life—studentship (*brahmacarya*), householdership (*gṛhastha*), forest dwelling (*vānaprastha*) and solitary peregrination (*saṁnyāsa*). Because of the inherent ambiguity in the term *puruṣa* (it can mean either human or male), the four goals have often been translated as the four goals of human life. But scrutiny of their description along with discussions of *strībhāva* (female nature) and *strīdharma* (the duties of women) suggests that the orientations of elite men and women had major differences.

Goddesses and epic heroines provided models for human wives. From the classical period, two of the most important divine models of the good wife have been Sītā and Satī-Pārvatī (though Lakṣmī, Sāvitrī, Damayantī, and Draupadī have also been popular). Wife-goddesses represented an 'ascetic sexuality', that is, a sexuality controlled by their husbands (parallel to the control of upper-caste human wives by husbands). Perhaps the most famous wife of all is Sītā, heroine of Vālmīki's epic *Rāmāyaṇa* (redacted between 200 BCE–200 CE?). The author's interpretation of this well-known story follows:

Because the name Sītā literally means a furrow of the earth, Sītā—who is said to be born from the earth and who returns to it—can be connected with agriculture (both earth and rain) and with royal rituals to make the fields fertile (it was, after all, King Janaka who found her in the furrow). Though the epic is supposed to be about the perfect kingdom (*Rāmrājya*) ruled by the perfect king (Rāma) and queen (Sītā), this never transpires, for as dutiful son, Rāma honours his father's fulfilment of a boon once promised to Kaikeyī, his second wife, which she exercises to make her own son Bharata king and his half-brother Rāma, the rightful heir to the throne, banished to the forest.

This provides the occasion for Sītā to insist that she accompany her husband to the forest for the next fourteen years. Even though Rāma, following his male role as protector, tries to dissuade her, asking her to await his return in the comfort of the palace, she threatens to kill herself to obtain her way. Rāma relents with this display of feminine will-power that not only underscores the ideal of female loyalty and courage but also the exercise of negative power by threat of self-willed death. In fact, although ostensibly she follows him and subjects her will to his, Sītā is the power-broker and moral exemplar through the pivotal episodes of the epic.

Rāma, sometimes caught by his own sense of duty and sometimes by his own weakness or ego, pales by comparison to her integrity, tenacity, and chastity by which she upholds feminine norms. Nevertheless, Sītā is subjected to a series of tests. First, she is abducted by the demon Rāvaṇa and held hostage in his palace, but avoids his attempts at seduction even in his disguise as Rāma. Her chastity is tested again when the monkey god Hanumān finds her and offers to take her to Rāma by riding on his shoulder. She refuses the offer and maintains her purity. Later, when reunited to Rāma, she undergoes another test, for he refuses to accept her innocence. And so she orders her funeral pyre to be made and enters it, calling upon the god of fire to protect her if she is indeed pure. When she emerges unscathed, Rāma accepts her back.

But then again, when he hears his citizens gossiping about her, he banishes her from the kingdom, even though he has just learned she is pregnant. Graciously she obeys. Later Rāma calls her back to the kingdom. But to eliminate the doubts of the citizens, he orders one more ordeal. Sītā, however, has had enough of vacillation. She requests Mother Earth to receive her if she has indeed been pure and loyal to Rāma. And so to the furrows from whence she came, she returns. Rāma then lives out his life mourning her disappearance.

Another important wife-goddess is Satī-Pārvatī. She appears by the epic period as the wife of Śiva. Her myths are elaborated in the Purāṇas. According to a story:

In one life, Satī undergoes a severe fast in order to attract the great yogi Śiva who is deep in meditation. When she is successful in awakening desire in him, she requests him to marry her. After their wedding, they retire to Śiva's mountain abode, where they enjoy their lovemaking. This is interrupted one year because Satī's father Dakṣa does not invite his 'uncivilized' son-in-law and his daughter to a great sacrifice he is holding. Insulted, Satī kills herself. Śiva then destroys the sacrifice and carries his wife on his shoulder about the universe, which causes the cosmos to tremble with his grief. Pieces of Satī's body are cut off and fall to the ground; they become sacred places (*pīṭhas*), where different goddesses are worshipped.

This paradigmatic myth suggests that women's asceticism can be extremely powerful and exert control over even the most powerful male yogi. It also suggests once again that women exercise negative power not only through denial of food but also by willing their own death for the sake of fulfilling the norms of womanhood and justice. In other words, they *take control* of their lives (not to mention acting altruistically to benefit others), but their power is acted upon their own bodies.

In another incarnation Satī is Pārvatī. This time, too, Pārvatī uses her ascetic powers, stronger than those of all the other gods, to force Śiva to marry her. Seed from their lovemaking spills into the Gaṅgā river and is incubated there, resulting in the child Kārttikeya. Pārvatī creates a second child, who is to guard her privacy, but this is quickly tested when the child stops her husband Śiva from entering her quarters. In fury, Śiva cuts the child's head off. Furious herself, Pārvatī enjoins her husband to restore the head, and so Śiva gives him the head of an elephant. Because the elephant-headed being is then put in charge of all the troops (*gaṇa*), he is called Gaṇapati or Gaṇeśa.

These origin myths describe how the power of asceticism must be tapped to call forth desire (kāma), which is necessary to maintain the very life of the cosmos. Other myths about Śiva and Pārvatī describe the poles of asceticism and domesticity that characterize the classical worldview of Hinduism. And still other myths describe the opposition between auspiciousness (*śubha*) and inauspiciousness (*aśubha*) that structure the lives of elite Hindu women.

Even the independent goddesses Durgā and Kālī (who have a bipolar nature representing creation/life and death/destruction) have been transformed into Śiva's consort (though they dominate him) between 300 BCE and 400 CE. They were then called Pārvatī, Umā, and Satī (though the name Durgā was also used), and were associated with benevolence under the control of the male god. The other aspect of the Devī's nature became a different (and categorically malevolent) deity as she who is out of control.[24]

The life-cycle of the wife of a twice-born (*dvija*) man, especially a brahmin, consisted of virginal maidenhood (*kaumārya*) and marriage (*vivāha*), which might involve the life-style change of vānaprastha in later years. All of this was epitomized in the idea that for a woman, her husband was her god (the very word *pati*, in fact, meant husband or god).[25] Although wives were also apotheosized as Lakṣmī, goddess of prosperity, in the home, especially during rituals, this was never so central to male rituals and psychology as the apotheosis of husband was for wives. At the same time, apotheosis as Lakṣmī served to validate women's own sense of self-worth and mitigate the hierarchy that favoured men.

Inauspiciousness (aśubha) was primarily the attribute of a woman whose husband pre-deceased her. This was by no means uncommon for a woman was to be married to a man at least three (and sometimes ten) years her senior. Many of her vows, in fact, were performed to ensure his health and longevity. When her husband died first, this was blamed on her bad *karma*.

An upper-caste woman then had two options. One was to undergo the rite of passage to widowhood (*vaidhavya*). This involved having her bangles (and other jewels) and her *tilaka* (the auspicious red dot on her forehead), both signs of her auspiciousness, removed. And it involved henceforth living a life of utmost simplicity akin to an ascetic's life-style —simple dress without adornment, minimum food, sleeping on the floor, and so on. Her other option to this dire existence was the act of sati (burning herself on the funeral pyre of her husband or following his cremation by her self-willed death). The antecedents of the custom were probably the act of self-willed death by burning, drowning, fasting, and so forth as a way to achieve salvation done by both men and women. The fact that self-willed death is described in both the northern Hindu epics and the southern Tamil *caṅkam* texts and the fact that fasting to death (*sallekhana*) is the ideal form of death according to Jainism suggest a common antecedent (perhaps, the archaic Indus civilization).[26]

The structure of the upper-caste Hindu woman's life cycle was visually marked by the presence or absence of a tilaka (also known as *potu/bottu* or *bindi*). Prior to marriage, a girl would wear a black or red dot; after marriage a red dot (like that of the goddess)—if a satī, a red dot; but if a widow, no dot whatsoever. The presence or absence of a dot signified auspiciousness or inauspiciousness, respectively. This same semiotics was expressed by the presence or absence of bangles. A woman wore tight bangles when her lover or husband was present; they become loose when she was love-sick, adulterous, or her husband was away; and she removed them when he died. The presence, absence, or fit of bangles (or other round ornaments such as toe-rings, necklaces, earrings, and belts) symbolized the dynamics of union and separation in the life of a woman.[27]

The presence of bangles on female figures—human but also goddesses and female spirits associated with water, trees and stars (the apsarās and yakṣinīs)—is omnipresent in the Indic religions. That these bangles have magical power is attested even today by the fact that their presence can ensure obtaining a good husband. Brides are given bangles at the time of marriage; these concretely represent their purity. Contemporary women still use bangles as votive offerings when they desire to become pregnant or when they want the birth of a male son. When they are actually pregnant, they are given bangles first made of *nim* (believed to have therapeutic and healing properties) and then green glass. Bangles have power to protect the husband and family as well. They are used by women as votive offerings when crises like smallpox or cholera affect the children. In addition, women tie red ribbons (like bangles) around the branches of a banyan tree to ensure their children's survival. Finally, the power of bangles can defy death and facilitate a better rebirth or even liberation (represented in the medieval period by images of a raised arm with bangles on sati stones).

Medieval to Early Modern Period (400–1947 CE)

A more inclusive orientation developed by the early medieval period. The Gupta Empire (fourth century CE) had furthered this, as had some of the Purāṇas. 'By the tenth century, the city culture of northern Indian had firmly established. Pataliputra, Kasi, Prayaga, and Ujjain were flourishing cities. Caste flexibility was at an end and the castes were clearly defined. The Greeks, the Huns, and the Gujar invaders had been absorbed ... It was a period of comparative peace and security.'[28]

In the early modern period, the link of women and śūdras took on a positive connotation in some texts. The elevation of śūdras might have resulted from the inter-religious competition among Hindus, Buddhists, and Jains in areas such as the Deccan and Tamilnadu. The old *varṇāśramadharma* system would have had little attraction for śūdra groups that had their own regional identity and power (as local warrior or land-owning elites). How could they be called low caste and barred from elite religious identities by migrants who were in the minority? Obviously, an adjustment had to be made, and so even some brahmanical groups became inclusive.

As a result, smṛti texts (such as the Epics and Purāṇas) were said to be equivalent for women and śūdras to the Vedas (*Mahābhārata* and Nāṭyaśāstra, for instance, were both called the fifth Veda and the Tamil devotional hymns the Tamil Veda). Some texts allowed śūdra males to receive Vedic education, be patrons for Vedic rituals, and achieve salvation.[29] (Curiously, Vedic sacrificial religion, while declining in the north, was revitalized for a time in the central and southern parts of the subcontinent, once it was made available to local elites and became a status symbol for them.) In this age of proselytism, how could Hindu women be considered of lower spiritual worth than Buddhist or Jain women when the religions were competing? Women, after all, were hostesses in the homes and often made decisions about which ascetics they should give food and other donations to.

Hindu *bhakti* sects had themes of universalism and their rhetoric was designed to actively recruit women and all castes (sometimes even outcastes). They made women and śūdras, for instance, the exemplars of humble devotion and service to God that was incumbent on all devotees (a positive spin on the old Mauryan service/slave ideology which had subjugated śūdras). It is striking that male poet-devotees themselves assumed the persona of a woman in love with a male god!

Hindu proselytism was also directed to local rulers, many of whom had Buddhist or Jain sympathies. With their conversion (there are many stories to this effect), or at least sympathy, the Hindu offensive gained an important political dimension (in Tamilnadu, for instance, this occurred after the seventh century).

In general, female Hindu devotees were to adjust their devotion to the deities Viṣṇu or Śiva to their domestic context. Women could, however, exploit the ambiguity of certain concepts such as heaven, understanding it as *svarga*—a paradise that could be enjoyed as a temporary reward for good deeds (and therefore was a woman's reward, so to speak, for her good service to her husband)—or supreme heaven such as the Vaiṣṇava Vaikuṇṭha or Śaiva Kailāsa.[30]

Many of the bhakti sects allowed salvation for householders. Because this bypassed the need for asceticism, it made salvation more accessible for women (and śūdras). But the fact that the ideal type of devotion was an *exclusive* love of God—compared to the ordinary woman's focus on two patis, her husband and her chosen God (unless, of course, she was the devotee of a goddess)—inspired some women to defy the marital system by refusing to marry or leaving their husbands altogether. Pati now was God, not a human husband. And with that change, these women were inspired to sing about their own spiritual experiences, expressing an authentic love outside of marriage.

Such acts of spiritual defiance turned women such as Kārikkāl-ammaiyar, Āṇṭāḷ, Mahādevī, Janabāī, Bahiṇabāī, and Mīrābaī into bhakti saints, often much more popular and remembered than their male counterparts (certainly the case with Āṇṭāḷ and Mīrābaī, who have inspired temples, festivals, reform movements, and musical renditions of their poems from bardic to high, classical style). Every region had its examples of unusual, norm-defying women, sometimes proud, sometimes humble, sometimes high caste, sometimes low, who surrendered to the Lord and took refuge in him. According to the hagiographies, their spiritual journey consisted of several stages: early dedication to God, denial of marriage, defying societal norms, initiation, and marrying the Lord.[31] Most of these medieval female saints were religious poets, whose hymns praising a deity have been preserved.

If bhakti sects utilized reversal symbolisms for popular appeal especially across caste and gender lines—occasionally inspiring devotees to take these reversals literally, thereby creating saints—*tantric* groups inspired an esoteric, counter-culture. The latter was small enough not to threaten the society but radical enough in its left-handed form to challenge all norms and in its right-handed form to leave its imprint on the arts.

The primary deity of left-handed tantra was Devī and the female had precedence in religious practices. By contrast, Śiva and the male have precedence in right-handed tantra. Left-handed *tāntrikas* literally partook of the five forbidden elements (wine, meat, fish, parched grain, and sexual intercourse). Regarding the latter, orgasm was postponed for the ritualized time of one hour and thirty-six minutes and then this energy was released up through the seven *cakras* or subtle energy centres of the body, culminating in the release of great joy and occult power. Tantra encouraged other reversals such as celebrating low caste status, adultery, or the female in the dominant position in intercourse. By contrast, the right-handed tāntrikas did their rituals with the forbidden substances only symbolically.[32]

But, tantra was mainly oriented to elite men's quest for liberation (female tāntrikas, remember, were generally from the lower castes). Its general support of feminine values did, however, have some influence in the society at large. Tantric texts prescribed, for instance, that men should not marry their daughters for money and should cherish their wives, avoiding rudeness and punishment; rape should be punished by death, and female animals should not be used in sacrifice.

Other women, not just bhakti saints and tāntrikas, rejected or circumvented the extreme norms of upper-caste women. Through the centuries, for instance, there had always been prostitutes (*veśyās*). Some women turned to this ancient profession when they encountered problems in their domestic life (lack of marriage, persecution in marriage, child widowhood and so forth). Another class of independent (Hindu) women were the courtesans (*gaṇikās*). They had specialized in the arts—dance, song and Sanskrit poetry. Both veśyās and gaṇikās were linked with kings. The status of a king increased with their presence in his kingdom, which made it fertile and prosperous. It also increased through his patronage of the gaṇikās' art. Two famous gaṇikās were Muddupalani (1730–1790) of the Tanjore court and Nagaratnammal (1878–1952), the daughter of a Mysore court gaṇikā, who started the Tyāgarāja festival in Tamilnadu.[33] Their 'style of non-confrontational resistance [was] ... not a part-time or sporadic activity, but a way of life'[34] as old as the profession, examples of which can be found through the centuries.

With a poignant reversal of fortunes, the son of a courtesan in the nineteenth century wrote:

> While I love and respect my mother and all my 'aunts' [other courtesans] and my grandmother ... my misfortune is that I was born a son and not a daughter in their house. When a boy is born in the *kothā*, the day is without moment, even one of quiet sadness. When my sister was born there was a joyous celebration that was unforgettable. Everyone received new clothes, there was singing, dancing, and feasting. My aunts went from door to door distributing *laddus* [a sweet traditionally distributed to mark an auspicious event]. ... My sister is, today a beautiful, educated, propertied woman. She will also inherit what my mother and grandmother own. She will have a large income from rents; she doesn't even have to work as a courtesan, if she so chooses. I am educated, but I have no money or property. Jobs are very hard to come by, so I live in a room and subsist on a small allowance ... Funny isn't it, how these women have made life so topsy-turvy?[35]

Closely related to the gaṇikās, according to the Āgamas, were the devadāsīs. 'The devadāsī, who served God through song and dance, was the pre-eminent member of this class, for not only did she enhance the prostitute's and artist's image through direct connection with the deity, but she also linked the fame and functions of the king with the temple.'[36] Women played a part in the culture of the monumental Hindu temples in the medieval period.[37] They were performers of dance and song as part of the temple ritual, especially at festival times. In addition to these specialized tasks, they took part in festival processions; they brought, lit, placed, and removed auspicious lamps; they waved flywhisks. They also served in the temple by preparing purifier threads (*pavitras*); making food offerings; plaiting garlands; and pounding substances to prepare ritual materials. Compared to men's roles, those of women were 'inessential, occasional, and optional';[37] aside from dancing and singing, they involved few skills. Nevertheless, these roles provided women with lifestyle options, and perhaps wealth.

Reform as Response to Foreign Critique

Because devastating critiques of Hindu womanhood had been a way that the British Raj legitimated its political rule (part of the 'white man's burden' was to rescue Hindu women) and because Christian missionaries had proselytized by attacking Hinduism's treatment of women, one of the major responses to colonization was to initiate reforms of the norms governing upper-caste women's life cycle, the devadāsī institution and the courtesans' *kothās*. Because brahmin men (who had been the creators of many of the repressive norms over the centuries) were blamed, because their own status was threatened by foreign moral critiques,[39] and because they recognized the grave injustices that many women experienced, they themselves took up the cause for reform. Mrtyunjaya Vidyalankar, M.G. Ranade, Raja Rammohan Roy, Ishwarchandra Vidyasagar, Dayananda Sarasvati, Keshab Chandra Sen and Behramji Malbari are a few of the many reformers who criticized upper-caste practices such as child marriage; early age of marriage; polygamy, domestic confinement; seclusion (*purdah*); lack of education, divorce, remarriage, and equal inheritance; and treatment of widows and sati.

Interpretive strategies (many based on Mīmāṁsaka ones pertaining to ritual) were used in this endeavour of reform. One was to consider the Vedas (śruti, the primary scripture) as the norm; if a practice such as sati or child marriage was not found there, it was deemed an accretion that could be eliminated. Another strategy was to use the behaviour of contemporary ethical or 'good people' (*ācāras*) or 'conscience'—also recognized sources of authority—rather than scripture per se as the norm. And still another was to argue that this, the Kali Yuga, had different norms than earlier periods. (Ironically, just as Hindus were using interpretive strategies for greater flexibility, the British were introducing greater rigidity).

This had another intriguing development. As Subramaniya Bharati, E.V. Ramaswami, and Jotirao Phule agitated for their rights (which created the non-brahmin movement), they drew attention to the fact that both they and women had suffered over the centuries because of brahmin male values. In modern feminist terms, sexism, and classism were deeply linked and the oppressed classes recognized this.

But where were Hindu women in this reform movement? Some women were outspoken critics, too. Take Pandita Ramabai (1858–1922). As her title suggests, she had a most unusual upbringing as a brahmin woman because her father, implementing the reform mood of the times, taught her not only Sanskrit but also the sacred Vedas themselves, making her an authority, a 'pandit'. Orthodox brahmins persecuted the family for this renegade education. When her husband died two years after her marriage, Ramabai campaigned for reform of widow norms. Eventually, after writing *Sthri* [sic] *Dharma Neeti* (Women's Religious Law), she turned against Hinduism, converting to Christianity. Many other widows such as Ramabai Ranade, Swarnakumari Devi, Subbalakshmi and Anandibai Karve instituted reforms in various parts of the subcontinent.[40]

It was only during the Indian independence movement, however, that women themselves began in large numbers to agitate for change and created their own organizations and publications toward this end. Along with seeking new laws to give teeth to the reforms of the nineteenth century, they fought for political enfranchisement. Now, ironically, British male rulers were not so keen on reform, arguing that Indian women were too conservative, largely illiterate, and could disguise their identities by the veil (purdah)—all this making enfranchisement dangerous or difficult to implement. But the real reason was that, after the Revolt of 1857, the British were fearful of enflaming Hindu sentiments (which might occur if they interfered with religion or women's norms). They were also trying to hide their hypocrisy. For even in England they were refusing to give women the vote and they definitely did not like the fact that Indian and English suffragette movements were developing their own links. Nor did they like the fact that all major Indian political parties supported Indian women's right to vote. The Raj avoided a showdown by turning the decision over to the new Indian Assemblies. In many of the provinces and princely states, Indian women were enfranchised before English women in 1928, though universal suffrage in India took yet more agitation.

Heroic Responses to Foreign Rule

Women who exercised military power were called *vīrāṅganās* from the words *vīra* (heroism, manliness, semen) and *aṅganā* (woman), therefore a woman who possessed the manly quality of heroism. With Muslim invasions and later British battles, vīrāṅganās fought heroically to protect their lands and identity. They had often been tutored by fathers, husbands, or fathers-in-law. Some were queens who refused to perform sati or to take on the ascetic-like regimens of widowhood when their husbands died, opting instead to rule as queen regents (often dressed as men) until their sons were old enough to assume the throne. Durma Devi, Tarabai, Ahalyabai Holkar, Lakshmibai and Rani of Jhansi are all examples of heroic women. The vīrāṅganā motif also appears in other contexts as well such as the tradition of Alli Rani in Tamilnadu, where the antagonist is the epic hero Arjuna. Although some references to the rule of women (*strīrājya*) were literary tropes, there is also evidence for female rule.[41]

What is particularly intriguing, given all the *pativratā* ideology of the elite Hindu tradition, is the fact that these women came to be eulogized by this religion. Even though some of the vīrāṅganās had paramours, this was ignored. In short, it was valour, not feminine loyalty, chastity, and fertility, that were recognized and praised as an exceptional value that had overridden the norm of *strīdharma*. It has been suggested that the popularity of the vīrāṅganā model by the nineteenth century, a time of reforms, was an attempt to dissipate the colonial critiques of norms for women by showing that Hinduism has had other models of womanhood (as it has had models of courageous men—like the Marathas or the Rajputs). The fact that these groups worshipped goddesses also contributed to a renewal of goddess worship.

There was a discontinuity between the vīrāṅganās and most female freedom fighters, however, for the former were willing to use violence whereas the latter, following Mahatma Gandhi, used non-violent means. As such, they were *satyāgrahinīs* (a feminine noun made from the term *satyāgraha* coined by Gandhi to mean grasping/insisting on that which is real and true or 'soul-force'). Gandhi realized the profound link between national liberation and upper-caste women's liberation. Because these women had been 'caged' [his word] in domestic spheres and prided themselves on maintenance of custom, he found that their mentality was insular, narrow, prejudiced, infantile, and petty. As he said when addressing a meeting of women: 'It is good to swim in the waters of tradition, but to sink in them is suicide.'[42] They needed liberation from the very tradition they so carefully protected.

Hindu women understood Gandhi's strategies because he had based them, in large part, on Hindu women's religious practices. Just as women performed vows, so did the freedom fighters vow to end foreign rule. Just as women's vows involved giving up salt or fasting, so the freedom fighters gave up salt or fasted. Just as women sometimes threatened to die (as did Sītā, for instance, when she felt it her duty to follow Rāma to the forest) so did Gandhi when he applied pressure on the British by fasting to the brink of death.

Self-denial created *tapas* or spiritual power that could be used to achieve mundane or supramundane goals. Gandhi found that traditional ideas of women's purity, chastity, self-sacrifice, moral courage, and idealism were useful for the cause of independence. Hindu widows were important for the movement because they had 'learnt to find happiness in suffering' and had 'accepted suffering as sacred'.[43] In fact, because many women had suffered in their lives (he often referred to Mīrabāī), they could make a deep emotional link to the suffering of the nation under foreign rule. Today, Gandhi has been criticized by some women for not going far enough. He continued to think of women primarily as wives and mothers.

The Post-independence Period

The Indian Constitution was based on the concept of a secular state, one that was to be supportive of all religions but partial to none. There was a curious exception to the latter, however, for although the state was not allowed to favour any one religion, it could single out one for reform. That was Hinduism, the religion of the majority. Exercising its constitutional power to reform Hinduism, the government (against the will of some Hindus) instituted the Hindu Marriage Act of 1955 and the Hindu Succession Act of 1956. Polygamy became illegal, the age for marriage was raised to eighteen for girls and twenty-one for boys, and women could file for separation and divorce. The following years witnessed a series of laws to address dowry deaths, assault, rape, wrongful confinement, cruelty, and sexual harassment. When an incident of sati occurred in 1987 (that of Roop Kanwar), women's groups agitated and new legislation was introduced even though it had been a criminal act in the lawbooks since the nineteenth century.

Reforms, Religious Identity, and Polarization

Despite major legal changes, the great discrepancy between progressive legislation and social practice has led many to the conclusion that good laws are no longer the issue. Rather, it is how to empower Hindu women to know about and use the law to eliminate abuses and create an equal society. Some critics have also argued that because women gained their entry into political life through the fight for independence and had the support of men, the process has been too easy and they have relied too much on political patronage rather than militancy for their rights.[44] Others have pointed out that male leaders have simply used women to further their own political projects[45] (though the idea that they were pawns does not do justice to the spontaneous and deep identification of women with the freedom struggle).

The development of Socialism and Marxism in post-independence India, especially in westernized, English-speaking circles, has led to attempts to bring reforms to the grassroots, not only in the rural areas and the villages but also in the urban ghettos of the poor. In Bombay, for instance, Jyoti Mhapasekara has led a movement called Strī Mukti (the liberation of women). Her play called 'A Daughter is Born' begins with homage to reformers such as Agarkar, Karve, Pandita Ramabai, Gandhi, and Nehru culminating in the call: 'Let us unite; we shall destroy the ancient traditions and make women free.' It goes on in pithy and humorous vignettes to address the problems women face, with choruses chanting 'we want equal opportunity'. Underlying its reform orientation, however, is its Marxist presupposition that real progress is the destruction of religion.[46] Socialists and Marxists have focused on women's solidarity with other marginal groups (Dalits, Adivasis and others labelled by law as Scheduled Castes and Tribes). Along with organizations for social change are magazines such as Delhi's *Manushi* dedicated to educating women for social change, providing networks and forums to spread the news of activism on women's issues around the country, and critically commenting on books, films, laws and other influences on the status of women.[47] Women, in fact, are social activists in many regions. These include village women. In the South, for instance, they have agitated for temperance.

Because Hinduism (more precisely, brahmanical male Hinduism) created and legitimated the norms for family and social life, it was heavily implicated when these appeared hierarchical, unjust and rigid. But reforms—especially those instigated by the Constitution, Congress, socialists and Marxists often have appeared to be sweeping attacks on the religion. For this reason, some Hindus have considered the secular state no longer a positive support of all religions, which are to be regarded as equal (*sarva dharma samabhāva*), but hostile to Hinduism (though critics have argued that governmental favouritism to Hinduism has been common).

Old hostilities between Muslims and Hindus, which had exploded at the time of Partition and periodic outbreaks of communalism came to a head once again with the 1992 conflict over the Babri Masjid, a no longer functional mosque which Hindus wanted to remove so that they could build a temple on this site believed to be the place where Lord Rāma was born. This communal and political issue spilled over into women's issues in several ways. The demand by Hindus that there be a uniform civil code of family law (divorce, custody, and so forth) was perceived as an issue of justice: if the government had had the right to interfere in Hindu family law, it should do the same in other religious communities so that all citizens of the country were under one law.[48] This has had the effect, however, of splitting Indian women's solidarity and contributing to the growth of fundamentalism in the various religions, including Hinduism.

Religious movements such as the Rashtriya Svayamsevak Sangh (RSS), and Vishva Hindu Parishad (VHP) and Bharatiya Janata Party (BJP) in the 1990s have often been called expressions of Hindu fundamentalism. On the one hand, the male leaders of these parties have rallied against the women's movement for causing disintegration of the Hindu family and they have honoured women's domestic roles. Consider the example of the BJP candidate Deepika Chikalia, who had the lead role of Sītā in the televised serial of the Rāmāyaṇa, was invited by the BJP to run in the 1991 parliamentary elections. Just as she had presented Sītā as extremely passive on film, so also she maintained the image of the passive woman during the political campaign. On the other hand, the male leaders have appealed to women by acknowledging their problems and grievances as a way of bringing them into the movement. But A.B. Vajpayee, then leader of the BJP, admits—'we have created only two roles for women: as either *devīs* or *dāis* (goddesses or slaves), to the exclusion of other roles.'[49] Nevertheless, according to one assessment, 'although the most powerful women in Hindutva (Hindu nationalist) movement are less powerful than the male leadership, they enjoy more prominence and exercise greater influence than women have in most other national and social movements in India ... the female leadership implicitly sanctions and indeed encourages women's use of violence.'

It is striking that three of the main female leaders of the BJP—Vijayraje Scindia, Sadhvi Rithambara and Uma Bharati—all present themselves as celibate with its associations of purity, spiritual power, and morality. Scindia, a widow, dresses in traditional white (although widowhood was traditionally inauspicious, after a century of reforms it has been reconstituted as an honourable form of asceticism), Rithambara and Bharati dress in the ochre robes that indicate an ascetic. These women have used the authority conveyed by iconic, religious symbols of chastity and asceticism (as well as allusions to religious myths and legends) to curse the corruption of political opponents (drawing on the traditional view that the spiritual is superior to the political or *saṁsāric* realm as women's morality is superior to men's).

These female leaders of the political right also have their differences. Scindia, from an upper-caste background, presents a more traditional image of Hindu womanhood. Bharati, from a lower-caste background, views the traditional oppression of Hindu women as a lack of education and knowledge about the complexity of the religion (for instance, Sītā was not subordinate but defied Rāma, in Bharati's words, by committing suicide).[50] She herself had helped her mother fight for land rights after her father's death. These differences surface on particular issues such as the 1987 sati of Roop Kanwar. Scindia defended voluntary sati in the past, though she was cautious on pronouncing whether the current one was voluntary or involuntary. By contrast, Bharati opposed any kind of sati, saying that the underlying reason was always to prevent women's inheritance.[51]

It has been pointed out that all these women are not under the influence of men in their personal lives, and this has contributed to their individualism.[52] As for the male leaders of these groups, they have found these female leaders useful (even though they do not maintain the subordinate Sītā role) because they can reach women in ways that men cannot. For instance, Rithambara and Bharati used cassettes to promote the building of the temple to Rāma at the site of the Babri Masjid as a way to connect with women who were still home-bound.

Other Indian feminists, of the Gandhian, Marxist, or Socialist traditions, think that the rise of female leaders such as Scindia, Bharati, and Rithambara does not bode well for the future of India in general and the women's movement in particular. The most appalling symbol of this communalism, they say, is the rape of Hindu women by Muslim men as symbol of the larger victimization of Hinduism by Islam. By extension, Muslims are being used as surrogate victims to achieve nationalist unity in Hindu terms (with its threat to the concept of the Indian secular state). For these critics of Hindu nationalism, this functions as a displacement of Hindu women's own anger against Hindu men on to Muslim men. But for defenders of Hindu self-confidence (if not nationalism)—and there are many in the middle class in the middle of the political spectrum—the Babri Masjid affair is more about Hindu esteem and exercise of Hindu power, which they think is now coming of age after being dormant since the tenth century.

Towards Greater Choice for Hindu Women

In general, many former high castes now belong to the Indian middle class. Here the ideal is no longer a gendered spatial division between the male public world and the female private world. On the contrary, the ideal is education and careers/jobs for women as well as men as the matrimonial advertisements in Indian newspapers reveal. (Unlike in the West, most young Hindus continue to view the family as an important institution; parents encourage their children to marry and most do.) Another development is that upper-caste girls (especially brahmin girls) are now the ones who are trained in singing and dancing according to the classical styles of the former gaṇikās and devadāsīs. Their first major performance is like a coming of age ritual, and their musical skills are important credentials for marriage (evidence that they are cultured and linked with religious tradition in an increasingly secular age).

Perhaps the most striking development at the end of the millennium is the convergence of the values of dalit women (once called *pañcama* untouchable, or *harijan*) and śūdra women with those of upper-caste women. Surely, this reversal could not have been consciously designed for the sake of reform. Rather, it so happens that modern values align with traditional, low-caste values in some basic ways. (Low-caste values, for instance, have been largely egalitarian and so are modern ones.) This has created a major shift in the religion.

Consider the following. Just as the status of low-caste women was not defined by concepts such as purity and pollution or auspiciousness and inauspiciousness, so too these are no longer operative as defining characteristics for modern, middle-class Hindu women (few, for example, practise segregation during menstruation, though they might avoid visits to the temple). Just as dalit and śūdra women always worked in the public realm, so now do many modern, middle-class women. Just as husbands of dalit and śūdra women helped with household tasks and childcare, so do some husbands of modern middle-class women, the division of labour depending more on time and skill than traditional gender roles. Just as dalit and śūdra women have always participated in major household decisions, so now do modern middle-class women. Just as dalit and śūdra women have always handled finances, now modern, wage earning women are doing the same. Just as dalit and śūdra women have usually lived in nuclear households, so now do more and more middle-class women. And just as dalit and śūdra women have had real authority, now middle-class women are enjoying the same. And just as most dalit and śūdra women allowed widow remarriage (in 1931 only 13.9 per cent refused it), so now does the middle class.[53]

This shift can also be seen in women's attraction to certain goddesses. Independent goddesses have existed in India since time immemorial and have been especially popular with the lower castes. These have included the village mothers manifested as stones, trees, animals, and independent women. Independent goddesses, for instance, are not married and their eroticism is not restrained;[54] they are portrayed as giving birth or making love. Although they have related to women's domestic concerns, they have also related to the community's concerns with rain, crops, and prosperity. They are benevolent when worshipped but punish those who have neglected them with disease or death. Their social status is more like that of humans than abstract and remote Sanskritic deities. The other major independent goddesses have, of course, been Durgā and Kālī. Especially in their more Sanskritized forms, they have been worshipped by the upper castes. But now, with women's growing independent spirit, it is no coincidence that they are looking to independent goddesses rather than wife goddesses for inspiration. The word *śakti* signalling the new power of women, is in; *pativratā*, signalling their subservience, is out.

Some modern Hindu women still face traditional pressures, such as bearing a son. This has led to pressure for sex selection and this, in turn, has been used to criticize Hinduism as a religion by secularists and others. It is important to capture the complexity of this phenomenon. It has been suggested that if care of the elderly members of the family is defined as the duty of a son (the traditional version of old age pensions), then there will be son preference and sex selection in the society, but if such care is viewed as the joint responsibility of all offspring, male and female, then there will no son preference and sex selection. A closer view of practices attributed to religion often reveals an underlying social or economic reason. Critics of modern Hinduism have also pointed to the fact that upper caste women sometimes face violent resistance if they attempt to marry lower status men. Certainly this does occur, but it should be remembered as well that marriage across status barriers is a problem in most societies. Today there is an increasing number of matrimonial alliances based on love or professional interests. If this trend continues, the choices for Hindu women will surely grow.

Modern Women as Ascetics and Religious Leaders

There have also been changes on traditional spiritual fronts. Although women had been bhakti saints and tāntrika adepts in the past, they had not been *brahmacāriṇīs* (at least for many centuries), *saṃnyāsinīs*, or spiritual gurus. This, too, began to change in the nineteenth century, for the Arya Samaj led by Lal Devraj began to teach girls how to recite the Vedas and perform Vedic rituals.[55] There are other groups that have promoted this tradition: Sarada Devi Mission, Brahma Vidya Mandir, Kanya Kumari Sthan, and Udyan Mangal Karyalaya.

An anthropological study of female ascetics in Varanasi[56] indicates that one-tenth of the city's thirteen hundred ascetics are women and girls. These can be divided into three types: brahmacāriṇīs, saṃnyāsinīs, and tāntrikās. The brahmacāriṇīs type is located in convent-style, sectarian establishments: *kanyāgurukulas* (schools for virgin, female students). Here girls and young women (with an average age of twenty-three, about two-thirds of all the female ascetics in the city) study Sanskrit scriptures in a traditional manner under a female teacher as preparation for renunciation. In addition, they perform Vedic rituals. To maintain an image of purity and orthodoxy (which seems to make them more acceptable when they move into non-traditional roles, they wear plain, white saris and cropped hair and are carefully chaperoned in public.

By contrast, the saṃnyāsinīs (about one quarter of the female ascetic population in Varanasi) are old women (widows?) who have undergone the ritual of initiation, consisting of symbolically performing their own funeral ritual (*śrāddha*), including burning an effigy of themselves. Their religious practices vary, consisting of pilgrimages, visiting other establishments associated with their sect, going to gatherings of ascetics (*melās*), repetition of mantras (*japa*), and meditation. Some cater to lay disciples by organizing communal singing of hymns (*bhajans*), telling of stories (*kaṭhās*), or worship (*pūjā*) of a deity (often a goddess). Some saṃnyāsinīs become the leaders of their orders or start new ones. They also run private schools and oversee their property. All, however, link their initiation with *mokṣa* (liberation) in this life; they are just waiting for the 'death' of their physical body.

The few remaining female ascetics are tāntrikās (also called *siddhās*, *sādhikās*, *tapasvinīs*, *yoginīs*). Few admit to full left-handed practices (saying that it is just a quick and inferior route), though they practice yogic postures, experience trances (*samādhis*), and cultivate occult powers (*siddhis*). They also use reversal images such as madness, intoxication, or wantonness when expressing their path and goal of bliss. Many of these tāntrikās are connected to shrines of non-Sanskritic deities. Because they have special channels of communication with the deity, they specialize in possession, divination, sorcery, spells and amulets.

The status of guru—linked as it was to leadership of institutions (ascetic lineages or *sampradāyas*) and the creation of philosophical systems of thought (*darśanas*), which often involved commentaries on the Vedas —had been firmly in the hands of men. The post-independence period has witnessed a dramatic change. Some leaders of important *sampradāyas* have transferred their spiritual mantle to a woman to make her their successor when they died. One of the first to do so was Ramakrishna who appointed Sarada Devi, his wife, to head the mission after his death. When this came to pass, she was helped by other women such as Sister Nivedita, Gauri Ma, Sudhira Basu, and Sarala Mukhopadhyaya. Similarly, Aurobindo appointed the Mother, Yogananda (Daya Mata), Upasani Baba (Godavari Mataaji), Paramananda (Gayatri Devi), Lakshmana (Mathru Srisarada), Dhyanyogi Madhusudandas (Asha Ma), Muktananda (Gurumayi Chidvilasananda) and Lingananda (Mate Mahadevi).[57] The other important context for this discussion is that of the Śaṅkarācāryas. Here the tradition seems to be split—the Śaṅkara of Kanchipuram initiated Jñānānanda as a saṃnyāsinī[58] and guru. Shankaracharya Kapileswaran and Saraswati said in 1994, however, that if women recite the Vedas, both they and their infants would have bad health.[59]

Some women have attained spiritual leadership on their own. One of the most interesting examples was Anandamayi Ma, a Bengali from a very poor, Vaiṣṇava brahmin family. She achieved national and even international recognition (though she did not cater to Westerners as did so many other modern gurus.[60]) In many ways, her spiritual biography reads like that of other saints (Śaṅkara, Rāmānuja, Caitanya, and Ramakrishna). Gradually, Anandamayi Ma attracted the attention of other well-known gurus of the day—Paramahamsa Yogananda, Maharishi Mahesh Yogi, Rajneesh, and Swami Chidananda.

With lateral peer recognition, her disciples claimed that she was superior to these gurus, for they had to struggle for their spiritual development whereas it came naturally to her. In other words, they were engaged in a spiritual discipline (*sādhana*), she in a play (*līlā*). They could only become *jīvanmuktis* (those liberated in life), she was an incarnation (*avatāra*) of the supreme deity. On some occasions, she identified herself with Viṣṇu, Śiva, or the Goddess as supreme divinity (thus, she was the comprehensive Hindu divinity). On other occasions, she identified herself (in the manner of Ramakrishna) with Muslim *fakirs* by reciting the *Qur'ān*, and with Christians by telling them to worship Christ as their chosen deity (as Hindus choose a particular manifestation of the supreme deity).

Anandamayi Ma heralded modernity in other ways as well. She appealed to the poor (with whom she could herself identify, having come from a poor family and married into one). Although she maintained her orthodoxy, she preached social equality, periodically ate with her servants, and gave her *darśana* (sight) to all castes. By generally maintaining gender and caste norms, yet periodically breaking them, she integrated hierarchy and equality in the transition between tradition and modernity. She also integrated the norms of the householder and the ascetic by remaining married and a good housewife (her skills in cooking, hospitality, spinning, and needlework were admired), yet practicing sexual abstinence (brahmacarya), a variant on the theme of *vānaprastha*.

Anandamayi Ma's skill of defining female power on the boundaries is evident in her relation with political figures. When Mahatma Gandhi desired to meet her in 1942, for instance, she repeatedly broke appointments and kept him waiting, until she finally graced him with her audience, at the same time excusing her bad behaviour by declaring she was crazy and taking on the role of a little girl, calling him 'father' (*pitāji*). She also rejected Gandhi's statement that she was a guru by her claim of being a little girl yet acknowledged her power to inspire God-intoxication in his associate. Kamala Nehru had a long association with Anandamayi Ma (in fact, it was she who had encouraged Mahatma Gandhi to make her acquaintance). Here at the heart of modern India, the seats of temporal and religious power, was the feminine connection. Moreover,

> Anandamayi Ma knew full well that her spiritual message was in tune with the grand project of national integration led by her political friends. Her role was to make sure that Hinduism maintained its elasticity for its role as good citizen in a modern nation state. Over the years, she acted as the ambassador of Hinduism. After independence, she was received by many state governments or officials, such as the governor of Gujarat, the chief minister of Andhra and the governors of Karnataka, Madras and Orissa. She always spoke for Hinduism but never at the expense of any other religion or the secular state.[61]

On Kamala's death, the rosary given to her by Anandamayi Ma was handed down to her daughter, Indira Gandhi. Indira herself frequently visited Anandamayi Ma and flew to Dehradun to join the crowd of mourners after Anandamayi Ma had died. Although Anandamayi Ma was not a saṃnyāsinī, she was buried like a realized being, 'the place of burial becoming a shrine, a place of worship and pilgrimage renowned for its spiritual power'.[62]

Women like Anandamayi Ma paved the way for Hindu women as spiritual gurus. If she was a product of the female oral tradition, more and more women today are learned in Sanskrit, the Vedas, and other scriptures. In fact, the joke now is that Sanskrit is *apauruṣeya*, not in its older meaning as *non-human* but as without *male* students (if the fact that women are more numerous in university Sanskrit classes is any indication of current trends).

From one point of view, the prestige of Sanskrit learning has been marginalized in modern India, and so it could be argued that women are simply taking over domains in which men are no longer interested. But from another point of view, women's expertise in Sanskrit learning can be construed as empowering in traditional terms. At the very least, it enables women to command the sources and offer alternative arguments to defend themselves when stereotypes are imposed on them in the name of tradition. By analogy, the British may have introduced English to produce of a class of English speaking people whom they could keep at the margins of their administrative structure as points of connection with the native people. This does not mean, however, that the introduction of such English education did not ultimately empower the Indians.

CONCLUSION

The end of the millennium will surely not be the end of Hinduism. Although in ferment, it is alive and well. But the end of the millennium certainly is the end of a long history of the subordination of some elite women for gender or caste or stress reasons (though despite this assessment that has led to many reforms, there must have been many women not recorded by history who were happy with their lives; most have always been proud to be Hindu).[63] More Hindu women now have real choices and multiple role models from which to choose, all of which can be integrated into the life cycle in addition to marriage and work: Vedic scholars, satyāgrahinīs, vīrāṅganās, saṃnyāsinīs, and the artistic performance aspect of the gaṇikās. Just what will they do next? Put otherwise, having come of age, what will the new age bring?

NOTES

1. Basham, A.L., *The Wonder That Was India* (New York, Grove Press, 1959: p. 1).

2. Little is known about the Indus civilization because the script has not been deciphered. Because this is true of religion as well, scholars have tended to interpret the history of Indian religions mainly on the basis of ancient texts beginning with the Ṛgveda. Major developments that seem to have no textual precedent have been attributed to vague indigenous or tribal factors. Given the extent and sophistication of the Indus civilization, it stands to reason that there

must have been greater continuity than meets the eye and that much of what goes under the scholarly label of indigenous or tribal are, in point of fact, fragments of the Indus civilization, which were maintained in pockets of the region or as the living practices of certain groups on the margins of Vedic culture. It is also possible that these archaic Indus traditions spread throughout the subcontinent through migrations.

3. The date of the Ṛgveda is currently the subject of great controversy. Until the issue is settled, the author prefers to leave the question open.

4. See the wedding hymn in Ṛgveda 10:85. Viśvāvasu, protector of virgins, transfers his role at the time of marriage to another.

5. Ṛgveda 8:31 mentions how husband and wife worship the gods to attain immortality.

6. Śatapatha Brāhmaṇa I.3.1.12.

7. Here are the author's reasons. (1) Because in the family books of the Ṛgveda, the rituals were relatively simple and education was in the home, women no doubt had the requisite knowledge. Several female ṛṣis, such as Lopamudra, composed Vedic hymns (see Ṛgveda 1:179; 5:28; 8:91 and 10:39–40). If women composed hymns, it is likely that they also recited them in an age of oral literature and home worship. (2) At the minimum, a wife in Ṛgvedic times participated in the rituals by tending the fire, preparing ingredients for the offerings such as thrashing and winnowing the grain and cleaning the sacred area, for the sacred fire was located in domestic space and these were activities generally performed by women (see Ṛgveda 5:28:1; 8:91). (3) When the husband was absent from home, the wife no doubt assumed the role of hostess to insure the mandatory daily offerings to the gods. In this case, she would have to repeat mantras and sing hymns of praise. The Gṛhyasūtras establish a hierarchy for one to do these tasks if the man could not. In some texts, it is the wife who is next in command [see Kane, Pandurang Vaman, *History of Dharmaśāstra: Ancient and Mediaeval Religious and Civil Law* (Poona: Bhandarkar Oriental Research Institute, 1974) vol. 2, part 2, 557;683f]. (4) Even after the Vedic rituals were elaborated and became the domain of priests, women still chanted mantras. And even when the priests took over some of these, they were still spoken in the first person as if the wife herself were chanting them [Jamison, Stephanie W., *Sacrificed Wife/ Sacrificer's Wife: Women, Ritual and Hospitality in Ancient India* (New York: Oxford University Press, 1996) 43]. Jamison also points out that 'there are some tantalizing but slender hints that women could undertake more (*śrauta*) ritual responsibility than the official party line allowed. For example, Manu forbids a Brahman to eat at a sacrifice offered by (among other people) a woman (MDŚ IV.205) ... If such a provision was necessary, it suggests that women had been known to offer independently' (37). She adds that MDŚ XI.36 forbids unmarried young women from acting as priests in the *Agnihotra*. Once again, the very presence of such a law suggests that the contrary practice had occurred.

8. The word 'elite' is used here to indicate the three upper castes (brahmins, kṣatriyas, and vaiśyas). Because their values were often informed by the

brahmanical concepts of *strīdharma* (duties of a woman), they are discussed here as a group. This orientation is sometimes termed brahmanical and the process by which these values are accepted by other groups is called Sanskritization.

9. Kāśikā on Pāṇini IV.1.59 and III.3.21.

10. Jamison, Stephanie W., 1996, op. cit., pp. 53–5.

11. Shastri, Sakuntala Rao, *Women in the Vedic Age* (Bombay: Bharatiya Vidya Bhavan, 1969) pp. 74–85.

12. A text probably written before the Buddhist period and attached to the Ṛgveda as an appendix.

13. Kinsley, David, *Hindu Goddesses: Visions of the Divine Feminine in the Hindu Religious Tradition* (Berkeley: University of California Press, 1986) p. 20.

14. One female symbol is a downward-pointing triangle (representing the mound of Venus). The earliest example of this is a triangle at the centre of a circular platform from an upper paleolithic site in Madhya Pradesh [Jayakar, Pupul, *The Earth Mother* (New Delhi: Penguin Books, 1989) p. 39]. A number of goddess figures have also been found at neolithic sites throughout the subcontinent. On one Indus seal, there is a female figure giving birth to a plant. The association of goddesses and fertility of the crops continues in modern, rural India.

15. The heroine of this epic is Kannaki, whose name literally means 'chastity'. As the chaste wife, she acts for justice (punishing the unjust Paṇṭiya king who wrongly accused her husband Kovalaṉ of stealing the queen's anklet). Women's chastity and morality were closely linked to the king, who, in turn, was responsible for the justice, harmony and fertility of the kingdom.

16. A late strata of the Ṛgveda (1.24.7) depicts a banyan tree in the middle of the sky, an image that is repeated in subsequent texts. 'King Varuṇa holds up the crown of the (heavenly banyan) tree in the bottomless space; those (branches) which hang down have (their) roots above: may these beams of light (*ketavaḥ*) be fixed on us?' (Ṛgveda 1.24.7). See also *Taittirīya Āraṇyaka* 1.11.5; Kaṭha Upaniṣad 6.1; Maitrī Upaniṣad 6.4; and *Bhagavad Gītā* 15.1 in Parpola, Asko, *Deciphering the Indus Script* (Cambridge University Press, 1994) p. 245. The branches of the banyan are compared to the rays of the sun and the invisible ropes that are said to connect the seven stars of the Great Bear to the Pole Star located in the north. The same Tamil word *vaṭa* means rope, banyan, and north (Parpola, pp. 240–5). If one of the languages of the Indus culture was Dravidian or vaṭa was a loan word into Dravidian, then this homophony explains these unusual symbolic connections.

17. According to the law-giver Yama (ca. 200 BCE), women were not to pronounce the vaidika (Vedic) mantras, yet another indication of women's growing marginalization in Vedic rituals. Manu (ca. 100 BCE–200 CE) said the same and equated the ritual of marriage with the ritual of upanayana for men, a woman's service to her husband with a male student's service to his teacher, and her household tasks with the public (śrauta) rituals performed by a man. Though

Manu allowed married women to perform the domestic rituals, he did not want those who did not know the Vedas and rituals to perform them for clients—presumably, in the capacity of priests. All of this is symbolized by the sacred syllable *om*. The texts where it first appears (Yajurveda and *Jaiminīya Brāhmaṇa*) make no prohibitions about women pronouncing it: *Taittirīya Brāhmaṇa* (2:11) associates the syllable with knowing Brahman as real (*satya*), knowledge (*jñāna*) and infinity (*ananta*). The Upaniṣads associate it with the three Vedas and Brahman beyond them, the bliss of salvation, as well as the fulfilment of desires in worldly life (children, cattle, long life, and fame). The Dharmasūtras and Gṛhyasūtras more explicitly connect it with the upanayana or sacred-thread ritual that marks the beginning of Vedic study and the *gāyatrī mantra* and *sandhyā* (the daily ritual performed at sunrise, noon and sunset). By the fourth century CE, it is possible that women were having trouble even with domestic rituals. Kātyāyana, for instance, suggests that if a woman cannot do it herself, then several women should try to do it together. See Young, Katherine K., 'Om, the Vedas, and the Status of Women with Special Reference to Śrīvaiṣṇavism' in *Jewels of the Vedic Authority* edited by Laurie Patton (Oxford University Press, forthcoming).

18. This is evident in five contexts; royal women who followed their husbands into exile in the forests and practised asceticism; royal wives who accompanied their husbands (former kings who in old age handed over their kingdoms to their sons and withdrew to the forest for penance, sometimes culminating in self-willed death by drowning or self-immolation); brahmanical wives who lived with their sage-husbands in the forest; female ascetics who lived in groups headed by brahmanical preceptors and independent, female ascetics (Young, Katherine K., 'Vaidika Images in the Hindu Epics and their Implications for a Sitz im Leben' (Paper presented at the American Academy of Religion, Chicago, 1994).

19. Yama, one of the authors of the Dharmaśāstras, for instance, spoke out against female ascetics.

20. In any case, until the modern period, Hindu female asceticism rarely developed an institutional basis in the sects that acknowledged the authority of the Vedas (though the Mitaksara on Yajñavālkya's Dharmaśāstras 3.58 quotes an aphorism by Baudhāyana that some ācāryas accept it. There were probably always a few ascetics such as the female wanderer Śaṅkarā mentioned by Patañjali in his *Mahābhāṣya*.

21. *Manu* 5.155.

22. *Manu* 5.147–148; cf. *Manu* 9.2–3.

23. Young, Katherine K., 'Om the Vedas, and the Status of Women'. Op. cit.

24. Gatwood, Lynn E., *Devi and the Spouse Goddess* (Riverdale, Maryland: The Riverdale Co., 1985) pp. 159–60.

25. Young, Katherine K., 'Hinduism' in *Women in World Religions*, 1987, p. 74. This can be explained from a psychoanalytic perspective as the projection of the girl's idealized image of father on to husband (and when that does not succeed, on to god or guru).

26. Self-willed death was antithetical to Ṛgvedic values, which viewed the ideal life to consist of one hundred years.

27. Bangles, a prominent feminine symbol, can be traced back to the Indus culture as well. One of the Indus female statues wears many bangles on her arms as do some of the figures on the seals. Descriptions of women adorned with bangles are also found in the earliest Tamil texts (from about 100 BCE).

28. Jayakar, Pupul, op. cit., p. 85.

29. See *Yajñavalkya* 1:121; *Mahābhārata* 12:319:87ff; 12:60:36; *Mārkaṇḍeya Purāṇa* 28.7–8; *Brahmāṇḍa Purāṇa* 3:12:19 and the texts *Vaijavāpagṛhyasūtra* and *Vajrasūci*.

30. Young, Katherine K., op. cit., p. 78.

31. Ramanuja, A.K., 'On Women Saints', *The Divine Consort Radha and the Goddesses of India* edited by John Stratton Hawley and Donna Marie Wulff (Berkeley: Graduate Theological Union, 1982) pp. 316–24.

32. Perhaps the most famous example of right-handed tantra was the nineteenth century Bengali brahmin man named Ramakrishna. Initiated by a wandering female (brahmin) member of the Shākta Bhairavi, he symbolically practised tantra with her. After he married Sarada Devi (a marriage that was never consummated), he worshipped his wife as a manifestation of Kālī in the temple at Dakṣineśvar, an act which prompted an hour-long *samādhi* (state of ecstatic bliss) by both him and his wife. Ramakrishna viewed Kālī as consisting of all qualities, who was ultimately pure love, though her outward appearance was frightening, an intriguing illusion (māyā) that had to be pierced to reveal the divine (and non-dual) love of the Mother of the universe. Despite his early tantric training, Ramakrishna approached Kālī primarily through the bhakti relationship of child to mother. As a result, he emphasized her maternal rather than erotic aspect. Even when she was Śiva's wife, she was dominant: 'Erect She stands on Shiva's bosom, and the earth trembles under Her tread' [Kinsley, David R., *The Sword and the Flute: Kālī & Kṛṣṇa: Dark Visions of the Terrible and the Sublime in Hindu Mythology* (Berkeley: University of California Press, 1975) p. 121].

33. Narayanan, Vasudha, 'Brimming with *Bhakti*, Embodiments of *Shakti*: Devotees, Deities, Performers, Reformers, and Other Women of Power in the Hindu Tradition' in *Feminism and World Religions* edited by Arvind Sharma and Katherine K. Young (Albany: State University of New York Press, 1999) p. 53.

34. Oldenburg, Veena Talwar, 'Lifestyle as Resistance: The Case of the Courtesans of Lucknow', in *Contesting Power: Resistance and Everyday Social Relations in South Asia* edited by Douglas Haynes and Gyan Prakash (Berkeley: University of California Press, 1991) p. 23.

35. Oldenburg, Veena Talwar, op. cit., p. 29 quoting a nineteenth century letter.

36. Young, Katherine K., op. cit., p. 89.

37. This discussion is based on the assessment of the Āgamas and Cola

inscriptions by Leslie C. Orr, 'Women in Hindu Temple Ritual', *The Annual Review of Women in World Religions* vol. III edited by Arvind Sharma and Katherine K. Young (Albany: State University of New York Press, 1994) pp. 105–41.

38. Orr, Leslie C., op. cit., p. 119.

39. The struggle of men over the status of women was related to their own status and courage. Many in Calcutta, for instance, took up wrestling to counter their fears of weakness and effeminacy, guilty that these might have contributed to foreign rule.

40. Narayanan, Vasudha, 1999, op. cit., pp. 57–62.

41. Hansen, Kathryn, 'Heroic Modes of Women in Indian Myth, Ritual and History: The Tapasvinī and the Vīrāṅganā' in *The Annual Review of Women in World Religions*, vol. II. *Heroic Women* edited by Arvind Sharma and Katherine K. Young (Albany: State University of New York Press, 1992), pp. 26–36.

42. *Narajivan* 28 June, 1925. *The Collected Works of Mahatma Gandhi*, vol. XXVII (Ahmedabad: Navajivan Trust, 1982), p. 126.

43. *Narajivan* 28 June 1925. *The Collected Works of Mahatma Gandhi*, vol. XXVII, p. 307.

44. Kishwar, Madhu, 'Gandhi on Women', *Economic and Political Weekly*, 5 October 1985.

45. Falk, Nancy A., '*Shakti* Ascending: Hindu Women, Politics, and Religious Leadership during the Nineteenth and Twentieth Centuries', *Religion in Modern India*, edited by Robert D. Baird, third edition (New Delhi: Manohar, 1995), pp. 298–334.

46. Young, Katherine K., 'Women in Hinduism', *Today's Woman in World Religions* (Albany: State University of New York Press, 1993), pp. 87–92.

47. Young, Katherine K., 1993, pp. 92–7.

48. Young, Katherine K., 1993, pp. 111–13.

49. Basu, Amrita, 'Feminism Inverted: The Real Women and Gendered Imagery of Hindu Nationalism', *Bulletin of Concerned Asian Scholars* 25/4 (1993) 3–4: 32.

50. Ibid., p. 31.

51. Ibid., p. 30.

52. Ibid., p. 35.

53. Narayanan, Vasudha, 1999, op. cit., p. 28.

54. Gatwood, Lynn E., 1985, op. cit., pp. 142–3.

55. Falk, Nancy A., op. cit., pp. 299–300.

56. Denton, Lynn Teskey, 'Varieties of Hindu Female Asceticism', in *Roles and Rituals for Hindu Women* edited by Julia Leslie (Delhi: Motilal Banarsidass, 1991), pp. 211–33.

57. King, Ursula, 'The Effect of Social Change on Religious Self-understanding: Women Ascetics in Modern Hinduism', *Changing South Asia: Religion and Society* edited by K. Ballhatchet and D. Taylor (London: Asian Research, 1984), 80. Also Johnsen, Linda, 'Women Saints of India', *Yoga Journal* (no. 81,

July/August 1988), 52. Also Clementin-Ojha, Catherine, 'The Tradition of Female Gurus', *Manushi* no. 31, 1985), pp. 2–8 and 'Feminine Asceticism in Hinduism: Its Tradition and Present Condition', *Man in India*, 61/3 (1981), pp. 254–83.

58. White, Charles S., 'Mother Guru: Jñānānanda of Madras, India', in *Unspoken Worlds: Women's Religious Lives in Non-Western Cultures* edited by N.A. Falk and R.M. Gross (New York: Harper and Row, 1980), pp. 22–37.

59. Narayanan, Vasudha, 1999, *India Today*, 15 August 1994, p. 26.

60. The following analysis is from Katherine K. Young and Lily Miller, 'Sacred Biography and the Restructuring of Society: A Study of Anandamayi Ma, Lady-Saint of Modern Hinduism' in *Boeings and Bullock Carts: Indian Civilization in its Local, Regional and National Aspects* (Delhi: Chanakya Publications), pp. 112–47.

61. Young, Katherine K. and Lily Miller, op. cit., p. 142.

62. Young, Katherine K. and Lily Miller, quoting Marlin, 1987, p. 5.

63. In fairness to brahmin men who, as the authors of normative texts, have been blamed for stereotyping and subordinating Hindu women, we should remember that this occurred in every major civilization and was often a function of unprecedented social problems such as the stress experienced by foreign invasions and rule that took time to understand or ameliorate. For that reason, we have been attentive in this chapter to historical changes and their underlying reasons and admit that it was not always possible for men to be self-conscious of what was occurring in society. Even patriarchal history has a human face (which is not to excuse such behaviour once society has become conscious of it).

Women and Buddhism in India

Nancy J. Barnes

Gautama the Buddha attained enlightenment more than 2000 years ago in north-eastern India after undergoing years of rigorous asceticism and intensive meditation. Men and women quickly gathered around him to learn the path he had followed to reach the ultimate goal, and to hear him explain the insight he had gained into the true nature of existence.[1] This group of dedicated followers practising what they had learned from their teacher became the core of the new religion that grew from the Buddha's own experience. Some of the followers left their homes and families to follow the Buddha's path, and the Buddha welcomed them as *bhikṣu* and *bhikṣunī*, male and female religious mendicants, thus establishing one of the world's first monastic orders.[2] The Buddha's community of disciples, the *saṃgha*, also included laymen and laywomen, the most pious of whom committed themselves to a particular set of disciplinary rules and came to be known as *upāsaka* and *upāsikā*, male and female devotees.[3]

To his disciples, the Buddha taught a middle way between asceticism and worldly indulgence, a life of moderation and moral responsibility. His insight into the nature of existence and into the possibility of liberation from the round of rebirths to which all beings are bound came to be formulated in Buddhist scriptures (*sūtras*) as the *four noble truths*: (1) pain and unhappiness are inherent in the experiences of all beings; (2) pain and unhappiness are caused by self-centred desire; (3) liberation (*nirvāṇa*) from desire, pain and unhappiness is possible; (4) the Noble

Eight-fold path of meditation and moral discipline is the way to liberating wisdom.[4] The Buddha could point out the path to his disciples, and inspire them by the example of his own accomplishment, but it was up to each of them to reach the goal through his or her personal efforts. It was not a question of faith, but of actively taking responsibility for one's own spiritual victory.

According to the scriptures, many of the disciples did attain nirvāṇa during the Buddha's own lifetime. When one of the many visitors who came to listen to the Buddha asked him skeptically whether any of his followers had ever really succeeded in freeing themselves from desire and attachment and had attained liberating wisdom, the Buddha declared that hundreds and hundreds had already done so, and that among these victors were as many nuns as monks, as many lay women as men.[5] Women, indeed, were just as significant as men among the avid followers of the Buddha's path, and among the dedicated supporters of the Buddha and his saṃgha.

Early Buddhism upto ca. 300 CE: Laywomen and Nuns

Laywomen

Lay followers of the Buddha provided vital economic support to his saṃgha. Lay benefactors mentioned in Buddhist scriptures, and those whose gifts are recorded in inscriptions at Buddhist monastic centers, were most often members of the prosperous landowning agricultural class, wealthy merchants, skilled artisans, or workers of various kinds. These were the socio-economic groups that formed the economic foundation of the prosperous new monarchical states that were forming during the Buddha's lifetime, and that flourished for centuries afterward. These groups were also strongly attracted to the Buddha's new religion.

Laywomen offered economic support to the monastic saṃgha and contributed funds to the construction of *stūpas* and *caityas* where they and their fellow Buddhists could go to venerate the Buddha.[6] Sūtras and *Vinayas* recount the generosity and piety of many such women, and hundreds of inscriptions recording the gifts of laywomen to Buddhist monuments and monastic communities all over India have been discovered by modern archaeologists. Such financial supports from the laity was required in order for the religion to flourish. Bhikṣunī and bhikṣu were religious mendicants, and although their life style in the early days was extremely simple, they were never expected to be self-supporting. It was the laity who gave them food when they went on daily alms rounds in the towns or villages near which they were staying, or invited them to their homes for special meals. Lay people also supplied them with new robes and other necessities at the end of the rainy season. The lay donors earned merit for their gifts, which would help them to better future rebirths. Frequent contact with monastics also provided the opportunity for lay people to hear them explain the Buddha's *dharma* (his teachings, the truth he had realized at the time of his enlightenment), which would aid their gradual spiritual progress towards the ultimate Buddhist goal of nirvāṇa. Texts and inscriptions show that men and women both gave generously to the saṃgha. But it was most often the woman of the house who met a monk or a nun at her door and offered them alms.

Laywomen also made gifts to building projects at Buddhist monuments, of or were members of royal families or of families sometimes very substantial gifts. Many of these donors were wives or daughters of merchants, court officials. They had ample resources and they controlled these resources themselves, for many of their gifts were made in their own names without the direct involvement of family members. In some cases, the husbands of these generous donors were probably not Buddhists; thus the women made their gifts individually. Such cases are easiest to identify when the donor is a queen, and it is known from other inscriptions that her husband made his own gifts to a Hindu or a Jain community.

Some of the gifts from women were very grand and costly. For example, most of the extant parts of the elaborate stone railing that once surrounded the caitya of the Bodhi Tree at Bodh Gaya, the place where the Buddha attained enlightenment, were gifted by a queen, Kuraṅgī, whose devotion to the religion seems to have finally inspired her to become a bhikṣunī in her old age (ca. first century BCE). At Mathura during the Kuṣāṇa period (first to fourth centuries CE) a respectable woman named Amohāssi dedicated a large image of the Buddha and also the *vihāra*, the monastic dwelling, where it was placed. The sister of the Ikṣvāku king Vāśiṣṭhiputra Chāṁtamūla (third century CE) contributed lavishly to the construction of the *Mahācaitya* at Nagarjunakonda in present day Andhra Pradesh.[7] Laywomen of more modest means also gave to Buddhist establishments, and their gifts of a paving or a railing stone were carefully recorded as well.

According to sūtras and vinayas, laywomen's full participation in the new religion was welcomed. As followers of the Buddha, no distinctions were made between their capacities and men's. As members of the larger society, however, women and men had different roles to fill, and Buddhist texts have no argument with the traditional ordering of society. There are some sūtras in the Buddhist canon that are explicitly directed toward laywomen or laymen; in them women and men are counselled to fulfil their social roles responsibly. Both genders are urged to adhere to the same standards of conduct in their different roles: be diligent and prudent in order to preserve the household's prosperity; be respectful and kind to family members and other dependants; be generous to religious mendicants; and in all things avoid jealousy, ill temper, vengefulness and lust.[8] Lay women appear often in the Vinaya, where they function as helpful critics of the conduct of monks and nuns. Visākhā, the wealthy, generous and intelligent matriarch of a prominent merchant family in the city of Śrāvastī, figures prominently in the Vinaya and in several other texts. She was born into a Buddhist family, and remained a major supporter of the saṃgha during her whole long life. On occasion, she also tactfully offered suggestions to the Buddha about ways to help the lives of Buddhist monastics run more smoothly in a society that was not predominantly Buddhist. Visākhā is the archetype of the devoted laywoman in Buddhist literature.[9]

The saṃgha depended on laywomen as well as laymen for their well-being, and the relations between monastics and laywomen described in the scriptures are mutually respectful. In general, the attitude toward women found in the scriptures is positive. But although the scriptures are traditionally believed to preserve the actual words and teachings of the Buddha and his immediate disciples, the texts were transmitted orally for a few hundred years, and even after they were committed to writing in the first century BCE, they continued to be modified and edited by generations of monk interpreters. It is impossible now to determine how much of the extant texts represent the Buddha's own views, and how much the views of monks of his own time and of the succeeding generations. Concerning women, the texts do reveal diverse judgements. There are some hostile passages that denounce women as deadly temptresses who are by nature addicted to sex, who are faithless and deceitful, greedy and foolish—in sum, a danger to men, above all a danger to men who strive to live the religious life and realize their own inherent spirituality.[10] Such viciously misogynist outbursts are relatively rare in the scriptures preserved by the early Buddhist schools, and seem to reflect a period after the Buddha's death when the monastic saṃgha was making itself into an organized institution with a strict hierarchical structure.[11] Within the saṃgha, leadership was reserved for men. This was also the value that prevailed in the larger society, and was sanctioned in the scriptures.[12] Even Visākhā, who, as she is depicted in the scriptures, would have been a natural leader, is shown to be always discreet and careful to recognize the superior status of the men in her family and in the saṃgha.

Nuns

Some women longed to leave ordinary home life altogether so that they could devote themselves completely to the religious life. The Buddha welcomed them to his saṃgha, just as he welcomed men who felt the same vocation. He clearly asserted that women's spiritual capacities were equal to men's and, according to the scriptures, many bhikṣunī were able to quickly attain liberating insight after diligent practice of meditation. Several of these women are said to have been praised by the Buddha for their learning and for their skill as teachers of lay people and other nuns. The opportunity to lead such a life of personal spiritual development, study and teaching, without time-consuming family obligations, offered possibilities to women that were unusual in the society of the Buddha's day. Life as a bhikṣunī was an extremely important addition to the choices open to women in ancient India.[13]

Although women were recognized to be no different from men in their spiritual abilities and attainments, as the saṃgha gained in popularity and found its place in the larger society, the structure of the organization became a matter of concern to the monastics and probably to their lay supporters as well. Questions about what should be the relative status of bhikṣu and bhikṣunī, and who would fill the leadership positions in the community, were raised. The answers arrived at were explained in a story of how the bhikṣunī saṃgha came to be founded. This story, although it was probably composed many generations after the first bhikṣunī was ordained and cannot be taken to be an accurate recounting of a historical event, came to be the accepted account of the founding of the bhikṣunī saṃgha and was incorporated into the canons of all the Buddhist schools. It is now the tradition that is believed by most of the world's Buddhists.[14]

According to this story, five years after the Buddha had attained enlightenment and had founded the bhikṣu saṃgha, he returned to the city of his birth to teach the dharma to his relatives and countrymen. Many people joined his saṃgha; several men became bhikṣu. Mahāprajāpatī, the Buddha's aunt and foster-mother, who had raised him after his mother died, came to him with a group of women and asked to be accepted into the monastic order. He refused her request three times; she went away dejected and in tears. But she and her friends did not give up. They shaved their heads as the monks did and put on saffron robes, then followed the Buddha for many miles as he journeyed on to another city. Mahāprajāpatī prepared to go to the Buddha again at the place where he had stopped, but hesitated outside the gate and began to weep.

The Buddha's attendant monk, Ānanda, who was her kinsman as well as the Buddha's, found the venerable lady there all tear-stained, dust-covered, and with feet swollen from walking so far. Surprised and alarmed, he asked why she was crying, and she told him she longed to follow the Buddha's path as a female mendicant, but he had rejected her plea. Moved by pity, Ānanda decided to intervene with the Buddha on her behalf, but his request, too, was rebuffed. Then Ānanda asked the Buddha whether women as well as men were capable of attaining spiritual perfection, and the Buddha affirmed that they were. Thereupon Ānanda reminded him how Mahāprajāpatī had nurtured him as a child, and then he repeated his request that she and her companions be accepted into the order. Finally the Buddha agreed, provided she would accept eight strict rules that would apply only to bhikṣunī: (1) that every bhikṣunī, even if she has been ordained a hundred years, shall rise and salute every monk, even if he was just ordained that very day; (2) a bhikṣunī must spend the rainy season only in a place where there is a bhikṣu; (3) every half month, the bhikṣunī must request the exhortation of dharma from the monks, and instructions as to when the fortnightly Uposatha ceremony is to be performed; (4) at the end of the rainy season, the bhikṣunī must report any misdeeds she might have committed, before the bhikṣu saṃgha as well as before the bhikṣunī saṃgha; (5) a bhikṣunī who has transgressed a Vinaya rule must submit to discipline by both the bhikṣu and bhikṣunī saṃghas; (6) a bhikṣunī must be ordained by both the bhikṣu and bhikṣunī saṃghas; (7) a bhikṣunī must never abuse or revile a monk; (8) a bhikṣu may formally admonish a bhikṣunī, but she may not admonish him.

Mahāprajāpatī gladly agreed to accept the eight rules. Her acceptance served as her ordination, and she thus became the first bhikṣunī. Her companions were soon ordained as well. The narrative concludes with the Buddha's prophecy that because women have been accepted into the order, the dharma will endure for only 500 years rather than the 1,000 it would have lasted with them.

The Buddha's initial unwillingness, in the story, to allow women to leave their family responsibilities with his sanction and his announcement that the presence of nuns in the saṃgha would undermine the future success of the religion appear to be concessions to prevailing ideas about the proper roles of men and women in society, and the danger that could result if those roles were undermined. But this compromise with social attitudes is balanced in the story by the Buddha's acknowledgement that, in spiritual matters, women are the equals of men. The fact that Buddhists did recognize the ability of women to reach the ultimate spiritual goal was what attracted women to the religion in the first place. Buddhism offered women a way of life that was not easily available in the larger Indian society. However, once women had been incorporated into the saṃgha as bhikṣunī, it became necessary to establish their position in it vis-ā-vis the bhikṣu. The eight strict rules establish a clear hierarchy in the saṃgha that requires nuns to defer to monks in all formal matters. The eight rules proclaim to monks and laity that leadership roles and superior status as practitioners of the Buddha's way are reserved for monks. Mahāprajāpatī's acceptance of the rules reiterates real nuns' agreement to this hierarchical structure. The story of the founding of the bhikṣunī saṃgha publicly proclaims that the formal structure of the saṃgha reflects that of the society around it: Buddhism would be no threat to the values that governed lay society.

Bhikṣunīs were not inhibited in their spiritual progress by the eight rules, or by the hundreds of other precepts the Vinaya requires them to keep. They quietly disciplined themselves, practised mental concentration, and finally experienced awakening, or nirvāṇa. Some of them proclaimed their struggle and their success in verses, that came to be collected in the *Therīgāthā*, the Songs of the Nuns.[15] After much striving, Paṭācārā's nirvāṇa was triggered by watching her lamp go out.

> I washed my feet, and paid attention to the waters; and seeing the foot-water come flowing downhill from the high land to the low land, then I concentrated my mind, like a noble thoroughbred horse.
> Then I took a lamp and I entered my cell. I inspected the bed, and sat on the couch.
> Then I took a needle and drew out the wick. The complete release of my mind was like the quenching of the lamp.[16]

Sīhā's vain struggle to free herself from sensual desire drove her to the point of suicide:

> Thin, pale, and wan, I wandered for seven years; being very pained.
> I did not find happiness by day or night.
> Then taking a rope, I went into a wood, thinking 'It is better to hang myself than to lead a low life again'.
> I made a strong noose, and tied it to the branch of a tree. I cast the noose around my neck.
> Then my mind was completely released.[17]

Bhikṣunīs were not prevented from studying the dharma either by the strict rules imposed on them. The scriptures contain traditions about some whose understanding reached the highest level, such as Dhammadinnā who was praised by the Buddha for her brilliant explanation of dharma to her own learned former husband, and Khemā who taught King Pasenadi of Kosala.[18]

The idea that such levels of understanding could be attained by women did not go unchallenged, however. A very old scripture puts the challenge into the mouth of the mythological figure of the god Māra, the personification of worldly attachment. Coming upon a bhikṣunī named Somā, who was resting alone in the forest, he taunted her with the charge that she lacked the ability to attain understanding:

> That vantage-ground the sages may attain
> Is hard to win. With her two-finger wit
> That may no woman ever hope to achieve.

She countered with a challenge of her own, that sent Māra away, defeated:

> What should the woman's nature signify
> When consciousness is tense and firmly set,
> When knowledge rolls ever on, when she
> By insight rightly comprehends the Dharma?
> To one for whom the question arises:
> Am I a woman, or
> Am I a man, or what not am I then?
> To such a one is Māra fit to talk.[19]

It is the conventional notion that women are intellectually and spiritually inferior to men that is rejected here. Buddhist scriptures like this one clearly affirm the equality of women and men in such matters; it is only the deluded who insist that gender distinctions should be made.

Women like Dhammadinnā and Khemā were not only very learned, they were skilled at teaching others. Paṭācārā was a teacher, but she is renowned in the Therīgāthā not so much for her ability to expound dharma as for being an inspiration and a compassionate guide to other women on the Buddhist path.[20] Learned women who were teachers and guides also appear in inscriptions found at Buddhist monuments. A second century BCE donor to the stūpa at Sanchi is called *sutatika* or 'one who knows the scriptures'. The nun Buddhamitrā, who was *trepiṭaka*, 'master of the three collections of scriptures', was, with her teacher, the monk Bala, the donor of the earliest known images of Buddha. Her name appears in three inscriptions on early images that are believed to date from the first century CE. At Sanchi, six female pupils honoured their women teachers in inscriptions recording gifts they made to the stūpas;

five teachers are named, and although they are not specifically called bhikṣunī, it is probable that they were nuns.[21] These inscriptions are evidence that real women outside the scriptural accounts were recognized for their learning, just as men were. However, most nuns' inscriptions simply call the women bhikṣunī, and make no comment about their accomplishments. By contrast, a great many of the monks' inscriptions call them by religious titles having to do with their status and their attainments. This does not prove that there were fewer accomplished nuns than monks active in early Buddhist communities, just as the fact that fewer learned bhikṣunīs than bhikṣus are named in the scriptures does not necessarily mean that women were less likely to attain success in the saṃgha. The scriptures were recorded and preserved by monks, and they gave prominence to their male monastic predecessors. Donative inscriptions from the second century BCE to the first century CE include roughly equal numbers by monks and nuns. So nuns were clearly very active as donors and supporters of the faith. It seems to have been the convention to identify a female monastic only by the term bhikṣunī and by the place of her birth or her residence—the same convention that was used for laymen and laywomen. A bhikṣu, on the other hand, would be honoured by a list of his religious titles, and the place he hailed from would often not even be mentioned, for it was his spiritual accomplishments that truly identified him—this was the convention for bhikṣu. In the hierarchy within the saṃgha, the bhikṣunī's status was between that of the bhikṣu and the laity. In short, the higher status of male monastics was regularly recognized in formal contexts like inscriptions, just as their higher status was insisted on in the scriptures.

Inscriptions of nuns and monks were recorded on the building stones they donated to stūpas or caityas at cult centres such as Sanchi, or on the images they gave to monastic communities. Scholars had long assumed that all Buddhist monastics had given up all their personal wealth and taken vows of poverty when they joined the order, for the scriptures say that they received their daily sustenance from the laity.[22] The abundance of nuns' and monks' donative inscriptions at sacred sites reveals, however, that they did not have to renounce their personal property—they could maintain control of what they had owned before their ordination, and many of them chose to make generous use of their wealth for religious purposes. Nuns were just as frequent donors at sacred sites as monks. Thus, just as the inscriptions show that Buddhist laywomen had control of their property and used it to support their religion, they show that Buddhist nuns did too; and all these women were every bit as active as donors as were men. The cult centres, the images, and the material well-being of the monastic communities were the creation of women and men, monastic and lay, working together.[23]

Stūpas were erected over the remains of some of the Buddha's most revered disciples, his contemporaries, such as Śāriputra and Mahāmaudgalyāyana. Later, stūpas were also erected over the ashes of respected local teachers and spiritual leaders. Surviving inscriptions have identified several such structures and the monks commemorated in them. No known inscriptions commemorate any stūpa erected for a revered nun. The *Theravāda Vinaya* recounts that once some nuns did build a stūpa for the remains of an especially venerated sister. But when a senior monk found them honouring her there, he was annoyed and demolished the mound before their eyes. It was not rebuilt.[24] Since inscriptions at major Buddhist cults centres like Sanchi clearly indicate that nuns had the will and the financial resources to support building projects, it may be that they were discouraged by the monks who led the local saṃghas from establishing stūpas that might become rival cult centres and divert the attentions of nuns and their female disciples from the monk's stūpas.[25] Evidence from the *Apadānas*, stories of the lives of great nuns and monks, has led at least one scholar to conclude that a cult focused on Mahāprajāpatī, the founder of the bhikṣunī saṃgha, did exist in the last few centuries BCE, and that nuns and monks participated in religious festivals honouring her and other renowned bhikṣunī and bhikṣu. However, no remains of a stūpa for Mahāprajāpatī, at which such celebrations might have been held, have been discovered.[26] It appears that, in real life as well as in the scriptures, the unity of the saṃgha and the relative hierarchical status of monks and nuns were carefully maintained under the monks' control.

BUDDHISM UP TO CA. 1500 CE: MAHĀYĀNA, TANTRA AND WOMEN'S PRACTICES

Laywomen, Nuns and Changes in Buddhism

Inscriptions and archaeological remains from ancient times right up to the disappearance of Buddhism from most of India demonstrate that laywomen continued to be important worshippers of the Buddha and supporters of monastic communities, sponsoring the construction of caitya halls and monasteries in both north and south India. Few inscriptions survive, however, that record donations by nuns after about the third century CE. In fact, nuns are occasionally mentioned as recipients of donations in inscriptions, and in literary works: the famous monk,

Vasubandhu, had a residence built for a group of nuns at Pataliputra in the fifth century; and a ninth century inscription commemorates a grant to a large monastery in eastern India that included a community of nuns living near the monks.[27] The Chinese pilgrim-scholars, Fa-hien and I-tsing, commented on nuns they saw during their travels in India in the early fifth and the late seventh centuries, respectively. I-tsing described their dress and customs, and noted that they seemed to live a poor and simple life.[28] During these centuries when the nuns left so few traces, however, the great Buddhist monasteries and centres of learning at places such as Nalanda and Valabhi exerted remarkable international influence, attracting scholars from all over the Buddhist world, and receiving the lavish support of foreign rulers as well as of Indian kings and queens. This is when scholarly Indian monks reached the apogee of their fame as masters of Buddhist philosophy, and the works of dozens of them have come down to us. Indian nuns were hardly noticed in documents and inscriptions from these brilliant centuries. Why is this so?

It seems that the hierarchical structure of the saṃgha that reserved leadership positions for monks and assigned nuns to secondary rank in all the formal affairs of the community did eventually impact the fortunes of women monastics after the third century. Wherever nuns were living, whatever they were doing in their own communities, they were evidently not at the centre of Budhhist intellectual life. Consequently, their activities were no longer recorded. This absence of documentation of nuns' activities is true throughout India, and in most communities about which any information has survived. Monks are known to have belonged to several different schools of Buddhism during these centuries, some of which differed in their interpretation of Vinaya rules, others differed in their philosophical commentary on doctrine. No evidence indicates that nuns played a role of any importance in the activities of any of these schools, not even in the new Buddhist school that became known as the Mahāyāna, the Great Vehicle that all beings can ride to enlightenment.[29]

Mahāyāna Buddhism

Sometime between about 100 BCE and 100 CE, a new movement emerged among Indian Buddhists, with new scriptures that their promulgators declared were the true words of the Buddha. The ideas in these sūtras had evolved gradually from the ideas and practices in earlier Buddhist scriptures. The new sūtras taught that a true disciple of the Buddha should aspire to more than personal liberation from suffering (nirvāṇa). A true disciple should become a *bodhisattva*, a heroic being committed to the future attainment of complete and prefect enlightenment: that is, he or she should aspire to become a Buddha. The motivation for such a commitment, which would take countless lifetimes to realize, was compassion for all the beings in the world who were overwhelmed by suffering but could be helped by a bodhisattva who had perfected his or her own wisdom to a high degree. Theoretically, the bodhisattva's way could be practised by both men and women.

The earliest of the new scriptures, the *Prajñāpāramitā Sūtras* (Perfection of Wisdom), explicitly taught that all conventional distinctions we ordinarily make between beings, including gender distinctions, are illusory. They are empty (*śūnya*) of real meaning, they are not the ultimate truth. To attain enlightenment, one must abandon all such distinction making. When one reads the Prajñāpāramitā Sūtras, one may conclude that this was a religion that openly recognized the perfect spiritual equality of women and men.

Although Mahāyāna scriptures were produced in India from about 100 BCE on,[30] there is no evidence in inscriptions from any Indian Buddhist archaeological sites that the new movement made any impact until the fourth or fifth century of the Common Era. When inscriptions of Mahāyāna followers do begin to appear in the fourth and fifth centuries, they almost exclusively record gifts of monks to Buddhist monuments. Nuns seem rarely to have been involved in recorded religious activities of Mahāyāna Buddhists.[31] Mahāyāna sūtras normally open with a description of the enormous audience that had heard the Buddha preach the contents of these scriptures, and bhikṣunī as well as bhikṣu and lay people are said to have been present . Thus the authors of the Mahāyāna scriptures self-consciously included women in the new dispensation, but evidence of any strong presence of Mahāyāna nuns in real Indian Buddhist communities is not to be found in inscriptions.

Mahāyāna sūtras and philosophical works (*śāstras*) do affirm that women as well as men can be bodhisattvas. However, although a bodhisattva will spend many lifetimes perfecting her or his compassion and wisdom, ultimately this being will become a Buddha. The question is, then, can a woman be a Buddha? It was a question that had been raised by monks in other Buddhist schools also, not just by followers of the Mahāyāna, and some had clearly stated that only a man could be a Buddha. A fully enlightened Buddha could only have a male body, for that body is the visible and inevitable consequence of a being's perfection of wisdom and virtue, gradually accomplished during countless rebirths in this world. To be born with a woman's body is proof that she has not advanced spiritually to the highest level.[32] The Buddha is the most perfect of beings, and his body is the epitome of male bodies. It alone bears all the physical marks (*lakṣaṇa*) of the Great Being, the *Mahāpuruṣa.*[33]

This argument that the male is spiritually superior to the female goes far beyond the views expressed in the sūtras, vinayas, and inscriptions discussed earlier. It is a symptom of a hardening of attitudes toward all women, even those who had dedicated themselves to the religious life. Women's secondary rank in the formal saṃgha hierarchy had already been established, and now women's spiritual status was declared inferior as well. In the light of such developments in Buddhists' thinking, it is not surprising to find that nuns were no longer at the centres of Buddhist religious activities, dedicating monuments, and studying and teaching at centres of learning. Suggestions can be made about why mainstream Buddhist thinking turned against women. Social changes connected with the rise of Hinduism and the reassertion of Brahmanic values probably played a role. As Hinduism expanded, Buddhism lost popular support, and debates among Buddhists about their own doctrinal positions were probably influenced by the Buddhists' public debates with leading Hindu thinkers. These are speculations, but whatever provoked the widespread Buddhist reaction against women's spiritual capacities, one result is obvious—nuns disappeared from the records, and thus from our view.

Mahāyāna monks relegated women to a secondary position just as surely as did monks of the Theravāda and other Buddhist schools. But the authors of some Mahāyāna scriptures, at least, did try to reconcile the non-dualistic thinking of the Prajñāpāramitā Sūtras with the controversy over women's bodies and women's spiritual aspirations and possibilities. The *Saddharmapuṇḍarīka* (*Lotus Sūtra*), the *Vimalakīrtinirdeśa*, and several less well known sūtras, introduce women who exceed all monks and bodhisattvas in wisdom and spiritual development, and become Buddhas on the spot.[34] In the Lotus Sūtra,the bodhisattva Mañjuśrī tells the other male bodhisattvas, who have assembled to hear the Buddha teach, that she has found one person who is supremely capable of understanding the message of Lotus Sūtra, can put it into practice, and as a result can immediately become a Buddha. This person is the eight-year old daughter of the Dragon King. The girl suddenly appears among the bodhisattvas.[35] The monk Śāriputra, the wisest of the Buddha's disciples, speaks for all the skeptics in the assembly and challenges her, saying that no matter what she has already accomplished, her female body will prevent her from reaching the ultimate goal, becoming a Buddha. Instead of answering him, she turns to the Buddha himself, and presents him with a precious jewel she has brought with her from her father's realm. He immediately accepts it. She says, 'Now you shall see me achieve Buddhahood even more quickly than the Lord accepted my gift.' And before their eyes her body changes into that of a male bodhisattva, and then at once she becomes a Buddha with all the characteristic marks of the Mahāpuruṣa, and begins to teach the Lotus Sūtra to others.[36]

The sūtra is not completely true to the non-dualism of the Prajñāpāramitā scriptures, that insists that all absolute distinctions we make between beings are the product of ignorance. The young female bodhisattva must give up her female body while still living and change into a 'properly' male Buddha. Still, she has advanced to the very final stages of the bodhisattva path as a female, and a very young one at that. Only at the last moment did she cease to appear as female and became a male. The solution is an attempt at a compromise between two opposing views about whether a woman can be a Buddha; it was the best the sūtra writers could do at the time. At least they made the attempt to argue for the validity of women's claims to spiritual equity and for their aspirations for the ultimate spiritual attainment. The other Buddhist schools, such as the Theravāda, continued to honour their own canons of scriptures, that already contained accounts of wise women who had attained nirvāṇa.[37] Prajñāpāramitā non-dualism, however, remained a major current in Mahāyāna Buddhist thought that was fully expressed in the doctrines and practice of Tantric Buddhism that flourished in India, especially in the north-east, after the sixth century of the Common Era.

Tantric Buddhism

Vajrayāna, the Diamond Vehicle to enlightenment, also known as Tantric Buddhism, is a branch of Mahāyāna. It is philosophically grounded in the teaching of non-dualism or emptiness(*śūnyatā*), the fundamental insight that no being and no thing possesses a unique essence that belongs to itself alone and endures for a lifetime and beyond. The sense of permanent personal individuality that separates one being from another is an illusion, the result of imperfect understanding of the true nature of existence. Each being and each phenomenon is inter-related with every other in such a way that everything that exists conditions everything else. Nothing, therefore, exists in and of itself, and nothing can be understood in and of itself. Each thing or each being can only be understood relative to everything else.

The difference between Tantric Buddhism and Mahāyāna is the practices employed to bring one to enlightenment. The tantric yogi or yogini practises highly ritualized techniques of meditation under the close supervision of a spiritual guide and teacher (guru), that enable the pupil to experience his or her own intrinsic purity here and now. There is no need to perfect oneself for aeons so that one will eventually become a fully enlightened Buddha. A pure Buddha is what we all are, without knowing it, right now. Tantric practice enables the yogi or yogini to open the mind and experience that reality now, in this body and in this lifetime. That means the Buddha's body may be female as well as male. In that Buddha body and Buddha mind, all dualistic experience is re-integrated. Female and male are no longer experienced as opposites or as unequal; they are united in the experience of enlightenment.

The Tantric approach to enlightenment is taught in a new collection of scriptures called Tantras, that claim, like the Mahāyāna Sūtras, to be direct revelations of the Buddha's thought. These texts were composed from about the sixth century to the twelfth. The texts and the practices became increasingly influential in several parts of India, and especially in the Pāla kingdom of Bengal that lasted from the eighth to the twelfth century.

Tantric Buddhism does appear to have arisen outside the great monasteries, largely among lay people,[38] and even today in countries where tantric practices are widespread it is not necessary to be ordained to receive instruction from a guru. Some nuns and monks did become *tantrikas* and, in countries like Tibet, monks eventually came to dominate all modes of Buddhist practice. But married couples, wandering lay adepts of both genders, and solitary hermits always claimed the right to employ the new techniques for opening the mind.

Recent scholarship has brought evidence to light that indicates that in India women practised and taught tantric meditations just as freely as men did. Yoginis were as numerous as yogis at pilgrimage centres and in meditation retreats. A guru sought out by a yogi or yogini for initiation into a powerful meditation ritual would be the individual who had gained renown as a master of that particular practice; it didn't matter whether the guru was a woman or man. There is a considerable amount of literary evidence that documents women's religious activities and attainments during the centuries when Vajrayāna thrived in India, and afterwards when Buddhism had faded away in its homeland but had been transmitted by Indian teachers to the Himalayan regions, especially to Tibet and Nepal. Most tantric yoginis were laywomen.[39]

In sharp contrast to what we find in the literature of other Buddhist schools, tantric women wrote assiduously of their own experiences; some produced instruction manuals on rituals they had originated or mastered.[40] Yoginis also composed 'songs of realization' that poetically expressed their own enlightened state, and sang them at tantric feasts.[41] In an especially beautiful poetic essay that describes her own realization of the ultimate enlightened state of mind and goes on to instruct others on how to attain the same realization, the yogini and teacher, Niguma, wrote:

> Don't do anything whatsoever with the mind—
> Abide in an authentic, natural state.
> One's own mind, unwavering, is reality.
> The key is to meditate like this without wavering
> ....
> In a pellucid ocean,
> Bubbles arise and dissolve again.
> Just so, thoughts are no different from ultimate reality.
> So don't find fault; remain at ease.[42]

For the first time in the history of Buddhism, then, we have an extensive body of literature that informs us of women's religious lives from the women's own point of view. Many of these texts are preserved, correctly ascribed to their women authors, in the Tibetan Buddhist canon.[43]

There were, then, women like Niguma who attained the ultimate realization, the perfect enlightenment of the Buddhas. In tantric Buddhism, the idea that only someone who had a male body could become a Buddha was finally rejected. There are female Buddhas in the tantric pantheon, and *sādhanas* (methods of practice related to a particular deity)[44] that a tantrika can practise to realize her or his identity with that enlightened being. Tārā, in her many forms, is the most famous and beloved female Buddha in the Tantric tradition. Some of the meditations and *maṇḍalas* (circular diagrams symbolizing the wisdom-emanated abode of the Buddha) dedicated to Tārā or to other female Buddhas were developed by women. Some of these practices were designed by women primarily for other women to use, for powerful and nourishing female Buddhas were certainly very appealing to yoginis who were striving to realize their own essential enlightened nature.[45] Female Buddhas, however, were objects of meditation and of worship by both men and women in India, just as they are today among Tibetans.

In Tantric Buddhism in India, there were no institutional barriers to women practising and to women teaching both male and female aspirants. Religious authority was based on what a yogi or yogini had accomplished, not on gender.[46] Most modern scholars writing about tantric Buddhism have misunderstood the true role of women in the tradition, and have assumed that women were subordinate figures just as they had been during much of the earlier history of Buddhism. It seems, however, that both women and men were leaders in this tradition that explicitly recognizes the complete spiritual equality of male and female from the beginning of their practice all the way to the ultimate attainment, the realization of one's own Buddhahood. Women and men together created tantric Buddhism, a form of practice and study that remains one of the most vital Buddhist traditions up to the present day.

BUDDHISM IN MODERN INDIA

For many centuries, Buddhist monastic communities and centres of worship flourished in India, and Buddhist lay people continued to devote themselves to the Buddha's dharma. But as Śaiva and Vaiṣṇava sects grew gradually in popularity, and as more and more worshippers were drawn to great temples of Hindu deities, the influence of Buddhism declined and so did its lay following. By the twelfth century, Buddhist vitality was largely concentrated in the huge monastic universities in the north. When Nālandā and the other universities were destroyed by invading Muslim armies, the monks fled, and little was left of institutionalized Buddhism in the land of its birth. Small pockets of Buddhists remained scattered and isolated in some places in the north-east and in the south, but by about 1500 Buddhism had essentially disappeared from India. In the twentieth century, however, it has undergone a rebirth. According to the 1971 Census of India, there were almost 4,000,000 Buddhists in India, the largest group being found in Maharashtra and adjacent areas, with other substantial populations present in the north and in the north-west.[47] The present population may be about 5,000,000. The majority are the new Buddhists who converted to Buddhism under the inspiration of Dr B.R. Ambedkar in 1956. Most of the rest are members of Tibetan-speaking populations in the border regions of northern and north-eastern India, including Tibetans who fled the Chinese invasion of their homeland in the 1950s. These people practise tantric Buddhism.

Tantric Buddhist Women in North India

A few of the Buddhists of the north-east may represent Indian Buddhist traditions that have survived in India until the present, but most are nineteenth or twentieth-century immigrants from Nepal or Bhutan, cultures that received their religion from Tibet.[48] More recent Tibetan arrivals have settled there also, and others have settled in the Dharamsala area in Himachal Pradesh which the Dalai Lama had made his residence, and elsewhere in that state. There is a large Tibetan group in Karnataka, too. The Buddhist populations of Ladakh and Zangskar in the state of Jammu and Kashmir, and Spiti in Himachal Pradesh, have been well established for a very long time and are the oldest intact tantric Buddhist culture areas in modern India.[49]

Monasteries dominate religious life in Ladakh and Zangskar, just as they did in Tibet, and consequently tantric instruction and practice are largely centred in monastic communities. A few married yogis and yoginis live in the villages, but most of the Tantric masters are monks. The laity, both male and female, maintain close relations with the monks and monasteries near their villages, visiting them frequently and supporting them with the most generous gifts they can afford. There are also nuns who have been initiated by monks into certain tantric practices.[50] Nuns in these regions are not the same as those in ancient India, however, for the saṃgha of fully ordained bhikṣunī was never established there or in Tibet. Some women do elect to shave their heads and live as renunciants, but since the bhikṣunī saṃgha does not exist in their land, they can only take the vows of a novice. Consequently, they do not have the prestige that bhikṣunī enjoyed in India. There are no more than five hundred of these novice nuns in Ladakh and Zangskar together.

There are few nunneries in Ladakh and Zangskar, not even enough to house five hundred nuns. Most of the nuns have no choice but to continue to live with their families even though they have dedicated their lives to religion. Life in these regions is hard, and families need as many labouring hands as possible to work in the fields and in the household. Women of the family who have chosen religion over marriage are a good source of labour, for they do not have husbands or children to look after. They work hard to support the household, and have little time for religious devotions. Those women who try to leave their families to go to a nunnery often run into serious opposition from family members, for their labour is very valuable. Even after she joins a nunnery, a woman still has obligations to her family, and will have to return home to work for them at intervals in exchange for their financial support for her religious calling. Some Ladakhi nunneries are daughter houses of great monasteries, and there the nuns labour for the monks rather than for their natal families. Whether they remain at home or live in a nunnery, few of them have received much religious education or training in religious practices, and thus have little opportunity for spiritual development. Their situation is very different from the monks', who are much more numerous, live in grand monasteries, and are highly venerated by the entire population. The promising possibilities that the tantric tradition offered to women has not yet been fulfilled in this part of the world.[51]

Since the invasion of Tibet by the Chinese in the 1950s and the resulting flight of the Dalai Lama and thousands of other Tibetans to India, the situation of Buddhist women in the exile communities[52] and among the indigenous populations in northern India has begun to change. Now these venerable cultures have been opened to new ways of thinking, due partly to the presence of Western converts who want to practise Buddhism without being limited by traditional strictures concerning women's religious possibilities. Consequently, older ideas about the social and religious roles of women are being re-examined. His Holiness the Dalai Lama and other high *lamas* have promoted and helped provide for religious training for nuns in the Tibetan exile communities, and have been seriously seeking an appropriate way to establish a bhikṣunī ordination lineage in the Tibetan tradition.[53] Until such a lineage comes into being, some of the lamas are willing to sanction bhikṣunī ordination in the Chinese tradition for their female disciples now. Because of their great reverence for the lamas, nuns would not be willing to seek advancement without their approval. Now that the lamas have given their support, nuns and laywomen leaders are emerging throughout the Buddhist Himalayas. This movement began among Tibetan exiles in India and Nepal, but has spread also to Ladakh and other areas within the last ten years. Advanced training in Buddhist philosophy, debating techniques, sacred painting, and initiation into core meditation rituals are again becoming available to tantric Buddhist women, as they were hundreds of years ago, with the lamas' blessings. The dignity and freedom of tantric women practitioners, that were unquestioned in India for hundreds of years, are now coming to fruition once again.

Dalit Buddhist Women

In 1956 Dr Bhimrao Ramji Ambedkar converted to Buddhism, and over the next few years three million Indians followed him into a new religious identity. Many of these converts were untouchables, for Dr Ambedkar was an untouchable himself and the leader of a strong and effective movement to bring civil rights and human dignity to these despised people. Dr Ambedkar had announced in 1935 that he would convert from Hinduism to another religion because he utterly rejected the caste system that had brought such suffering and injustice to untouchables, and the caste system was thoroughly enmeshed in Hindu customs, beliefs, and religious practices. Over the next twenty years, he studied and evaluated a number of religions. At conferences held to support his decision to convert, his followers, both women and men, spoke out about their need to find a religion that would recognize their dignity and freedom. With their concurrence, he ultimately chose Buddhism because he found this ancient Indian religion to be rational, ethical, egalitarian, and able to support the idea of social justice for all people. Dr. Ambedkar, who had been independent India's first law minister and was the principal author of India's Constitution, sought to effect fundamental changes in Indian civil law and society. He decided that Buddhism was the religion that validated and upheld his views and the hopes of his followers. Millions of ex-untouchables, now called *Dalits* (the oppressed), regard him as their saviour, their great *bodhisattva*, and practise Buddhism as he understood it.[54]

Dr Ambedkar 'made it a point', as he said, 'to carry women along with men' as equal participants in the just society he envisioned. He urged each woman to 'stand up to her husband, claim to be his friend and equal and refuse to be his slave.'[55] Since his death, however, men have most often acted as leaders of local Buddhist communities, following long-standing Indian custom. But many Dalit women have felt empowered by Ambedkar's socially progressive Buddhism, and practise the religion proudly. Women uphold the ideal of social equality for themselves and their daughters, they want their daughters as well as their sons to be educated, and they can be as strong a force for social and political change as men, sometimes stronger.[56] Madhumaya Jayant and her sisters in Sujata's *Vahini* (army) are such forces for change.

Madhumaya is the leader of Sujata's Vahini in Agra. She and the army are actively asserting their liberation from patriarchy, caste hierarchy, and educational backwardness by entering public places to argue for their views.[57] Most recently, the army women have become an active and vocal presence in the Liberate Bodh Gaya Movement, the effort to gain control of the Mahabodhi Temple, which was built on the spot where the Buddha attained enlightenment and where the religion began. The temple and its environs passed under the control of Hindu priests after the demise of Buddhism there in the twelfth century, and although governance of the temple's affairs and funds was transferred to an appointed committee of five Hindus and four Buddhist monks in 1949, the Dalit majority in the Liberate Bodh Gaya Movement agitated for total control by Buddhists. None of the four monks who sat on the committee was a Dalit, and that, too, was a situation that required change since Dalits are the majority among Indian Buddhists.[58] Agitation for change has gone on since 1992, but was upgraded in 1995 from public protest to sit-down strikes, in which groups of Dalit women from many cities in India have been the mainstay. By late 1997, Dalit monks[59] had replaced the non-Dalits on the committee, and one of them now heads the temple's managing committee. But control of the temple is still shared with Hindus, so the movement for change continues. Madhumaya and Dalit women from all over India continue to play a significant role in it, and theirs is a commitment that is based on Buddhist values as well as the assertion of Buddhist rights.

The Liberate Bodh Gaya movement is concerned with a specifically Buddhist issue, but Madhumaya and her associates, and other Dalit women, Buddhist and non-Buddhist, have publicly confronted social problems that pit the women against their men. A significant case was their effort to ban the lottery in Agra. Many Dalit men were spending most of their money on lottery tickets, hoping for wealth, while their families went hungry. So, in 1995 a group of Dalit women went to make a protest at the market where tickets were sold—a public place where women, especially Dalit women, never go—and they were beaten by the vendors. The moral outrage that erupted in response in the Dalit communities and far beyond led to the arrest of the vendors, and brought women from all castes into the movement. For perhaps the first time in the experience of Dalit women, they had not only publicly 'stood up to their husbands', as Dr Ambedkar had urged them to do, but they had initiated an inter-caste movement in the public arena.[60]

The Buddhism of the Dalits is an overwhelmingly lay religion. Religious leaders and teachers are mostly lay men and women, although some young men have been trained and ordained as bhikṣu. It has been reported that there are a few nuns as well.[61] Since the Buddhism of the Dalits differs in this respect, and in its emphasis on social justice, from earlier Indian Buddhism, critics of Dr Ambedkar and his Buddhist followers have charged that their religion is primarily a political movement, that they are not serious about it as a spiritual way of life, and that they will soon abandon it. However, there were few Buddhists in India at the time of the first conversions, and no living example of a Buddhist society that they could emulate. So the converts had to create a meaningful religious life that met their needs. In their communities they have established vihāras[62] which are community meeting places where people can gather to hear lectures on Buddhism, where they can make reverence to the Buddha, and where children can receive religious instruction. Learning about Buddhism is very important to these people who are new to the religion. Each year, four great observances replace the Hindu festivals in their religious calendar—the Buddha's birthday, and the anniversaries of Dr Ambedkar's birth, conversion to Buddhism, and death. The Buddhists' observances, and their life rituals, are fewer and simpler than the Hindu practices they had known, and that is very satisfying to them.[63]

Their new religion has given many women precisely the sense of dignity and social and gender equality they had longed for. They say that Buddhism has given them self-respect and the confidence to rely on themselves. They find Buddhism to be a rational religion, free of superstition, a religion that takes the intelligence of women as well as men seriously. Buddhist women, both educated and illiterate, speak very proudly of the fact that they do not worship gods; they venerate the Buddha and Dr Ambedkar, but do not treat them like gods. To many women, Buddhism is primarily about morality, a clear and direct guide to living peacefully and responsibly with others. That, too, gives them a sense of great satisfaction.[64] In short, although most Dalit Buddhists remain poor and live with hardship, their opinions of themselves have changed significantly. As a result, they no longer believe they are ritually obliged to perform degrading duties, and they work confidently for better futures for themselves and their children. Buddhism has freed them from any sense of inferiority. Psychologically, they have been liberated by their strong new identity as Buddhists. Positive social change will be slower to come, but now they have hope.[65]

CONCLUSION

Buddhism is one of the world's major religions, an immensely rich Indian contribution to world civilization. It began as a religion that treated women as equal to men in their capacity for personal spiritual development. As it blossomed and grew over the next few centuries, it fulfilled women's desires for full participation with men in vibrant religious observances, in the creation of great monuments, the development of religious imagery, and even in the creation of original meditation practices and rituals. Buddhism also opened to women a new lifestyle as full-time religious practitioners (bhikṣunī) that freed them from women's traditional family and social roles and obligations. Women's religious horizons were extraordinarily broadened by the establishment of a nuns' order for women, and for the thousand and more years that Buddhism flourished in India countless women took full advantage of the possibilities this vocation offered to them. In return for all of this, nuns and laywomen gave their full support to the religion and contributed as significantly as men did to its success, especially in the earlier centuries of its existence in India.

There were tensions, however, within the saṃgha of monks, nuns, and lay people, between the scripturally sanctioned recognition of women's full spiritual equality with men, and the questions of leadership, of control of cult centres, and of creative direction of intellectual developments within the Buddhist communities. Monks institutionalized their right to leadership in all saṃgha matters, and nuns were permanently relegated to lesser ranks in the religious hierarchy. Despite their secondary status in the saṃgha, as in the larger society, nuns and laywomen did accomplish much. We know this was true at certain periods in Buddhist history, for there is documentation to prove it. But because women's activities were largely ignored by the monk leaders of the saṃgha and of religious institutions, the very presence of women in monastic and lay communities was overlooked by the men who kept the records of the faith. Buddhist women were effectively marginalized, and consequently it is difficult now to assess what their lives were like and what they were able to contribute at any level to the sustenance of their religion in India. They were there, however, to the end, and fortunately current research by modern historians, textual scholars, and archaeologists is now opening new windows into the lives of Buddhist women of the past.

In the second half of the twentieth century, Buddhism has arisen in India once more, after a disappearance that lasted hundreds of years. Buddhists are a small percentage of the total current population of India, but the numbers of adherents continue to grow at a modest rate, and the ancient religion is once again a significant presence in the land of its birth. For women, the old conflict between the freedom to pursue spiritual realization and restrictions on the scope of their religious activities persisted into modern times. But in this modern environment, Buddhist women have begun to clearly assert their claim to equity as practitioners and devotees, and some of them are becoming articulate leaders in the Himalayan regions and in Dalit Buddhist communities.

Buddhism has always had the potential to become a catalyst for social reform in India, because those who join the monastic saṃgha abandon their former caste identities, and because women and men are recognized as equals in their capacity for highest spiritual development. There is no evidence that, in the past, Buddhists ever sought to apply scriptural teachings to bring about reforms in lay society. The Buddha offered a spiritual path to his followers, not a revolutionary philosophy for social change. In the late twentieth century, however, perhaps for the first time in the history of the religion, Buddhist teachings are being used to justify major changes in Indian society, including the improvement of the situation of women inside Buddhist communities and beyond. Such re-evaluation and application of Buddhist ideas to issues of social justice is occurring throughout the Buddhist world at present. It is particularly notable in India, because it is Dalit women and men who are calling on Buddhist ideas to help them emerge from the miserable conditions to which they have been bound for centuries. Such constructive actualization of the full potential of Buddhist thinking holds great promise for the future. Buddhist women have already begun to change their own lives. There can be no doubt that they will continue to take responsibility as Buddhists for their own destiny in India and wherever the ancient Indian religion is seriously practised.

NOTES

1. The widely accepted traditional dates of the Buddha are 566 or 563 to 486 or 483 BCE. Recently, however, many scholars have re-examined the basis on which those dates were determined, and have suggested other possibilities, ranging from about 600 to 350 BCE. Research and debate continue on this issue. Whatever the Buddha's precise dates, this period of the sixth and fifth centuries BCE was one of great religious exploration and innovation. Wandering spiritual seekers, called *śramaṇas*, promulgated new paths leading to the realization of ultimate truth, that were independent of Brahmanical traditions. The Buddha was one of the *śramaṇas*, and he, like many of them, attracted followers and eventually established a new religious community. This happened at a time in Indian history when the whole political, social, and economic situation was changing radically. See Warder, A.K., *Indian Buddhism*, Delhi: Motilal Banarsidass, 1970, pp. 28–42.

2. As is conventionally done by modern scholars, the English terms *monk* and *nun* are used in this essay for bhikṣu and bhikṣunī, although the way of life of Buddhist monastics is quite different from that of Western monks and nuns. Bhikṣu and bhikṣunī (*bhikkhu* and *bhikkhunī* in Pali) follow a code of discipline consisting of 227 precepts for the monks in the *Theravāda* school, and 311 for the nuns. The Theravāda, the school of the Elders, was one of the Buddhist schools founded sometime after the Buddha's death, and is the one that still thrives in Sri Lanka and in most of South-East Asia. The precepts are preserved in the *Vinaya*, the Book of the Discipline. The *TheravādaVinaya* and the scriptures are written in Pali, but the texts of some of the other early Buddhist schools were written in Sanskrit. Vinayas of five of these other early schools survive in Sanskrit, or in Chinese or Tibetan translations. The code of discipline is very similar in all the extant vinayas, although the number of precepts to be followed by monks and nuns varies somewhat from school to school. For the nuns, there are always more rules to follow than for the monks, and the number of rules for them varies from 290 to 380 in the six Vinayas.

3. Upāsaka and Upāsikā took on themselves five to ten precepts that are also observed by bhikṣu and bhikṣunī. The ten precepts are: to abstain from killing, stealing , sexual relations, lying, using intoxicants, eating after mid-day, dancing and other worldly amusements, self-adornment, using comfortable beds and chairs, touching gold and silver (*The Pali Text Society's Pali-English Dictionary*, ed. T.W. Rhys Davids and William Stede, London: Luzac and Company Ltd., 1966, p. 708: *sikkhāpada*). An upāsaka or upāsikā must observe the first five of

the precepts, but could elect to observe more of them, either permanently or for a designated period of time. Pious lay devotees still follow this practice in Sri Lanka and South-East Asia.

4. The Four Noble Truths are traditionally believed to have been the first matters taught by the Buddha to his first five disciples, and this 'first sermon' became part of the body of teachings preserved orally by the Buddha's followers and eventually committed to writing in the first century BCE. It is known as the *Dhammacakkaparivattana Sutta*, the Scripture of the First Turning of the Wheel of Truth, and can be found in the Theravāda canon of scriptures in the *Saṃyutta Nikāya* 56.11.5–8 and in the Vinaya, Mahāvagga 1.6.17–29.

In this essay, texts from the Theravāda canon will be most frequently cited because this canon is the most completely preserved in an Indian language, and it is also the most accessible to most readers. The Theravāda canon was published (with English translations) over a period of several years for the Pali Text Society by Luzac & Company Ltd., London. When they are relevant, the author will cite texts belonging to other Buddhist schools, regardless of the languages in which they are currently preserved.

5. *Majjhima Nikāya*, 73, *Mahāvacchagottasutta.*

6. On politics, economics and society at the time of the Buddha, see Chakravarty, Uma, *The Social Dimensions of Early Buddhism*, Delhi: Oxford University Press, 1987. A stūpa is a reliquary mound erected to house a part of the cremated remains of the Buddha, or of one of his revered disciples. There is archaeological evidence that Buddhist stūpas began to be built as early as the third century BCE. Scriptures claim that stūpas were built during the Buddha's lifetime and even before, but so far no remains of such early structures have been found. The earliest stūpas were simple earthen mounds; later stūpas were faced with stone or brick, surrounded by massive stone railings, and adorned with sculptures. Among Buddhists, the term *caitya* referred to places and objects that were venerated, and caitya halls with stūpas or images inside were excavated into cliffs during the last few centuries BCE; later, free-standing halls were built. Buddhist lay followers and monastic disciples would visit stūpas and caityas to venerate the Buddha by circumambulating the holy place, and by making offerings of flowers or perfumes.

7. Law, B.C., Bhikshunis in Indian Inscriptions, *Epigraphia Indica*, XXV, January 1939, 33; Sharma, R.C., *Buddhist Art of Mathura*, Delhi, 1984, pp. 52, 59, 178; Sarkar, H., and B.N. Mishra, *Nagarjunakonda*, New Delhi: Archaeological Survey of India, 1987, pp. 31–2. Remains of ancient stupas, temples, viharas, and cave excavations dating from the third century BCE to the twelfth century CE have been found all over India, and new sites continue to be discovered. The greatest concentrations of archaeological sites known thus far are in northern India, and along the western and southeastern coasts.

8. Examples of sūtras directed specifically to laywomen or men in the canon of the Theravāda school are *Anguttara Nikāya* II.202–5; III.3–37; IV.91–93; *Saṃyutta Nikāya* IV.238–51; and *Dīgha Nikāya* III.180–93.

9. Visākhā's story is concisely summarized by I.B. Horner in *Women Under Primitive Buddhism*, Delhi: Motilal Banarsidass, 1990 (originally published 1930), pp. 345–61.

10. Some of the most inflammatory excoriations of women can be found in the *Kunālajātaka*, edited and translated by W.B. Bollee, London: Luzac and Co. Ltd, 1970, verses 24ff. *Anguttara Nikāya* III.67–8 is also extremely harsh toward women.

11. See Sponberg, Alan, 'Attitudes toward Women and the Feminine in Early Buddhism', in *Buddhism, Sexuality and Gender*, edited by José Cabezon, Albany: State University of New York Press, 1992, pp. 3–36 for a good discussion of this issue.

12. In a short scripture in the *Anguttara Nikāya* (II.80), the Buddha is asked why it is that women do not sit in courts of justice or embark on business ventures, and he replies that it is because women are uncontrolled, envious, greedy, and weak in wisdom. Whether the Buddha ever said such a thing or not, this text must reflect a view prevalent in Indian society that women were not suited to take positions of leadership and responsibility in secular affairs outside the home. The monks who included this passage among the scriptures saw the matter just as non-Buddhists did.

13. Buddhists and Jains both formed orders of religious renunciants at about the same time in ancient India, the first such communities known to have been instituted anywhere in the world. The Jains, like the Buddhists, permitted women as well as men to live the religious life.

14. This account of the founding of the bhikṣunī saṃgha is taken from the *Theravāda Vinaya, Cullavagga*, X.1–3, translated by I.B. Horner in *The Book of the Discipline*, Volume V (London: Luzac & Co. Ltd., 1963), pp. 352–8. A Sanskrit version of the story, belonging to the Sarvāstivāda school's Vinaya, can also be read in English translation by Frances Wilson: see Paul, Diana, *Women in Buddhism* (Berkeley, California: Asian Humanities Press, 1979), pp. 82–7. The *Mahāsaṃghika Vinaya* account, which now exists only in a Chinese translation, is also available in English translation by Akira Hirakawa, *Monastic Discipline for the Buddhist Nuns, An English Translation of the Chinese Text of the Mahāsāṃghika-Bhikshunī-Vinaya* (Patna: K.P. Jayaswal Research Institute, 1982).

15. The poems of the *Therī*, or senior nuns, are part of the Theravāda canon. There are seventy-three poems in this collection that are believed to have been the utterances of some of the first nuns to join the saṃgha. There is similar collection of 264 monks' poems, the *Theragāthā*, that is also part of the Theravāda canon. Although the traditional ascription of these poems to particular individuals well known from other Buddhist scriptures may not be accurate, the poems are testimony to the joy and triumph of women and men who had realized the ultimate goal. *Therīgāthā* and *Theragāthā* were translated into English by C.A.F. Rhys Davids as the *Psalms of the Early Buddhists*, volumes I and II (London: Luzac & Co. Ltd., 1909 and 1913). K.R. Norman translated them into

more modern English as *Elders' Verses*, volumes I and II (London: Luzac & Co. Ltd., 1969–1971). A recent study of the content of the poems is by Kathryn R. Blackstone, *Women in the Footsteps of the Buddha, Struggle for Liberation in the Therīgāthā* (Surrey: Curzon Press, 1998).

16. *Therīgāthā*, verses 114–16, translated by K.R. Norman.

17. *Therīgāthā*, verses 79–81, translated by K.R. Norman.

18. Dhammadinnā: *Majjhima Nikāya* I.299–305; Khemā: *Saṃyutta Nikāya* IV.374–80.

19. *Saṃyutta Nikāya*, V. *Bhikkhunī Saṃyutta*, 2 (volume I, pp. 128–9).

20. I. B. Horner discusses in detail the accomplishments of women according to the Theravāda canon in her *Women Under Primitive Buddhism* (London: Routledge & Kegan Paul Ltd., 1930; reprinted Delhi: Motilal Banarsidass Press Pvt. Ltd., 1989).

21. On these inscriptions, see Barnes, Nancy J. 'The Nuns at the *Stūpa*: Inscriptional Evidence for the Lives and Activities of Early Buddhist Nuns in India', in *Women's Buddhism Buddhism's Women*, edited by Ellison Banks Findly (Boston: Wisdom Publications, 2000), pp. 17–36. See also Schopen, Gregory, 'On Monks, Nuns, and Vulgar Practices: The Introduction of the Image Cult into Indian Buddhism', in *Bones, Stones, and Buddhist Monks, Collected Papers on the Archeology, Epigraphy, and Texts of Monastic Buddhism in India* (Honolulu: University of Hawaii Press, 1997), pp. 238–57, especially pp. 242–50.

22. It is true that food, robes, medicines, and much larger gifts were and are made to monastics by the faithful laity. This practice fulfils two goals for the saṃgha as a whole: it means that monastics can devote all their time to their religious duties since they do not have to labour to support themselves, and it means that the laity can earn religious merit that is of great value to them by giving to the monastics. Many of the men and women who renounced worldly life and joined the saṃgha could doubtless have supported themselves without further labour, because they were not required to renounce their worldly property. They changed their way of life completely, but they were still able to use their own wealth for religious purposes.

23. For discussions of the evidence from inscriptions and from a correct reading of the Vinayas, that monks and nuns did indeed possess personal wealth, see Schopen, Gregory, 'On Monks, Nuns, and Vulgur Practices', in *Bones, Stones, and Buddhist Monks*. See also his 'Archaeology and Protestant Suppositions in the Study of Indian Buddhism', and 'Ritual Obligations and Donor Roles of Monks in the Pali *Vinaya*', in *Bones, Stones, and Buddhist Monks*, pp. 1–22 and 72–85; and also 'What's in a Name: The Religious Function of Donative Inscriptions', in *Unseen Presence, The Buddha and Sanchi*, edited by Vidya Dehejia (Mumbai: Marg Publications, 1996), pp. 58–73.

24. Schopen, Gregory, 'The Suppression of Nuns and the Ritual Murder of Their Special Dead in Two Buddhist Monastic Texts', *Journal of Indian Philosophy* 24 (1996), pp. 563–92.

25. Ibid., pp. 564 and 583.

26. Jonathan S. Walters has written several articles on the Apadāna stories as a source of information on the stūpa cult in early Buddhism, and on nuns' efforts to preserve traditions about their great female predecessors. See his 'A Voice from the Silence: The Buddha's Mother's Story', *History of Religions* 33, no. 4 (1994), pp. 358–79; 'Gotamī's Story', in *Buddhism in Practice*, edited by Donald S. Lopez, Jr. (Princeton, New Jersey: Princeton University Press, 1995) pp. 113–38; '*Stūpa*, Story, and Empire: Constructions of the Buddha Biography in Early Post-Aśokan India' in *Sacred Biography in the Buddhist Traditions of South and South-east Asia*, edited by Juliane Schober (Honolulu: University of Hawaii Press, 1997), pp. 160–92.

27. Takakusu, J., 'The Life of Vasubandhu by Paramārtha', *T'oung Pao*, ser. 2, vol. 5 (1904), 286; Barua, D. K., *Vihāras in Ancient India* (Calcutta: Indian Publications, 1969), p. 191. Nancy Falk cites these references in 'The Case of the Vanishing Nuns: The Fruits of Ambivalence in Ancient Indian Buddhism', in *Unspoken Worlds, Women's Religious Lives in Non-Western Cultures*, edited by Nancy A. Falk and Rita M. Gross (San Francisco: Harper & Row, 1980), pp. 210 and 223–4, notes 6 and 23.

28. Fa-hien, *A Record of Buddhistic Kingdoms*, translated by Lames Legge (New York: Dover Publications, 1963; originally published Oxford, 1886), pp. 44–7; I-tsing, *A Record of the Buddhist Religion as Practised in India and the Malay Archipelago* (AD 671–95), translated by J. Takakusu (Delhi: Munshiram Manoharlal, 1966; originally published in London, 1896), pp. 78–82. Hsuan-tsang (his name is also transliterated into English as Yuan Chwang) spent two decades in India in the first half of the seventh century; he repeats Fa-hien's brief observations about nuns, but has nothing to add of his own. See Waters, Thomas, *On Yuan Chwang's Travels in India* (Delhi: Munshiram Manoharlal, 1961; originally published in London, 1904–5). These scrupulous records by Chinese monks are among the richest sources of information we have on Buddhism in India during the 'medieval' period. These monks were eager to learn all they could about Buddhist sacred places and their traditions, local religious practices and celebrations, monasteries and monastic life, scriptures, scholarship and centres of learning, and countless other details about Buddhist life in India. Nuns were apparently of no great interest to them, although the little information they communicate about religious women is very precious.

29. Gregory Schopen has been able to document that all but a few inscriptions by monastic adherents of the Mahāyāna were made by monks. He has suggested that 'the presence of these [Mahāyāna] monks is related to the decline or disappearance of nun donors' at several Buddhist sites: 'On Monks, Nuns, and Vulgar Practices, The Introduction of the Image Cult into Indian Buddhism', in *Bones, Stones, and Buddhist Monks*, p. 250. But there is no reason to believe that Mahāyāna monks were ever the majority in the Buddhist monastic population in India. Even if Mahāyāna monasticism had little space for nuns, they cannot be singled out and blamed for ignoring nuns since this was a pan-Buddhist phenomenon throughout India from the fourth century onwards.

30. Mahāyāna scriptures were taken by Buddhist monks and merchants to China and began to be translated into Chinese in the mid-second century CE. These translations survive, although few early manuscripts of their Indian-language originals do. Scholars working with these first Chinese translations have concluded that the Indian originals of some of them were composed as early as 100 BCE. See Zurcher, E., *The Buddhist Conquest of China* (Leiden: E. J. Brill, 1972). Such an early date for the emergence of the Mahāyāna movement accords also with Buddhist historical traditions.

31. Schopen, Gregory, 'On Monks, Nuns, and Vulgar Practices', in *Bones, Stones, and Buddhist Monks*, p. 250; and 'Mahāyāna in Indian Inscriptions', *Indo-Iranian Journal* 21 (1979) 1–19. In inscriptions the term 'Mahāyāna' is used only occasionally. Monks who belonged to the Mahāyāna referred to themselves as *śakyabhikṣu*, according to Schopen. From the Gupta period there is at least one record of a gift from a *śakyabhikṣunī*, but this is a rarity; See B C. Law, 'Bhikshunis in Indian Inscriptions', *Epigraphia Indica*, 25, January 1939, p. 34.

32. The Theravāda school's position on these issues is discussed by Sharma, Arvind 'Can There Be a Female Buddha in Theravāda Buddhism?' in *Women, Literature, Criticism*, edited by H.R. Garvin (Lewisburg, Pennsylvania: Bucknell Press, 1978). On Mahāyāna views, see Kajiyama, Yuichi, 'Women in Buddhism', *Eastern Buddhist*, new series 15, no. 2 (1982), pp. 53–70; Schuster, Nancy, (Nancy J. Barnes), 'Changing the Female Body: Wise Women and the *Bodhisattva* Career in Some *Mahāratnakūṭasūtras*', *Journal of the International Association of Buddhist Studies* 4, no. 1 (1981), pp. 24–69; Paul, Diana Y., *Women in Buddhism* (Berkeley, California: Asian Humanities Press, 1979), pp. 166–243, 281–302.

33. The thirty-two major and eighty minor lakṣaṇāni of the Mahāpuruṣa are catalogued in several scriptures belonging to different Buddhist schools. See Schuster, Nancy, 'Changing the Female Body'. Buddhists are believed to have borrowed this concept of the Great Being with unique physical marks on his body from Brahmanic tradition.

34. For a full discussion of several of these Mahāyāna sūtras, see Schuster, Nancy, 'Changing the Female Body', op. cit.

35. The Dragon King's daughter who is supreme in wisdom and about to become a Buddha is, of course, not a nun but a lay person. Most of the wise women in Mahāyāna sūtras who triumph in debate over supposedly wiser monks and bodhisattvas are laywomen. Although Mahāyāna texts proclaim that the Great Vehicle is open to everyone, and scholars had long assumed that the Mahāyāna originated as a lay movement, there is no evidence that laywomen, or laymen, were any more prominent among Mahāyānists than they were among other Buddhists. Lay people had important functions to perform as worshippers and donors, but it was always the monastic saṃgha that was the centre of Buddhist life in India. For that reason it is especially troubling to see that bhikṣunī recedes further and further into the background in the later history of Buddhism in India, even in the Great Vehicle. For a discussion of wise children in Mahāyāna sūtras, see Schuster, Nancy, 'Changing the Female Body', op. cit.

36. *Scripture of the Lotus Blossom of the Fine Dharma*, translated by Leon Hurvitz (New York: Columbia University Press, 1976), pp. 199–201.

37. Nirvāṇa and Buddhahood are not the same thing. The scriptures of the older Buddhist schools had already agreed that women were just as able to attain nirvāṇa as were men, but there was no discussion about whether either men or women could become the equals of the Buddha. Only several generations after the Buddha's death did the question arise of whether any but a few highly perfected individuals could become Buddhas.

38. Shaw, Miranda, *Passionate Enlightenment, Women in Tantric Buddhism* (Princeton, New Jersey: Princeton University Press, 1994), pp. 20–1 and 74.

39. Recent research is revealing how active women were in Indian Tantric Buddhism, and is correcting traditional scholarly interpretations of tantric practice as dominated by men, with women present only as their less significant partners. Miranda Shaw has argued this new interpretation forcefully in her book, *Passionate Enlightenment*, which is an exhaustive study of Indian and Tibetan materials on tantric women. Shaw cites works by the seventeenth century Tibetan historian, Taranatha, and other sources, for information on specific women tantrikas and their practices.

40. Shaw, Miranda, *Passionate Enlightenment*, pp. 80–1, 84–5, 87–8, 101–39.

41. Several of these songs are translated by Shaw, Miranda, *Passionate Enlightenment*, pp. 89–97.

42. Shaw, Miranda, *Passionate Enlightenment*, pp. 87–8.

43. After the decline of Buddhism in India following the Hindu renaissance and Muslim invasions, Tibet became the principal centre of tantric study and practice in the Buddhist world. Tantric texts composed in India were carefully preserved there, translated, and incorporated into the Tibetan Buddhist canon along with translations of non-tantric sūtras and śāstras, and original compositions by Tibetan masters.

44. Concise definitions of tantric technical terms can be found in the excellent book by Lama Yeshe, *Introduction to Tantra, A Vision of Totality* (Boston: Wisdom Publications, 1987), pp. 159–68.

45. Shaw, Miranda, *Passionate Enlightenment*, pp. 102–7 and 110–17, describes the meditation on Wrathful Red Tārā originated by Vajravatī Brāhmaṇī in north-west India (Uḍḍiyāna) in the eleventh century, and the Indian princess Lakṣmīṅkarā's meditation on Severed-headed Vajrayogini. Both these female Buddhas are accompanied only by female figures in their *maṇḍalas*.

46. Shaw, Miranda, *Passionate Enlightenment*, pp. 97 and 195–205.

47. Ling, Trevor, 'Buddhism in India: Residual and Resurgent', in *Studies in Pali and Buddhism, A Memorial Volume in Honor of Bhikkhu Jagadish Kashyap*, edited by A. K. Narain (Delhi: B.R. Publishing Corporation, 1979), p. 277; Bechert, Heinz, 'Buddhist Revival in East and West', in *The World of Buddhism, Buddhist Monks and Nuns in Society and Culture*, edited by Heinz Bechert and Richard Gombrich (New York: Facts on File Publications, 1984), p. 273.

48. Ling, Trevor, 'Buddhism in India', pp. 229–41.

49. The Himalayan regions bordering Tibet have not always been part of India; Ladakh, for example, was first conquered and annexed by the rulers of Jammu in 1834. The culture of Ladakh and the other mountain areas is Tibetan, and although Buddhism was known in these regions before it reached Tibet, the Tibetan form of tantric Buddhism pervaded the entire area after the eleventh century. See Bechert and Gomobrich, *The World of Buddhism*, p. 268.

50. Information on nuns in Zangskar is taken from two papers by Kim Gutschow: 'The Women Who Refuse to be Exchanged: Celibacy and Sexuality at a Nunnery in Zangskar, North-west India' (in press); 'A Nunnery in Zangskar', Paper presented at the IV Sakyadhita International Buddhist Women's Conference, Leh, Ladakh, 1995. Information on nuns in Ladakh is taken from a Paper presented by Venerable Bhikṣunī Amchi Jamyang Palmo at the same conference, entitled 'Nuns of Ladakh, their Conditions and Problems'; from Grimshaw, Anna, *Servants of the Buddha: Winter in a Himalayan Convent* (London: Open Letters Press, 1992); and from the author's visits to Ladakhi nunneries and interviews with nuns.

51. All that we know about modern Buddhist women in northern India comes from the testimony of the women themselves and from direct observation of the way they live. The information, therefore, is very reliable. The data available on medieval Buddhist women is derived from literary sources, and is thus of a different kind. This should be kept in mind when we attempt to evaluate the religious roles and accomplishments of women who lived several hundred years ago.

52. The status of nuns in Tibet was by no means equal to the monks', but they did have their own nunneries and were recognized as genuine monastics, although they were not fully ordained bhikṣunī. They had possibilities for a religious life that were rare for their sisters across the border in northern India.

53. Barnes, Nancy J., 'Buddhist Women and the Nuns' Order in Asia', in *Engaged Buddhism, Buddhist Liberation Movements in Asia*, edited by Christopher S. Queen and Sallie B. King (Albany, New York: State University of New York Press, 1996), pp. 259–94.

54. This summary of Dr Ambedkar's Buddhism and social philosophy is taken primarily from Zelliott, Eleanor, *From Untouchable to Dalit, Essays on the Ambedkar Movement* (New Delhi: Manohar Publishers, 1996); and from Lynch, Owen M., *The Politics of Untouchability: Social Mobility and Social Change in a City of India* (New York: Columbia University Press, 1969). Dr Ambedkar died in 1956, less than two months after he formally became a Buddhist. Not all Dalits have converted to Buddhism—many remain Hindu, or have converted to other religions.

55. Lynch, Owen M., 'Sujata's Vahini (Army): Dalit Buddhist Women and Self Emancipation', in *Women's Buddhism Buddhism's Women*, edited by Ellison B. Findly (Boston: Wisdom Publications, 2000), pp. 247–57.

56. Zelliott, Eleanor, 'Buddhist Women of the Contemporary Maharashtrian

Conversion Movement', in *Buddhism, Sexuality, and Gender*, edited by José I. Cabezon (Albany, New York: State University of New York Press, 1992), pp. 92–3. See also Bhave, Sumitra, *Pan on Fire, Eight Dalit Women Tell Their Story*, translated by Gauri Deshpande (New Delhi: Indian Social Institute, 1988).

57. Lynch, Owen M., 'Sujata's Vahini'. Madhumaya was the founder of Sujata's Vahini, the National Women's Union, in 1994. She named the organization after Sujata who, according to early Buddhist scriptures, encountered Gautama, the Buddha-to-be, just after he had given up his ascetic practices, and offered him the food that gave him the energy to make the final assault on enlightenment. In Madhumaya's eyes it was a woman, and by extension all women, who had made the enlightenment possible.

58. Lynch, Owen M., 'Dalit Buddhism: The Liberate Bodh Gaya Movement', *Dalit International Newsletter*, vol. 3, no. 1 (February 1996), pp. 4, 6.

59. These monks do not identify themselves as Dalit, or ex-untouchables, for anyone who has been ordained as a bhikṣu has cut off identification with any caste. Lynch, however, states that the recently appointed monks at Bodh Gaya were Dalits ('Dalit Buddhism', 11). At present there are about twenty-five or thirty bhiksus who come from Maharashtra, where the largest group of Dalit Buddhists live, and they probably were untouchables before ordination: Zelliott, Eleanor, 'Buddhist Sects in Contemporary India: Identity and Organization', in *From Untouchable to Dalit*, p. 243.

60. Lynch, Owen M., 'Sujata's Vahini', op. cit.

61. Moon, Meenakshi and Urmila Pawar, 'We Made History Too: Women in the Early Untouchable Liberation Movement', *South Asia Bulletin*, vol. 9, no. 2 (1989), 70. This article is a synopsis in English of the author's original study written in Marathi and published in Pune in 1989. The synopsis gives no further details about the nuns the authors met, such as where they were trained, or where and in what tradition they were ordained.

62. Vihāra is the term used in Buddhist scriptures for a monastic residence, or monastery. It is a distinctively Buddhist term that modern Buddhists have adopted for the religious centres that function in their communities. The term vihāra distinguishes these centres from Hindu temples, which they do not resemble.

63. Zelliott, Eleanor, 'Tradition and Innovation in Contemporary Indian Buddhism: Activities and Observances', in *From Untouchable to Dalit*, pp. 222–34.

64. Zelliott, Eleanor, 'Buddhist Women of the Contemporary Maharashtrian Conversion Movement', in *Buddhism, Sexuality, and Gender*, pp. 95–100; Bhave, *Pan on Fire*, pp. 97–100, 137–46, 187–90.

65. Zelliott, Eleanor, 'The Psychological Dimension of the Buddhist Conversion', in *From Untouchable to Dalit*, pp. 218–21.

Women and Jainism in India

Nalini Balbir

To Charuben, Rohiniben, Rakshaben and Kalyaniben, in memory of shared pleasures during ladies' trips for the *darshan* of Jain *sādhus-sādhvīs* or *tīrthas* of Gujarat

One of the world's oldest religious traditions, Jainism is still claimed today as their faith by about three and a half million followers in India and in countries where Jains are settled (mainly United Kingdom, United States, Canada and some African countries). The observation of present day practice and a vast body of literature handed down in the course of time are our main source of knowledge. Jainism has never excluded women as such, since one of its key concepts is that of the 'four-fold *sangha*' comprising monks and nuns, laymen and laywomen. Nevertheless, religious status of women is a crucial issue in the history of the tradition, being one of the main points at the background of the oldest sectarian division between the Śvetāmbaras and the Digambaras (79 CE; see below). In order to rightly understand the originality of Jainism with respect to the women's status, one should not overlook the fact that this tradition knows of all the same despising beliefs about them that other (Indian) traditions do, and that, on the other hand, it shows high care to integrate them in its own ethical and spiritual patterns. On the other hand, it must be kept in mind that, except in recent times when a few prominent Jain nuns have spoken of their own lives, Jain women have not been able to speak for themselves: almost all the texts we have inherited from the past are written by monks or are male-oriented, and no really innovative dogmatic treatise is known to have been composed by any woman of the tradition.

JAIN IMAGE OF WOMAN AND ITS THEOLOGICAL CONSEQUENCES

General Beliefs

The pan-Indian (universal) prejudices against women, who are said to be weak-minded, fickle, treacherous, and impure, are shared by the Jains and expressed in several passages of the canon, as well as in later texts, especially in the form of maxims (*subhāṣitas*) interspersed in the rich story literature the Jains developed in order to propagate the basic values of their faith.[1] Taste for deception and acts of deception (*māyā*) can be sorted out as the main characteristic of women, to the extent that rebirth as a woman as a consequence of deceitful behaviour in a former life becomes a stereotyped motif, especially among the Śvetāmbaras, and is adduced as an explanation for sex-differentiation:

> As the result of manifesting deception a man in this world becomes a woman. As for a woman, if her heart is pure, she becomes a man in this world.[2]

Except harsh criticisms against the woman's body, said to host innumerable subtle beings in constant danger of being crushed, which are obviously due to the specific importance ascribed to *ahiṃsā* by the Jains, these common ideas are not of much interest as such. What is relevant, however, is the way these prejudices are exploited by a religion that advocates renunciation as the highest value, the way they are inserted in religious debates and used as arguments therein, and their consequences. To put it in a nutshell: the point is to know whether the Jains are ready to admit the statement that 'The status of men and women [regarding the vow] is equal,' as one of their writers puts it,[3] or not. In other words, supposing there is some fundamental inequality between men and women as such, can it be neutralized and transcended through religious practices?

Woman as a Symbol of Attachment

In a religion like Jainism where asceticism is the central value and the quickest path to salvation, the woman is bound to be represented negatively: as connected with sexuality she is a living and insidious threat to the monk's fourth 'major vow', the vow of chastity (*brahmacarya*), which among the five 'great vows' (*mahāvrata*) taken by mendicants is said to be very difficult to comply with. Therefore, it is even prohibited to indulge in any talk connected with this taboo topic. This is conceptualized in the Prakrit term *itthīkahā*, talks with or about women, one of the four forms of 'bad talks' (*vikahā*)—thus it is forbidden to talk anything concerning their castes (*jāti*), their families (*kula*), their physical appearance (*rūpa*) and their clothes or ornaments (*nepathya*).[4] On the other hand, because it is emphasized that there exists a fundamental inter-connection between the different vows, not observing chastity would mean going against the resolution to renounce possessions and against the vow of ahiṃsā, sexual intercourse implying injury to 'great number of single-sense creatures, thought to dwell in the generative organs of the female and the ejaculate of the male.' (Jaini 1979: p. 176). Hence one comes across the vehement outbursts from the oldest texts onwards against women as temptresses:

> (A monk) who leaves mother and father (and his) former (family) connection, (resolving:) 'I will live alone, without companion, as one for whom sexual pleasure has ceased, seeking solitary places'—him approach, with crafty, stealthy step, sweet-spoken women; they know how to contrive that some monks will suffer a (moral) breakdown. They sit down closely at his side, they frequently put on holiday dress, they show him even the lower part of their body and the armpit when lifting their arm ... . He should not fix his eye on those (women), nor should he consent to (women's) inconsiderate acts, nor should he walk together with them: thus his soul is well-guarded [*Sūyagaḍanga* (*Itthīparinnā*) 1.4.1,1–3; 1.4.1,5: translation Alsdorf 1974: 202–3].[5]

The denunciation could be directed against the man's attitude more than against external causes, but this does not seem to hold true for Jainism where the account of the fourth vow generally forms a starting point for lengthy reflections on women's innate wickedness (Williams 1963: p. 176). At the same time, however, some writers probably felt that these were overstatements that should not be understood literally, since they indicate that their purpose is only to warn monks against danger and help them.[6] In fact, the aim is to make one understand that women (as well as children) are aliens; as such, they are to be given up. Negative outbursts also have to be viewed within the doctrinal frame: sexual differences are only external, the main thing is the soul (*jīva*), which is the same and can improve.

Women and Emancipation

It has been argued that the period between 300 BCE and 200 CE witnessed the eruption of 'a doctrinal crisis wherein the spiritual capacities of women were challenged and a real effort was made to prove theologically that women are inferior to men'.[7] This had an impact on Jainism as it had on Mahāyāna Buddhism at a similar time. As a matter of fact, the first evidence in support of men's and women's spiritual inequality is found in one of the religious poems ascribed to Kundakunda, one of the most revered Digambara teachers said to have worked toward the beginning of the Christian era. By establishing a direct connection between the fact that a woman (even as a nun) cannot go naked and the affirmation of nudity as *sine qua non* for the attainment of emancipation, Kundakunda put forward the central argument of debate that subsequently became a *locus communis* of the Digambara/Śvetāmbara doctrinal rivalry, which has continued to the present day:

> According to the Teaching of the Jina, a person wearing clothes cannot attain mokṣa even if he be a Tīrthaṅkara. The path of mokṣa consists of nudity (*nagna*); all other paths are wrong paths.
>
> In the genital organs of women, in-between their breasts, in their navels, and in the armpits, it is said [in the scriptures that] there are very subtle living beings. How can there be the mendicant ordination (*pravrajyā*) for them [since they must violate the vow of ahiṃsā]?
>
> Women have no purity of mind; they are by nature fickle-minded. They have menstrual flows. [Therefore] there is no meditation for them free from anxiety. (Kundakunda, *Suttāpāhuḍa* vss. 23–25; translation Jaini 1991: p. 35).

While the Digambaras advocate that a woman cannot attain emancipation, implying that rebirth as a man is a prerequisite, the Śvetāmbaras say that this transitory stage is not necessary. Copious primary literature on the topic comes from both schools and, interestingly enough, is often inserted in treatises devoted to the discussion of philosophical or logical matters as if the need was felt to lead the debate beyond mere postulates with the help of closely argued reasoning.[8] The first exhaustive book on the topic is apparently the *Strīnirvāṇaprakaraṇa*, composed in the ninth century by Śākaṭāyana, a member of the now extinct Yāpanīya sect whose positions side with the Śvetāmbaras (Jambuvijaya 1974; Jaini 1991: 41ff.; Shanta 1985: 490ff.), whereas most other texts date from the eleventh century onward.[9]

Among the arguments expressed by Digambaras in favour of their position, a first group is based on pan-Indian beliefs (or prejudices) against women whose inborn nature is supposed to be bad. Birth as a woman can be due only to a great sin and to pre-eminence of wrong belief. Women's nature is weak. Treachery is a woman's prerogative. Women are inferior to men with respect to glory and they are not shown respect by men. In such cases, the Śvetāmbaras answer by referring to counter-examples that invalidate the general value of the thesis, quoting, for instance, names of women who proved their energy, or saying that some of the criticisms levelled at them could be levelled at men as well.[10] In reply to the Digambaras who contend that the inability of women to be reborn in the lowest hell is a sign of their general lack of excellence (*prakarṣa*), the Śvetāmbaras say that since there is no adequation (*avyāpti*) between this well admitted inability and the inability for emancipation, it cannot hold as a cause.[11] However, as stated earlier, the major discussion centres around the question of clothing. According to the Digambaras, emancipation means total rejection of all belongings and giving up the satisfaction of physical needs (such as eating). But wearing clothes would mean transgressing the fifth vow of non-attachment and an inaptitude to observe self-control (*saṃyama*). Because of her innate physical impurity, a woman needs clothes in any case. Hence, since she cannot fulfil the precondition, she is not fit for emancipation. The other party says:

> If women cannot attain mokṣa because [they wear] clothes [then] they may abandon them. But surely it is not permitted to abandon them. [Let clothes be considered] a requisite for *mukti* [i.e. mokṣa], like a whisk broom. Otherwise, the teachers would be at fault. The teacher allows clothes for nuns, even though they are a possession, because in abandoning clothes there would be a total abandonment [of all the mendicant restraints], whereas in wearing clothes there is only a minor defect. This [objection] can apply to food and so forth. The title *nirgranthī* [a woman without possessions], which appears throughout the scriptures [referring to a nun], would not be appropriate if her requisites were considered to be possessions. By the same token, even a male could not be called a *nirgrantha* [a man without possessions]. Even though a man be adorned with clothes and ornaments, if he is free from a sense of possession, he would indeed be considered possessionless. But, even though naked, a man who retains a sense of possession would be considered one with possessions. (*Strīnirvāṇaprakaraṇa*, vss. 10–12 and a quotation from the commentary on vs. 12; translation Jaini 1991: pp. 56–59).

Thus, followers of this opinion seem to favour a spiritual interpretation of the concept of non-attachment rather than a literal understanding of the term. This appears to be a general feature of theirs in the present debate, as can be seen by their clear statement that the only way toward emancipation is the combination of 'right faith, right knowledge and right conduct' (the three *ratnas*) and that nothing shows women's inability to behave accordingly and annihilate karmic matter:[12]

> (Suppose that) a karman leading to femininity is acquired. As a matter of fact both women and men are emancipated when their individual karmas are

destroyed. Since the *ātman* is exactly the same in both women and men, woman is fit for emancipation.[13]

Nuns versus Monks: Laywomen versus Laymen

Once man's and woman's inequality on the religious level was questioned and led to a clear sectarian cut through the specific issue of emancipation, it could easily be extended. This resulted in two kinds of discussions.

The first finds support in the ambiguity of language, where masculine forms generally prevail. Thus the question arises whether words such as *sādhu* or *śrāvaka* are used in a generic meaning without any reference to sexual distinction and thus include both male and female ascetics/layfollowers, or whether they are exclusive of the feminine.[14] The interpretation highly depends on the groups concerned, the Śvetāmbaras showing a tendency to follow the first understanding, the Digambaras the second. Occasionally writers are aware of this situation: commenting upon the lesson called *Itthīparinnā* (Skt. *Strīparijñā*) of the *Sūyagaḍanga*, Śīlānka (ninth century) explains that the various inconveniences coming from interaction with women which could endanger a man's chastity would also be reversible and equally able to endanger a woman's chastity, in which case the chapter would be named *Puruṣaparijñā*![15]

Secondly, such a situation, which reached its climax in the Middle Ages, implied that in case both the masculine and the feminine (sādhu/sādhvī, śrāvaka/śrāvikā) are mentioned, the feminine part of the pair has to be justified. Thus, when dealing with the benefits of generosity, the Digambara Āśādhara (thirteenth century) cannot just take for granted that everybody is equal, and feels the need to devote a specific stanza for the women:

> (The layfollower) should consider as worthy recipients of generosity also the laywomen and the nuns who are endowed with qualities, because something sown in the fourfold *sangha* as a whole yields a lot of fruit.[16]

In such a context, even those who always supported the equality of women (the Śvetāmbaras) could not just state it as self-evident. They had to try to *prove* it. This takes place, for instance, in the books dealing with the layfollowers' duties (the *śrāvakācāras*), starting with Hemacandra (twelfth century) onward when the concept of the 'seven fields' (*saptakṣetrī*) in which a Jain should sow wealth is adduced: four of them are, respectively, the monk and the nun, the layman and the laywoman, but the fact that no difference should be made between them has to be discussed in the form of a fictitious logical argument. Interestingly enough, the solution lies in refusing one-sidedness (*ekānta*) and the recognizing the manifoldness of reality (*anekānta*) as Jains fundamentally do. Thus, even if there are 'two opposing poles of prejudice: the reverence shown to a few individual idealized women ... and the contempt shown to women in general' (Leslie 1989: p. 272), the Śvetāmbaras at least consider the existence of a positive pole more important and sufficient to support extension to laywomanhood as a valid general concept:

One should destine his own wealth to nuns respectful of the three jewels, as one does it for monks. Objection: but, because of their lack of physical and spiritual strength (*sattva*) and because of their wicked character, etc., women are not entitled to emancipation, so how can one give alms to them as he gives to monks?

Answer: Lack of energy is not proved in nuns like Brāhmī and others who gave up the life of housewives and followed the ascetic rules. In energetic beings absence of energy is impossible. As it is said:

'The chief nuns—namely, Brāhmī, Sundarī, Rājīmatī, and Candanā—were worshipped even by gods and demons, and are famous on account of their good conduct and sattva. Even in the household life, there were ladies like Sītā and others who were the best of those having good conduct and were known for their great sattva. How could such women be deficient in sattva for performing austerities (*tapas*) and lacking in holy conduct (after they have become nuns)? Having abandoned the royal fortune, as well as their relationship with husband, sons, brothers, and relatives, Satyabhāmā and others have borne renunciation. How can you say that this is being devoid of sattva?'

Objection: Rebirth as a woman is caused by big evil along with wrong faith. Somebody who has the right faith will never bind a karman leading to womanhood. So how can somebody who has a female body get emancipation?

Answer: Don't talk like that. Just at the time of acquiring the right faith, since there is the possibility of destroying all karmas (that which cause wrong faith and the obstructing ones) which last for less than *koṭikoṭis* with sincerity, the possibility of bad karmas together with wrong faith is without cause.

Objection: But it is appropriate to say that there is a drawback in causing emancipation as far as women are concerned.

Answer: This is not so. Because: 'A nun understands the Jina's words, believes in them, and practises them faultlessly; therefore there is no incompatibility between being a woman and the Three Jewels'. Thus it is proved: destining one's own wealth to the nuns who have the necessary means to reach emancipation is proper, as it is for monks.[17]

... Affection to be shown to laywomen should be inferred as being exactly the same as the one shown to laymen, not more and not less. Since they too are endowed with right knowledge, right faith and right conduct, since their chief characteristic is to be satisfied with chastity (*śīla*) whether they are widows or not, since their hearts are devoted to the Jain doctrine, they must be considered as co-religionists too.

Objection: But in the world as well as in the Teaching women are well known to be receptacles of bad points. They are indeed poisonous flowers without earth, Indra's thunderbolts without being produced from the sky, diseases without remedy, death without cause, prodigies without signs, female snakes without hoods, tigresses without a cave, real ogresses, destroyers of affection between relatives and elders, full of untruth and deceit (*māyā*). As it is said: 'Untruth, violence, deceit, stupidity, excessive greed, impurity and cruelty are the innate negative points of women. When heaps of infinite sins arise comes womanhood, know that well, Gotama.' In all treatises, almost at every step, they are criticized. Hence they should be avoided from far. How then can the fact that they should be objects of charity, respect and consideration be justified?

Answer: There is no invariability (*ekānta*) in the fact that women only are full of bad points: the same is true of men too. They also are very often seen to be cruel, full of bad points, unbelievers, ungrateful, perfidious against their masters, destroyers of trust, liars, attracted by women or others' wealth, without pity, deceivers of their kings or their elders. And all that does not justify that great men be despised. Similarly in the case of women. Even if some of them are found to be full of bad points, there are also some who are full of good points. As a matter of fact, even though they are women, the Tīrthaṃkaras' mothers are worshipped even by the highest gods and praised by the best sages because of the importance of their qualities .... Thanks to the power of their chastity, some of them change fire into water, water into earth, wildcats into jackals, a serpent into a rope, poison into nectar. In the fourfold *sangha*, the fourth part is the laywoman indeed. The fact that women are very often criticized in the treatises is only meant for the emancipation of those who are strongly attached to them.

In the treatises we hear about (the following things): the qualities of laywomen such as Sulasā and others are praised even by Tīrthaṃkaras. In heavens they are eulogised even by the best of gods as able to teach the Law. The right faith they have cannot even be shaken by strong holders of wrong faith. Some of them are in their last incarnation. Some others will come to emancipation after two-three births. Thus, as mothers, sisters, or daughters, laywomen are absolutely entitled to affection. That's all.[18]

Construction of Gender Through Mythology

Theological debates on women and emancipation are mirrored in the construction of gender in mythology, which centres around the twenty-four Tīrthaṃkaras.

The Twenty-fourth Jina, Mahāvīra

Representation of woman as a threat to the monk's chastity and complete renunciation of the world accounts for a discrepancy between Śvetāmbaras and Digambaras as far as the life of the twenty-fourth Jina, Mahāvīra, is concerned. Digambaras' position suffers no compromise: women are a threat for all, especially as they may prevent the monks from strictly observing the vow of chastity, everywhere said to be the most difficult to comply with. Under these circumstances, it seems impossible to conceive Mahāvīra as subjected to these temptations in any way. Albeit the young handsome son of a princely family, at the age of thirty he renounces the world as perfectly chaste and never surrenders to the delights of love, thus embodying the perfect ascetic. On the contrary, it is quite clear that women play a central part in this Jina's biography as told by the Śvetāmbaras. As far back as their canonical scriptures, they state that Vardhamāna was married. But whereas the *Kalpasūtra* merely gives the information, the later biographies try to justify it, and, one must admit, it is quite an embarrassing exercise. Therefore, they feel the need to advocate instances taken from the past, saying that the first Jina Ṛṣabha married, or insistingly indicate that the would-be Jina accepted marriage reluctantly after many negotiations and only to comply with his parents' wishes, which, when in his mother's womb, he had already pledged never to disobey. Here the attitude towards women might symbolically serve to highlight a fundamental difference in the importance ascribed to the layman's and the mendicant's path by the two sects: renunciation (implying perfect chastity) is the only way to salvation and can be reached *directly* according to the Digambaras, whereas a passage through the state of a perfect householder is a preliminary condition for the Śvetāmbaras.

Other questions are raised by the place of women in Mahāvīra's genealogy. How to explain in the Indian context that Śvetāmbaras literary sources *unanimously* show him as the father of a girl and mention her name as well as the name of the Master's granddaughter? The question is of some importance if we consider that this girl married a certain Jamāli, who in turn was Mahāvīra's nephew through his elder sister, and that the couple was responsible for the first schism in the church. Whatever the interpretation may be, this probably intentional stress on feminine lineage may be a part of a strategy meant to underline sectarian identity against the Digambaras (and perhaps also against the Buddhists since Gotama is said to have fathered a son). The desire to describe Mahāvīra as a perfect householder before he renounced the world is perhaps a way to make the ideal he represents closer to the ordinary man and is a less extremist view more in accordance with the accepted current social patterns.

The Nineteenth Jina Malli

The debate about women's ability to gain salvation and the answers given by both sects are best evidenced by the narrative literature relating the human existence of the nineteenth Jina. According to the Śvetāmbaras, who narrate this Jina's biography already in their canon, Malli was the feminine rebirth of the ascetic Mahābala, who, in spite of the agreement made with six of his companions to observe fasts of identical lengths, observed longer fasts. This had a double effect: Malli had to be a woman as a kind of atonement for an act of deception committed in a former birth, but, at the same time, she was deemed able to lead the same life as the other twenty-three Masters and to reach equality with them through emancipation, since asceticism is recorded among the twenty causes leading to Jinahood (the so-called *Tīrthaṃkaranāma-karman*).[19] As a young lady, she refused the six suitors who were the rebirths of her former companions, showing them by the device of a statue filled with food and thus emitting a putrid odour, that the body was disgusting and should be rejected. In short, she entered monastic life directly without going through the intermediate stage of married life, choosing renunciation and independence from the social function expected from her. Thus this narrative enhances the ambivalence of the woman-status as seen by the Śvetāmbaras. According to the Digambara versions (Jaini 1979: 40 n. 93; *Mallī-jñāta*: pp. 49–57), Malli (or Mallinātha) was born as a boy and thereafter lived the ordinary career of a Jina. Except for perhaps a doubtful and apparently unique gloss, which could lead us to think that even among them Malli could have been a woman before the time salvation was denied to this sex (*Mallī-jñāta*: pp. 53–4), this represents a unanimous tradition.

The interesting question about Malli's femininity is raised for the first time by Bhāvasena, a Digambara writer of the fourteenth century (Jaini 1986) who cleverly adduces indisputable iconographic observations as support for his position that Malli could not have been female:

> For example, no one in the world has ever perceived the (alleged) femininity of the images of the Lord Malli; on the contrary, those images are always depicted in masculine gender ... . The Lord under debate must be a man, because he is never portrayed as female in his images. This is like the images of Vardhamāna Mahāvīra, which are well known to be male in the traditions of both parties. (Bhāvasena's *Muktivicāra* 20; translation Jaini 1986: p. 217).

Nevertheless, one could wonder whether discussing the depiction of sexual characteristics in Tīrthaṃkaras' images is of any meaning, since these stereotyped standing or sitting images are conceived as material aids for meditation, basically supposed to show emancipated souls and not their physical features. As the author of the *Strīnirvāṇaprakaraṇa* flatly puts it:

> The Siddhas are neither male nor female (vs. 26). Your statement that a woman's

status is inferior to that of a man is valid only so long as the body exists as either male or female in the world. [This view] is not valid in the new state of the soul where both these genders have been abandoned (Jaini 1991: p. 70).

This conception can well explain that no representation of Malli with any feminine sexual characteristic has come down to us, except for a unique doubtful instance.[20] Anyhow, the fact that the Śvetāmbaras include in their canon a specific text narrating the life of Malli, whereas all Jinas are not provided with a fullfledged individual biography in this literary stratum, surely indicates their desire to stress their sectarian specificity regarding this point.

Mothers and Female Goddesses

The ambivalence of the Jain image of woman is best seen in the fairly high status ascribed to women as mothers or protective entities, and the development of a specific worship in connection with them *among both sects*.

A first instance of this trend is provided by the rather ancient respect shown to the parents of the Tīrthaṃkaras, and especially to their mothers as iconography proves (Shah 1987: 47ff.; *Śrāddhavidhiprakarana* quoted above). In the Śvetāmbara literary tradition a particular place is given to Marudevī, the mother of the first Jina, Ṛṣabha, since she is said to have been the 'first emancipated soul of the current descending era' and represents a special surprising case (*āścarya*) of spontaneous enlightenment not depending on any hearing of the teaching (Jaini: forthcoming). In fact, all the Jinas' mothers (e.g. Vāmā and Triśalā as Pārśva's and Mahāvīra's mothers) are very important as identifying models for today's Jain laywomen because they are embodiments of the continuity of the tradition and show that attainment of the goal comes from perfect fulfilment of their role as mothers (Kelting: forthcoming). Jain narrative literature also provides numerous instances where a man's mother is seen to act as a spiritual guide (*dharmācārya*) to whom much reverence is shown.[21] Canonical evidence is available to indicate that already at an early period learning could be identified with womanhood. Sarasvatī is revered as an embodiment of the Jinas' teaching that she protects (Cort 1987: p. 236). Thus her name is often quoted at the end of the five-fold homage-formula to the masters (*pañcanamaskāra*). There are also several groups of goddesses who are connected with the Jain doctrine, or with knowledge in general: what the Jains call 'the eight mothers of teaching' (*aṭṭha pavayaṇamāyāo*),[22] an expression that includes the fundamental categories formed by the five *samitis* and the three *guptis*, could be viewed as a conceptualization at an ethical level (and perhaps an adaptation) of the broader anthropomorphic *mātṛkās*. Similarly, the *vidyādevīs*, known at least from the fourth to fifth centuries, became codified in a list of sixteen which their iconographic representation on the ceilings of several Śvetāmbara temples (in Mt. Abu, for instance) made popular. They occupy an interesting status: they were first seen as magical powers, the acquisition of which was disapproved, and then held in rather high esteem. They are both concepts and deities provided with a personal identity through the names given to them. Influence of the general religious Indian background was obviously instrumental in the diversification of cults in Jainism and the development of goddess cults: the impact of tantric and Śakti worship and of bhakti cults acted as a challenge to Jainism; the response had to be specific, in order to prevent attraction towards Viṣṇuism and Śivaism. This process developed along an extended period of time and reached its climax in the Middle Ages, so as to result in a full-fledged pantheon where female deities play an outstanding role (Cort 1987: 241ff; Tiwari 1989: p. 5; Qvarnström 1998: pp. 36–7). Being mostly 'approached to assist (the devotee) in worldly affairs' (Cort 1987: p. 248), on given occasions when a specific problem arises (illness, need to protect a pilgrimage place, need of assistance in a religious debate, etc.), they do not endanger the Jina's top position, because the latters' main role is to guide along the path of emancipation. These deities are mainly the female attendants (*yakṣiṇīs*) of the Jinas, especially of the major ones. Together with their male counterparts (the *yakṣas*) they are grouped under the significant expression *śāsana-devatā*, 'deity of the Doctrine' (eighth century onwards: Tiwari 1989: p. 11). The most important of these *yakṣiṇīs* gradually developed an independent cult around themselves: Cakreśvarī, and even more Ambikā and Padmāvatī. Ambikā, whose name means 'mother', appears as a benevolent maternal figure connected with fertility and an inclusive deity par excellence:

> The Jaina Yakṣī Ambikā, riding a lion and sitting under a mango tree with a bunch of mangoes and child (*putra*) in her hands and her second son standing nearby, is a wonderful creation of the Jains combining in her both the Mother and Śakti aspects which the Jaina devotees hail from all walks of life (Tiwari 1989: p. 19).

As a protective deity, Ambikā possesses a terrific form too. In that case, she has to be pacified through various rituals and *mantras*. The same also holds true for Padmāvatī, a very prominent deity whose cult has given rise to a rather vast literature of mantras and *yantras* (yet to be explored), especially but not exclusively in South India.[23] In the Śvetāmbara temples of western India, Padmāvatī has often her own independent image, dressed in gorgeous red and golden clothes and worshipped by devotees expecting that she will provide wealth. Among Digambaras from South India the goddess Jvālamālinī is ascribed a rather high status and gives rise to much devotion.[24] Jain families also generally worship non-Jain *kuladevatās* (clanic deities), often females, associated with their castes or the villages where they belong. Boundaries between both groups of deities are not always hard and fast, as is proven by the case of Sacciyāmātā from Osian (Rajasthan) who has evolved from a local personal deity associated with all types of social groups into a goddess connected with extended communities of Osvāl Jains.[25]

Literary Representations: Famous Female Figures

In Jainism, story-telling is an extremely important means for communicating the Law to the followers and providing them with incitative models of conduct. Jain *dharmakathā* has a rich, old and multilingual tradition, conveyed in Prakrit, Sanskrit, Tamil, Kannara and all the Indo-Aryan vernaculars (especially Gujarati and Hindi). For the Jain women of the past as well as for those of today, lives of the female legendary protagonists, whether they are positively connotated or not, supplement the living examples of the nuns they meet and provide identification patterns to be imitated or to be avoided. Talking of them all is virtually impossible, but a non-exhaustive tentative typology can be attempted in order to stress the fundamental virtues, defects or functions emerging from stories having women as their main characters. Apart from the mothers (see above), another group familiar to most women is formed by the sixteen *Mahāsatīs*, namely Brāhmī, Sundarī, Candanabālā, Rājīmatī, Draupadī, Kausalyā, Mṛgāvatī, Sulasā, Sītā, Damayantī, Śivādevī, Kuntī, Subhadrā, Celanā and Prabhāvatī and Padmāvatī (Kelting: forthcoming), but there are also numerous other female names which are significant to the Jain minds. Salient episodes of their lives, which give them their outstanding role, have been transmitted by a long literary tradition, starting with the canon itself in Ardhamāgadhī (e.g. Rājīmatī, see below), going on with the rich exegetical literature in Māhārāṣṭrī Prakrit (especially the commentaries of the *Āvaśyaka-niryukti*, where the stories of Canadanabālā, Mṛgāvatī, Subhadrā and others appear for the first time), and continuing until today through recasts in numerous old Gujarati *rāsas*, *stotras*, *vratakathās*, etc., or adaptations in modern languages, not to mention dramatic adaptations of these same stories performed by youth-groups in India and outside among the Jain diaspora.[26]

All these famous figures correspond to different roles:

— Role as a donor of alms to a Jain monk is exemplified by Candanabālā and Revatī, who both fulfilled extremely important and difficult missions; the first one was the only one who was able to allow Mahāvīra to break his fast by offering him the food which was according to the conditions he had defined, whereas the second one was the only one who could offer the food which served as a proper medicine when Mahāvīra was ill at the time of his conflictual encounters with Makkhali Gosāla.[27] Later on, both Candanabālā and Revatī became nuns in Mahāvīra's community. Conversely, reluctant female donors who are unwilling to perform their duty when a monk comes to their house for alms because their mind is occupied by something futile also form a productive narrative pattern; the consequences they have to suffer in their future lives and rebirths are so negative that one is easily convinced that they should not be imitated: whether they are named Nāgaśrī (*Nāyādhammakahāo* 16), Rohiṇī (*Āvaśyaka*-commentaries: Balbir in Granoff 1990: p. 65) or Sugandhā (Digambara *Sugandhadaśamīkathā*) makes no difference.[28]

— Firmness and faith in the Jain *dharma* exhibited by pious practice are the themes of several stories where women are the heroines: Ārāmaśobhā is a famous young lady who always had a magical garden following her, because she quietly and carefully attended to a garden attached to a Jain temple (e.g. Granoff 1998: 264ff.). Sometimes the faith has to be claimed and manifested against the background of a hostile environment. In this case, the narrative pattern is that of an inter-religious marriage (Jain wife/Hindu, especially Śaiva, husband) and obviously acts as a translation of historical or socially rooted ideological conflicts which result in the triumph of Jainism: one lady defends the practice of abstaining from eating at night and setting a canopy (Guj. *Candarvo*) above the cooking-place, even though she is mocked at by her Śaiva in-laws, until it is proved that she is right.[29] Others convert their non-Jain husbands to Jainism by various means.[30] The lady of this kind who is probably the dearest to the Jains' hearts is Mainasundarī: this princess remained a strong Jain, in spite of her father's harsh opposition, placed all her faith in the goddess Cakreśvarī, performed a hard fast, and taught the Jain faith to Śrīpāla, the leper her father had given her for a husband so that he was finally cured and all the family became prosperous. All these women are active militants of Jainism.

— Models of moral virtue (*śīla*), mainly materialized in faithfulness to one's husband, encompass a vast scope of situations. Rohiṇī is a simple and classical instance of a lady who is desired by the king, while her husband has gone far away for business, and succeeds in turning him away, just through a moral discourse addressed to him (Jain in Granoff

1990: pp. 75-83). Subhadrā is the prototype of the faithful wife (*satī*), whose faithfulness can operate miracles: she is the only one who is able to open the shut gates of the city after having sprinkled them with water carried in a sieve from where not a single drop will fall.[31] Similar motifs of very strange conditions which can be fulfilled only by virtuous women or woman's chastity successfully put to test are numerous and not specific to Jain literature (e.g. Padmāvatī, who could revive a dead young man through her touch; Celanā, wrongly suspected by her husband Śreṇika, etc.).[32]

— But the ultimate value actually praised in almost all stories, whether explicitly or not, is undoubtedly renunciation. This is what Jain versions of the lives of pan-Indian heroines such as Sītā, Damayantī or Draupadī demonstrate:[33] more than models of true wives (*pativratās*), which they are anyway, they show an extraordinary steadiness and conviction in Jainism. Once they have fulfilled a pious life as laywomen, they are ready to finally become nuns. Rājīmatī, who had virtually no marital life, and immediately followed Neminātha after he decided to renounce the world, is an extreme example and one which is cherished by the Jains since its first appearance in the beautiful ballad of *Uttarādhyayana* (chapter 22). One of the earliest and most sensitive literary accounts of the process leading a female individual to renunciation is that of Tarangavatī who, being invited to explain why she became a nun, narrates her full autobiography and explains how renunciation is a consequence of her realizing that life and attachments are empty and cause suffering.[34] South Indian counterparts to Tarangavatī are provided by the figure of Kavuntī (from the *Cilappatikāram*), a complex human character who sets an example both by her teaching and her actions, or by the heroine of the *Nīlakeśī*.[35]

The Jain Nuns' Order

Early History

It is quite likely that the place to be assigned to women was a point of disagreement between early Hinduism—which denied women access to the religious scriptures—and the ascetic movements born in the sixth to fifth century BCE which, on the whole, defended egalitarian attitudes. Women's ability to reach liberation was recognized by the Buddha, and even though the account relating to the entrance of women into the Buddhist *sangha* at the time of the Buddha is problematic and seems to show that granting permission to them was perhaps not immediate, one has to consider the fact that its redactors were men in order to interpret it correctly.[36] Available data about the Ājīvikas show that women were admitted into the order (Basham 1951: p. 106). Jain scriptures also do not bear any trace of hesitation or restriction concerning this point. Ṛṣabha, the mythic founder of Jainism, as well as, more recently, Pārśva and Mahāvīra, all had among their followers numerous female ascetics and laywomen, some of whom became famous as paragons of virtue and were extolled in narrative literature of all periods. The number of ascetics given in the canonical texts (e.g. *Kalpasūtra*) cannot be taken literally, but there is no reason not to believe the ratio of female/male ascetics, all the more so since it is corroborated by contemporary statistics (below): the number of nuns is always more than twice the number of monks. This is probably a distinctive feature of Jainism.

Nuns' Status

Now the question is whether the probably massive initiations of women had any effect on the nuns' rank within the religious order. Data provided by Digambara sources on the organization of the church are so scanty that they can hardly be used. The disciplinary books of the Śvetāmbaras, the so-called *Chedasūtras*, which form part of the canonical scriptures, on the other hand, contain a whole set of rules stating what is allowed or what is prohibited for both monks and nuns in their daily routine. Although no statement seems to record any fundamental inequality between them, the redaction of the code points in a different direction and rests on the underlying thought that a woman needs more control. In many cases, prescriptions are similar and are then phrased 'a monk or a nun is allowed to ...', but there are also special regulations for nuns, in which case rules are phrased separately 'a monk is allowed to ..., a nun is allowed to ...', and stricter restrictions imposed upon nuns, corresponding to the phrasing 'a monk is allowed to ... , but not a nun' or 'nuns are not allowed to ..., only monks are'. They concern, for example, the type of alms that nuns can accept, the places where they are allowed to stay, or the implements they can use. Further:

> A nun is not allowed to be alone. A nun is not allowed to enter alone the house of a layman for food or drink, or to go out from there alone. A nun is not allowed to enter alone a place to ease nature or a place for stay, or to go out from there alone. A nun is not allowed to wander about alone from one village to the other. A nun is not allowed to be without clothing. A nun is not allowed to be without superior. A nun is not allowed to stand in [the ascetic posture called] *kāyotsarga* (*Bṛhat-Kalpasūtra* 5.15-21: Schubring 1977: pp. 31 and 55).

While there are eighteen causes forbidding religious initiation for men, there are twenty for women, the two additional ones being pregnancy or having a small child to support.[37] Generally speaking, the nuns are more dependent than their male colleagues, so that the pattern of ascetic relationship in a way reproduces the patterns at work in the worldly society. Thus it is admitted in some texts that a man can take ordination according to his own will without having been granted the permission to do so by his parents 'because men are not dependent on others', while 'a woman, who depends on others' cannot do so without having received the permission of her father, her husband or other males from the family.[38] Nuns are also subordinated to the monks' authority: 'The male-ascetic is governed by two persons: the teacher and the preceptor ... . The female ascetic is governed by *three* persons: the female superior [*pavattiṇī*], the preceptor and the teacher' (*Vyavahārasūtra* 3.11; 3.12). In the *Chedasūtras*, the rules are simply stated. But from the justifications expressed in the explanatory literature, it seems that most prohibitions are motivated by the wish to avoid all objects and conditions of life that could endanger the vow of chastity. Although it is not always clearly stated, the belief that women are more fragile creatures in this respect seems to be all-pervading.

The inferior status of nuns results in the fact that, even when they have had a longer religious life, they may be subordinate to monks who have been initiated only a few years. Moreover, nuns require more years than their male counterparts to attain high positions in the religious hierarchy. To judge from the literary tradition, nuns probably never reached the same positions as monks. The author can find no record of such high titles as *ācārya* and *sūri* being used for nuns. They have their own titles such as *gaṇinī*, 'head of a *gaṇa*', of a small unit of nuns, *pravartinī*, and *mahattarā*. Vardhamānasūri's *Ācāradinakara*, for instance, distinguishes between three degrees in the hierarchy: *vratinī* for the ordinary nun, *pravartinī* and *mahattarā*. He explains that, whereas some *gacchas* consider the last two designations identical, some take them separately, and opts for this solution. The fact that *mahattarā* is a special designation conferred on a restricted number of very learned, disciplined and highly respected nuns is clear, to the extent that some gacchas are of the opinion that only women who became nuns as celibates (*kumārī*) can ever get it.[39] Moreover, in such treatises as Vardhamānasūri's work as well as in the chronicles that record the lives of Śvetāmbara orders in the Middle Ages (thirteenth to fifteenth century), it is evident that both the decision and the act of conferring titles upon nuns always fell to male dignitaries who were instrumental in the process.

Theoretical literature does not really provide any argument against equality between monks and nuns as far as learning and teaching are concerned. The only passage often quoted in the secondary literature as proving that nuns (and women in general) were forbidden to study the texts included under the heading *Dṛṣṭivāda*, because they are 'empty, given to haughtiness, sensual and inconstant', cannot be relied upon. It has been convincingly shown that these commonplace remarks about feminine nature and other statements

> merely testify to a firmly established if somewhat naive belief that 'the Dṛṣṭivāda contains *everything*'—a belief obviously betraying complete ignorance of the real contents of the long lost text and, on the other hand, conveniently permitting to derive from 'the Dṛṣṭivāda' or 'the Pūrvas' any text or subject which it was desired to invest with canonical dignity (Alsdorf 1974: p. 256).

From the literary evidence it is not possible to draw any conclusion about the general educational level of nuns in the past. Compared with the large number of monks who are known to us as scholars or writers from the often very detailed colophons of Jain manuscripts, the number of nuns who did not remain anonymous is quite small: the most famous one is probably Yākinī Mahattarā, whom Haribhadrasūri (eighth century?) recognized as his 'spiritual mother'. Very few are those who have signed a work, or even who have collaborated with monks in the writing of a book, or who have inspired them; Gaṇa Sādhvī who seems to have cooperated with Siddharṣi (ninth century), Mahānanda Śrī Mahattarā and Vīramatī Gaṇinī who helped Hemacandra Maladhārin in writing the commentary on the *Viśeṣāvaśyakabhāṣya* are the few prominent names which can be mentioned in this context. On the other hand, testimony to the nuns' role as copists of manuscripts is available, albeit scanty.[40] Nuns' activity as mediators and convincing teachers of the Law able to take more members into the *sangha* is evidenced in the legendary biographies of some *Kharataragaccha* leaders, who took their decision to become monks after they heard them preach.[41] This could be explained as a literary motif, influenced by the famous pattern of Yākinī Mahattarā and Haribhadrasūri; the general Indian patterns of the female as an initiator could also have played its part in such cases. Anyway, statements of this kind are perhaps a means to express the specific stress of this gaccha on nuns' ability to preach (see below). Other testimonies showing that teaching activity was a defining characteristic of 'religious women' (in Tamil called *kuratti*) come from early Tamilnadu (eighth-ninth century), where they formed an intermediate category between nuns and laywomen (Orr 1998: 187ff; Shāntā 1985: 171ff.).

Statistics

Important statistical data about the number of Jain ascetics is provided by the *Samagra Jaina Cāturmās Sūcī*, a yearly published directory, co-ordinated by Bābulāl Jain 'Ujjval'. Although it is primarily to inform the Jain laity about the places where the various groups of ascetics will stay and be available during the monsoon months, it contains a lot of precious information, with some observations, about these groups. A comparison of the successive issues enables one to get an idea of the evolution over the years.

	1994		
	Monks	*Nuns*	*Total*
Śvetāmbara Mūrtipūjaks	1356	4884	6240
Sthānakvāsins	505	2422	2927
Terāpanthins	147	547	694
Digambaras	275	219	494

	1998		
	Monks	*Nuns*	*Total*
Śvetāmbara Mūrtipūjaks	1474	5420	6894
Sthānakvāsins	536	2638	3174
Terāpanthins	147	538	685
Digambaras	415	350	765

The Digambara group is the only one where nuns are less numerous than monks. The theological image of women among Digambaras has probably something to do with this situation. However, comparative statistics for the last decades show that the gap between male and female ascetics tends to reduce so that the ratio becomes more balanced:

	Monks	*Nuns*	*Total*
1986	318	48	366
1990	225	130	355
1995	295	250	545
1998	415	350	765

In other groups, the ratio is rather unbalanced in favour of nuns: four times more among the Sthānakvāsins, three-and-a half times more among the Terāpanthins and the Mūrtipūjaks. This ratio is even increased when considering separately some of the groups belonging to the Mūrtipūjaks: ten times more nuns than monks in the Kharataragaccha, five times more in the Añcalagaccha. In these last two groups, the number of monks becomes lower each year, while the number of nuns grows in significant proportions.

	1986		*1994*		*1998*	
	Monks	*Nuns*	*Monks*	*Nuns*	*Monks*	*Nuns*
Tapāgaccha	1382	3765*	1296	4479	1322	4714
Kharatara	19	193	20	201	20	207
Añcala	40	184	40	204	36	220

* See note 42.

Although the question should be examined further, factors related to social environment and restraints imposed upon women play an important part in the women's decision to become nuns. The impossibility for a widow to remarry or the prospect of a very hard life for women living in less developed areas of India are among those factors.[43] But in recent years it has also been observed that the number of women who have never been married when they enter into the *sangha* is increasing (Cort 1991: p. 660; Flügel: forthcoming). The fact that religious life is an opportunity to develop one's own personality through study and live as an individual not defined in terms of others is sometimes adduced as a strong motivation (Holmström 1988: p. 36), but whether such a plan is fulfilled depends on the organization of the gaccha and on the positions of the group concerning female education.

Organization

In most ascetic groups (gacchas), the basic unit around which daily life centres is the 'family' (*parivāra*), a kind of 'informal grouping' liable to change under the circumstances. These small units are subdivisions of the larger one called *samudāya*, where all the ascetics claiming an identical spiritual affiliation to a given teacher belong. While nuns are grouped together in parivāras for the daily monastic life, they are not necessarily allowed to wander alone (Misra 1972: 37ff.); they are not known to be authorized to form independent samudāyas, which would suppose that the leader of the lineage would be a nun, but they are attached to the samudāya of a monk. Hence the following has been rightly observed and can be taken as generally valid:

> [...] Ascetic institutions reflect the agnatic values prevailing in the wider social world : monks constitute the core of these entities, and nuns are attached to monk's lineages, just as women become attached to the families and lineages of their husbands by marriage (Babb 1996: p. 54).

Beside a certain amount of nun's subordination towards monks, there are also well defined seniority rules which define the relationship between nuns.

An interesting example of the way the nun's order is structured is provided by the vigorously organized Terāpantha sect, which originated in the eighteenth century in Rajasthan, as a reaction to the 'lax' discipline of the time. In the beginning, the patriarchal structure was centred around a single ācārya. He was the head of monks and nuns who were almost equally proportionate. But the regular increase of nuns led to the institution of a so-called *pramukhā*, 'a female head' who became the religious superior of the smaller units. She is, however, by no means the equal of the ācārya, who makes all the important decisions, but is rather a coordinator subordinate to him. It will remain to see in future years or decades whether the nun's numerical pressure along with undercurrents in favour of protests against excessive monks' supervision (increasing among Sthānakvāsins) will lead to any real change.

Instances of Crucial Issues in Today's Community

Nun's Education

Today this question is becoming a central point. There appears to be sectarian differentiation with regard to the canonical texts accessible to nuns. While the Sthānakvāsins and the Terāpanthins make no distinction between monks and nuns, and profess that everybody can learn everything if he or she has the capacity for it, the Tapāgaccha group of the Mūrtipūjaks spreads among its female followers the idea that their abilities are less than those of men. As a result, they study a very small number of the canonical texts and are, in any case, forbidden to have access to the *Chedasūtras* where faults and their punishments are recorded, lest it would give them bad ideas (Shāntā 1985: p. 377). A related question pertains to the nuns' permission to preach and have public sermons (*vyākhyāns*). This is a motif of disagreement between the various groups. Thus, nuns are generally not allowed to preach in the Tapāgaccha, whereas in the Añcalagaccha they are allowed to do so only if no monk is available, and are readily allowed to do so in the Kharataragaccha (one reason being that monks are much less numerous; Babb 1996: p. 55). However, this is a point giving rise to evolutions or reforms. The Tapāgaccha monk Ācārya Vijayavallabhasūri, for instance, has been a strong advocate for the uplift of nuns and has encouraged them both to read the sacred texts and to communicate their knowledge in public, be it among layfollowers or in the presence of monks.

The same tendencies broadly hold true for general education. The Sthānakvāsins and the Terāpanthins avowedly consider the nuns' education as a priority and have a modern position on the subject. Among the former, there is a tendency to encourage nuns to pursue in the line of higher education and to get degrees; lists of MAs and PhDs are regularly published in the *Samagra Jain Cāturmās Sūcī.* The steps taken by the Terāpanthins for improving nuns' education are rather specific. Before initiation the girls have to undergo a period of probation during which they have the status of *mumukṣus* (candidates for emancipation). They attend a full course in a boarding school and become familiar with religious scriptures (Holmström 1988: 46ff). The daily routine of the Terāpanthi nuns probably includes more time effectively devoted to the study or in copying of texts. Finally, for about fifteen to twenty years, the Terāpanthins have initiated within the order a particular category mainly consisting of women who are released from some of the strictest rules (such as that of going exclusively on foot) and whose main function is to read and write or to spread the Jain teaching: this is the so-called *samaṇa śreṇi* which counts 88 females for only 4 males.[44] Those who are sent outside India (to Great Britain and United States) have an important responsibility, as they are in charge of educating Jain devotees who are cut from the motherland, settled in a very specific environment (somewhat alien to their faith). They also have to face the interrogations of a demanding youth who occasionally has to be convinced of the intellectual truth of the basic principles of Jain ethics. The innovation of the samaṇa śreṇi is a part of the claimed objective of the Terāpanthins who, under the powerful guidance of the late Ācārya Tulasi, considered the improvement of women's condition as one of their main mottos.

Other groups (Mūrtipūjaks and Digambaras) are more discrete about nuns' education, which they do not seem to favour equally. The vast number of Tapāgaccha nuns generally do not receive much incentive for study, except for the basic texts, hymns and prayers required for the performance of the daily rituals. But there are, of course, some exceptions who, having benefitted from intellectual uplift, would also like their colleagues to do so. Under the impulse of Ācārya Vijayavallabhasūri from the Tapāgaccha and his positive approach towards female education, nuns belonging to his tradition such as the late Mahattarā Mṛgāvatīśrījī, for instance, clearly articulated the importance of nuns being knowledgeable, lest a valuable potential be wasted, and recommended that before young nuns are initiated, they pass through a five-year curriculum where they would study Jain basic texts as well as grammar, literature and the like, with some learned pandits (Mṛgāvatī 1989: p. 51). Whatever the situation and the turn it will take, prominent nuns who contribute to research on Jainism by translations, writing of educational pamphlets and other type of literature are not lacking in the present time: Āryikā Jñānamati (Digambara) is one of the most active in this respect, having several publications to her credit. Literary activity is not the only manifestation of nuns' spiritual and moral weight. They also often act as incentives (*prerikā*) for the establishment of institutions of learning and research or the development of pilgrimage places: whereas Mṛgāvatīśrījī impulsed the foundation of the Vijayavallabha Smārak (and the B.L. Institute of Indology) located in the periphery of Delhi, Āryikā Jñānamati was the main person behind the Trilok Śodh Saṃsthān of Hastinapur (UP), devoted to Jain cosmology, and the erection of the famous Jambūdvīp monument which partly accounts for the recent renaissance of this Jain *tīrtha*. In recent years, the desire to do full justice to the multifarious contributions of Jain nuns to the community and the faith as a whole has come to light and expressed itself through the publication of a few books, among which the bulky *Jin śāsan nāṃ śramaṇīratno* (The nuns, a jewel of the Jain teaching, 1994), which contains ample biographical material about the lives of several nuns of this century and the preceding ones.[45]

Nuns' Worship and Images

A Jain layfollower is expected to pay his respects and perform the ritual salutation (*vandana*) in front of a nun as he would do for a monk. But it seems that the strength of the sex boundaries sometimes encourages nuns to spontaneously impose restrictions, so that the laymen do not accomplish exactly the same gestures towards her as the laywomen would do (Jain 1997: p. 85).

The worship of deceased nuns and the question of their iconographic representation is another issue in point. The depiction of ācāryas in stone and to a lesser extent in painting is deeply rooted in the tradition, and has developed in some Jain groups such as the Kharataragaccha, where temples containing *mūrtis* of the earlier teachers (*dādāgurudevs*) are fairly numerous and increasing in recent years (*dādābāṛīs*: Babb 1996: 111ff.).

On the other hand, it is also a common practice for today's monks to keep photographs of their teachers and pay respect to them; and walls of the *upāśrayas* covered with photographs of the deceased gurus are also an ordinary sight. *Mūrtis* of nuns seem to be admitted, at least in some later texts such as Vardhamānasūri's *Ācāradinakara* (fifteenth century) where temple rituals and installation of images are dealt with at great length: the heading concerned with the procedure of installing monk's images (*yatimūrtipratiṣṭhāvidhi*) includes a sub-heading concerned with stūpas and images of monks and nuns (sādhu-sādhvī) and gives the formula to be recited for the installation of both.[46] In practice, however, although they exist, nuns' images were clearly much less frequent than those of their male colleagues.[47] In today's India, they are still exceptional. A recent case provides a good illustration of the tensions between different currents on this issue: in the beginning of 1997 a statue of the late Mahattarā Mṛgāvatīśrījī was installed in great pomp in the precincts of the Vijayavallabha Smārak near Delhi.[48] The fact that this prompted a Jain follower to write about it and to adduce evidence justifying the practice and underlining its antiquity shows that it was perhaps controversial and not readily accepted by all corners of the Jain community (Jain 1997). As a support for his point of view, the author mentions two famous nuns' images, one in the main Śvetāmbara temple of Rajgir, and another in the fort of Chittor. However, there is a fundamental difference between these statues, where the nuns are shown in a position of reverence towards a Tīrthaṃkara or a monk (the Chittor image is that of Yākinī Mahattarā visible beside Haribhadra's big statue) and the Delhi image, where the nun stands all by herself as an independent object of worship. Such novelties and the positive reactions they provoke may speak in favour of the emergence of a new tendency, which could lead to other comparable cases: impressive memorials for two leading nuns from the Kharataragaccha have also been constructed in Jaipur and attract a lot of people (Babb 1996: p. 55). In view of the always growing importance of the teachers' cult and the development of new *tīrthas* connected with places centred around their biographies, this is certainly not a minor point. One should follow the question and see how nuns will find their place in this process.

Jain Laywomen: Female Areas of Religiosity

The importance given to the laity was always an essential element of Jainism and is often said to partly explain the survival of the movement in India in contemporary times. As a matter of fact, the laity is the economic foundation of the religious mendicant order, which it supports by its gifts, receiving in exchange the teaching of the law. Laywomen contribute to the sustaining of the community no less than laymen do, so that it has been argued that they are those who could have been determining in the continuity of the Jain tradition because they build a kind of religious middle-class that consolidates the system and insures its stability (Tkatcheva 1996: p. 99). The Jain diaspora outside India is well aware of this fact and is conscious that the woman's role in pursuing the tradition is fundamental. Thus the Executive Committee of the 10-year Plan For Developing the Jain Way of Living in North America established by the Federation of Jain Associations of North America (JAINA) states:

> Women: Our women represent half the adult population. To them goes the credit of retaining and carrying from generation to generation our Indian culture in general and Jain religion in particular. So, their active involvement is a must. Following activities are suggested:
>
> 1. Women's club at each centre to discuss various issues relating to them.
> 2. Appointment of women directors from different centres on the JAINA board. JAINA board should not be male dominated.
> 3. Practising non-violence and respect for different views at home, at community activities and in dealing with outside world. Set example before children.
> 4. Camps about leadership in community activities.
> 5. Camps about studies in Jainism.[49]

Jainism developed an immense corpus of texts devoted to the code of conduct of the laity (*śrāvakācāra*: Williams 1963). In these treatises, however, 'the male is invariably taken as the paradigm' (Leslie 1989: p. 431) as can be seen from the wording of the fourth minor vow, which prescribes 'contentment with one's own wife' and 'avoidance of the wives of others' (Williams 1963: p. 85). Except for a few passages quoted above, no discussion is found on the question of whether the term *śrāvaka* also implies the feminine and how the *śrāvikā* should practice her faith. Thus 'Jain laywomen are the experts at being Jain laywomen'.[50]

As being obviously largely dependent on the Indian (Hindu) environment, Jain women (especially wives) have some general duties which they share with any other of their Indian colleagues. Although discrimination and submission are not inscribed in the doctrine, they are part of their lives, and their dharma is summed up by the word *śīla*, which designates the virtues of a perfect wife.[51] As has been shown by Reynell (1987: p. 340), 'physical chastity is believed equivalent to spiritual purity', and to some extent removes the boundary between a woman in the world and a woman outside the world.

'The social construction of gender' (Reynell 1987: p. 313) accounts for a certain distribution and complementarity of religious roles between men and women. As a general rule, men work outside to earn money, while women remain at home. Men manifest their prestige by giving money to the temple. Women are best fit to master all that is connected with food and, provided rather serious limitations, with the field of worship and rituals. Thus their place in the community is mostly practically directed towards two areas where the otherwise prevalent gender hierarchy is at least partly reversed. On the other hand, they insure 'the reproduction of the Jain Community' through marriage-organization and religious teaching imparted to their children (Reynell 1991: 59ff.). The level of education of Jain women largely varies, but is periodically encouraged by the Jain conferences (Cort 1995: p. 11). Mostly, they have access to the doctrine through encounters with monks, or even more with nuns, who often act as spiritual guides but also as general advisors on family matters. It is quite common that laywomen will visit the neighbouring nuns' upāśraya and have rather informal and intimate conversations with one of them. These visits are also an occasion to revive their memories about famous females of the past and keep alive the rich stock of legendary material. Knowledge about it can also come from the numerous magazines or small pamphlets in vernacular languages easily available, or from the immensely rich hymnic literature (*stotras, stavans*) which they know by heart.

Food

In a doctrine such as Jainism, which lays so much stress on dietary rules (Williams 1963: 50ff., 110ff.; Mahias 1985: 100ff.), the part played by women is obviously of primary importance (Reynell 1991: p. 54). Observation of such rules is one of the clearest means to insure sectarian identity. Thus the woman at home functions as a guardian or modifier of the tradition through the various roles ascribed to her. She is in a good position to obey the rules or transgress them, as well as to make others do the same. The first and foremost responsibility of a laywoman is to prepare food that is acceptable to monks and nuns though not specially meant for them. This is no easy task considering the number of prescriptions to be observed. Correct fulfilment of this role implies that she masters a minute sequence of actions and rules. When the canonical texts describe the donor, they use the feminine gender, because, as a commentator remarks, 'she is the one who mostly offers alms' and is the donor par excellence:

If a woman of the house wastes the food when distributing it, (the monks) should refuse (it, saying to) the (alms-)giver: 'I may not accept such (alms)'. (When he notices that) she crushes living beings, seeds (and) plants with her foot, he should avoid such (a house), knowing that she performs that which is not suitable to (his) self-control. ... She brings food and drink having put her hand into the vessel and poured out (that which was inside). (In all these cases) he should refuse. ... If she brings food and drink having put down her crying boy or girl to whom she is giving the breast, that food and drink is not allowed (*Daśavaikālikasūtra* 5.1.28–29, 31.42–43; translation Schubring 1977: pp. 208–9).

Popular stories telling how a woman caused the death of a sādhu because she had offered him some rotten vegetable, which he was obliged to eat in order to avoid the death of numerous ants attracted by its foul smell and examples of famous female donors have already been mentioned earlier. The woman is also the one who prepares the meals for the family and decides whether a rule like the one which forbids eating after sunset will be observed or not. Even if normative literature prescribes the avoidance of eating or drinking at night for all, whether men or women, a perusal of narrative literature seems to show that it is actually observed mostly (if not only) by women, for they are the sole protagonists of stories devoted to this topic.[52] Today Jain men who are proud of their wives for their respect of this prescription, while they themselves are unable to observe it for practical reasons, are frequently met (Laidlaw 1995: p. 356). It is remarkable that, while no specification is generally given about women in the case of other religious themes, some texts include a separate account listing the miseries or happiness awaiting any girl who would break this vow or keep it. Modern evidence shows the same trend (Misra 1972: pp. 44–54) and, as has been argued by Mahias (1985: pp. 108–11), it may result in inverting the normal sequence of the meals, since the wife would then take food *before* her husband. Similarly, the woman is also the one who will know which type of food has to be cooked, depending on the day (festival/ordinary) and will have a full command on the complicated calendar and typology of fasts which regulate the Jains' lives.

Fasting

As constituting the penance (*tapas*) par excellence because it also implies sexual purity, abstaining from food in the form of fasts in indeed 'one of the most important expressions of female religiosity' and 'one of the key ways through which women demonstrate family honour',[53] or at least the way males from the community want them to display it.[54] There is a large variety of fasts (Mahias 1985: 111ff.; Reynell 1987: pp. 320-1), either implying total restriction (water allowed, food forbidden) or partial restriction regarding the type of food or the frequency of meals. The aims of all the fasts are also not identical: while some of them (the *vrats*) are meant for worldly purposes, others (*upavāsas*) are a way to affirm the Jain ideals. The literary tradition, whether ancient or modern, shows that fasting for women is widely encouraged: female protagonists are dominant in the so-called *vratakathās*, and fasting women are among models to be imitated. Stories very often emphasize the quasi-miraculous power of fasts, which are liable to yield unexpectedly positive results and end in sudden cures, wealth, etc.[55] Some types of fasts, such as the *Rohiṇī-tap* and the *ravivār vrat* (Sundays' fast) among Digambaras, are specific to women.[56] The more fasts they perform during their life, the higher is their reputation of religiosity. Fasting women always arouse great respect among their relatives and are surrounded by great care (Misra 1972: p. 491). To quote Reynell (1987: p. 347), 'through her fasting a woman makes a public statement about herself. Fasting becomes a statement of a woman's inner purity and by extension becomes a statement about the honour of her family.' As a matter of fact, the breaking of a fast always involves a group celebration or a feast of some kind, which contributes to social cohesion (Misra 1972: p. 50; Reynell 1987: pp. 348–51).

Sphere of Ritual

The question of worship is rather intricate with regard to the position of women. Except for the followers of the non-idolatrous sect of the Sthānakvāsins who pray or meditate privately in their houses, all Jains must go to the temples daily and worship the Jinas as 'human beings who have achieved omniscience and final liberation and who teach the path of liberation to others' (Babb 1988: p. 67). The doctrine prescribes it for all, and actual observation shows that women do it more regularly and more at leisure, adding to it the performance of other rituals at home (Reynell 1987: p. 319). Ethnographic observation shows that they are those who are really conversant with knowledge of the praxis, who lead the men in this respect and manifest a certain type of power. As a matter of fact, pūjā is very often an organized social activity where women gather together in maṇḍals for chanting, worshipping, etc., and is an extremely important means of expressing the faith: performing the correct gestures with sincerity is the way to earn knowledge. Singing of hymns is highly creative, as the women do not necessarily use stotras available at hand, but may compose new ones. Through this medium they may express, in their own ways, some fundamental and conflicting issues of the doctrine. Thus

the way the laywomen used their knowledge to explore theological questions (within their own idiom) makes it clear that women have a 'voice' in the development of contemporary and future Jainism (Kelting 1999).

Moreover, Jain laywomen also assert themselves as a group respecting identical values when they go among themselves for trips to the main pilgrimage-centres, an activity which is often organized by local colonies in the big cities.

On the other hand, it is well known that in Śvetāmbara temples the right to perform different sorts of pūjās first is determined by a system of auction. Though nothing theoretically prevents women from raising bids, there seems to be a kind of consensus that they can do it only along with their husbands (Reynell 1987: pp. 327–8). Moreover sporadic statements also imply that their rights possibly differ from those of men as far as the performance of rituals is concerned, or that women are submitted to more restrictions. Whatever its divisions, daily worship generally implies two categories of rituals: the first takes place in the cella of the temple and requires a perfect physical and mental purity from the worshipper since it implies direct contact with the image, which has to be washed or anointed with paste of sandalwood and flowers. The second ritual requires less purity since it takes place in the main hall, in front of the image but at a distance from it (Babb 1988: 70ff.). Woman being the paradigmatic 'impure' creature, it happens that among Digambaras she may not be allowed to wash the image (Mahias 1985: p. 254). To quote a Digambara work: 'If a woman performs worship to the Jinas, she should follow the same injunctions (as men) but she is not entitled to touch the image. Thus do the knowledgeable people say'.[57] Among Śvetāmbaras she may be excluded altogether from the first category of rituals (Stevenson 1915: p. 251). The followers of the Kharataragaccha do not allow women to worship images of the Jinas (Deo 1950: p. 25). In front of a modern temple dedicated to the god Ghaṇṭākarṇa Mahāvīra (in Lodurva, Rajasthan), a board says that no woman should enter the cella, and that no menstruating woman should enter the main hall (see also Babb 1988: p. 69). Restrictions connected with menstrual periods are very important and often emphasized in talks of Jain women and nuns.[58] The belief is that a woman will not be able to 'communicate spiritual energy' and that recitation and other religious activities will have opposite consequences than those desired. Thus she is advised to remain aloof from the community, not to read sacred books or even touch them. Such details are important insofar as they represent an undercurrent tendency rather than a general line. They embody the conflict between the fundamentally egalitarian religious doctrine of Jainism and the pan-Indian beliefs about womanhood.

CONCLUSION

Whatever the way we consider the problem of womanhood in Jainism, we see two irreconcilable theologies at work as far as the soteriological level is concerned. The 'theology of subordination' is supported by the Digambaras. It is based on the idea that woman is ontologically, intellectually, and morally inferior to man, which contends that she will never be able to reach emancipation—the main goal for which the teaching of the law is meant. The 'theology of equivalence' is supported by the Śvetāmbaras. It admits that man and woman are human persons of equal value even if they are *different*, and thus that both are equally entitled to reach the final goal.

There are, however, two types of limitation to this bipolarization. The first one is the *law of karma*. If one's birth depends on one's own conduct, womanhood (which is due to specific karmic matters) will never be a permanent feature of the individual through the cycle of rebirths. Thus, no one is excluded from emancipation for good. The 'failure' will last as long as womanhood lasts. Secondly, even if the theology of equivalence advocates *theoretical* equality of men and women, it in fact also shares the postulate of the theology of subordination regarding the inferiority of women, although it is expressed through insinuations and not given the same extension. This contradiction probably translates difficulties in solving the conflict between the general Indian environment, including the negative ideas it conveys about womanhood, and the attempt to go beyond them through religion. Whatever the theology espoused, until now nuns have had a less important position than monks in the religious hierarchy and have been mostly denied leadership roles in spite of their large numbers. Thus, at an institutional level, Jainism is man-centred. However, the interesting fact is that whether they belong to one or the other of the two theologies (Digambara/Śvetāmbaras), Jain laywomen exhibit the same conviction in their faith and the same determination in its translation into acts in their daily lives.[59] Thus, on the whole, history as well as present time show that the construction of gender is a complicated process which constantly fluctuates between two extremes.[60]

BIBLIOGRAPHY

(All primary sources used are not listed here. They appear with corresponding references in the notes).

Alsdorf, Ludwig, 1974, *Kleine Schriften*, Herausgegeben von A. Wezler. Wiesbaden: F. Steiner Verlag.

Babb, Lawrence A., 1988. 'Giving and Giving up : The Eightfold Worship among Śvetāmbar Mūrtipūjak Jains', *Journal of Anthropological Research* 44, no 1: pp. 67–86.

—— 1996, *Absent Lord. Ascetics and Kings in a Jain Ritual Culture*, University of California Press.

Balbir, Nalini, 1982, *Dānāṣṭakakathā*. Paris: De Boccard.

—— 1983, 'Observations sur la secte jaina des Terāpanthin', *Bulletin d'Etudes Indiennes* (Paris) 1: pp. 39–45.

—— 1993, 'Women in Jainism' in *Religion and Women*. Edited by Arvind Sharma. SUNY: 121–138 (bibliography, 251–3).

Basham, Arthur L., 1951, *History and Doctrine of the Ājīvikas, A Vanished Indian Religion*. London, Luzac & Co.

Bhatt, Usha, 1997, 'Jain Women Saints in the 20th Century: Challenges and Response', *New Dimensions of Indology* (Dr Praveen Chandra Parikh Felicitation Volume). Delhi–Varanasi: Bharatiya Vidya Bhavan Prakashan: pp. 103–5.

Bhattacharya, Hari Satya, 1967, Edition and translation of *Vādidevasūris Pramānayatattvālokālaṃkara*, Bombay: Jain Sahitya Vikas Mandal.

Boradiyā, Hīrābāī, 1991, Jain dharma kī pramukha sādhviyāṃ evaṃ mahilāeṃ, Varanasi: Pārśvanāth Vidyāśram Śodh Saṃsthān (Pārśvanātha Vidyāśram Granthamālā 57). [The introduction includes Sargarmal Jain's contribution '*Jain dharma meṃ nārī kī bhūmikā*'].

Caillat, Colette, 1997, 'Code religieux et narration. La légende de Karakaṇḍu': *Lex et Litterae. Studies in Honour of Professor Oscar Botto*. Turin: Edizioni dell' Orso: pp. 101–13.

Chojnacki, Christine, 1998, 'Connaissance scripturaire et rituel chez les jaina: la *Jñānapañcamīkathā* de Maheśvarasūri': *Bulletin d'Etudes Indiennes* [Paris] 15, 1997: pp. 31–113.

Cort, John E., 1987, 'Medieval Jaina Goddess Traditions'. Numen 34, no. 2, December: pp. 235–55.

—— 1991, 'The Śvetāmbar Mūrtipūjak Jain Mendicant': *Man* 26.4: pp. 651–71.

—— 1995, *Defining Jainism: Reform in the Jain Tradition*. University of Toronto, Centre for South Asian Studies (The 1994 Roop Lal Jain Lecture).

Deo, Shāntā Ram Bhalachandra, 1950, 'Jaina Temples, Monks and Nuns in Poona', *The Jaina Antiquary* 16, no. 1: pp. 17–33.

—— 1956, *History of Jaina Monachism from Inscriptions and Literature*. Poona: Deccan College.

Desai, Kumarpal, 1998, 'Role of Women in Jaina Religion', *Jainism in a Global Perspective*. Ed. Sagarmal Jain and Sriprakash Pandey, Varanasi: Pārśvanātha Vidyāpīṭha: pp. 184–91.

Dineś Muni, 1987, *Sādhvīratna Puṣpavatījī Abhinandan Granth*, Udaipur: Śrī Tārak Guru Jain Granthālaya (pp. 237–300).

Dundas, Paul, 1992, *The Jains*, London: Routledge.

Flügel, Peter, (forthcoming), 'Protestantische und Post-Protestantische Jain Reformbewegungen: Zur Geschichte und Organisation der Sthānakvāsi Jains', *Berliner Indologische Studien*.

Granoff, Phyllis (ed.), 1990, *The Clever Adulteress and Other Stories*, A Treasury of Jain Literature. Oakville, New York–London: Mosaic Press.

Granoff, Phyllis, 1998, *The Forest of Thieves and the Magic Garden*, An Anthology of Medieval Jain Stories, selected, translated and with an introduction, Penguin Books.

Holmström, Savitri, 1988, *Towards a Politics of Renunciation: Jain Women and Asceticism in Rajasthan*. Unpublished M.A. Thesis, University of Edinburgh.

Jain, Mahendra Kumar 'Mast', 1997, 'Jainoṃ meṃ sādhvī pratimā kī pratiṣṭhā, pūjā va vandan. Itihās va prāmāṇikatā ke sandarbha meṃ', *Śramaṇ* [Varanasi], July–September, pp. 82–5.

Jain, Sagarmal, 1990, 'Jain dharma meṃ nārī kī bhūmikā', *Śramaṇ* [Varanasi] 41, 10–12: 1–48 (see above Boradiyā).

Jaini, Padmanabh S., 1979, *The Jaina Path of Purification*. Delhi, Motilal Banarsidass.

—— 1986, 'Muktivicāra of Bhāvasena: Text and Translation', *Indologica Taurinensia* 13: 203–19.

—— 1991, *Gender and Salvation. Jaina Debates on the Spiritual Liberation of Women*', University of California Press.

—— (forthcoming), 'From Nigoda to Mokṣa'. Paper read at the International Conference *Jainism and Early Buddhism in the Indian Cultural Context*. Lund, June 1998.

Jambuvijaya Muni (ed.), 1974, *Śākaṭāyana, Strīnirvāṇa-prakaraṇa*, edited by Jambuvijaya Muni. Bhavnagar.

Jin śāsan naṃ śramaṇīratno, 1994, Prerikā: Pu. Vātsalyamūrti Sā. Sarvodayāśrī ma. sā., ed. Śrī Nandalāl Devaluk. Bhavnagar.

Jñānamati, Āryikā, 1990, *Merī smṛtiyāṃ*, Digambar Jain Trilok Śodha Saṃsthān. Hastinapur.

Das Kalpa-sūtra, *Die alte Sammlung jinistischer Mönchsvorschriften*. Einleitung, Text, Anmerkungen, Übersetzung, Glossar, von Walther Schubring, Leipzig, 1905. [English translation by May S. Burgess in *The Indian Antiquary* 39 (1910), pp. 257–67].

Kelting, Mary Whitney, 1999, 'Jain Women's *Maṇḍals* and the Authority to Recreate Jain Theology', *Approaches to Jaina Studies: Philosophy, Logic, Rituals and Symbols*, ed. N.K. Wagle and O. Qvarnström. Toronto, pp. 275–90.

—— 1996, *Hearing the Voices of the Śrāvikā: Ritual and Song in Jain Laywomen's Belief and Practice*, Ph.D. Dissertation. University of Wisconsin, Madison [unpublished; the author has kindly made two chapters of her work available to me].

—— (forthcoming), 'Construction of Femaleness in Jain Devotional Literature', Paper read at the International Conference *Jainism and Early Buddhism in the Indian Cultural Context*, Lund, June 1998.

Kulkarni, V. M. (ed.), 1994, *A Treasury of Jain Tales*, Ahmedabad, Sharadaben Chimanbhai Educational Research Centre.

Laidlaw, James, 1995, *Riches and Renunciation*, Religion, Economy and Society among the Jains, Oxford, Clarendon Press.

Leslie, Julia I., 1989, *The Perfect Wife. The Orthodox Hindu Woman According to the Strīdharmapaddhati of Tryambakayajvan*, Delhi, Oxford University Press.

Leumann, Ernst, 1921, *Die Nonne*, Ein neuer Roman aus dem alten Indien, München (reprinted in *Kleine Schriften* [ed. by Nalini Balbir], Stuttgart: F. Steiner Verlag, 1998: pp. 578–681).

Mahattarā Śrī Mṛgāvatīśrījī Commemoration Volume, 1989, ed. Ramanlal C. Shah. Bombay: Śrī Vallabhasūri Smārak Nidhi.

Mahias, Marie–Claude, 1985, *Délivrance et convivialité. Le système culinaire des Jaina*. Paris: Maison des Sciences de l'Homme.

Mallī–Jñāta. Das achte Kapitel des Nāyādhammakahāo im sechsten Aṅga des Śvetāmbara Jainakanons, 1983, Herausgegeben, übersetzt und erläutert von G. Roth. Wiesbaden: Franz Steiner Verlag.

Mette, Adelheid, 1991, *Durch Entsagung zum Heil*, Eine Anthologie aus der Literatur der Jaina. Zürich: Benziger.

Mishra, Laxman Prasad, 1974, *Di alcune divinità femminili minori della bhakti jaina*, Torino: Istituto di Indologia dell' Università di Torino 8.

Misra, Rajalakshmi, 1972, 'The Jains in an Urban Setting [The Ascetics and the Laity among the Jains of Mysore City]: *Bulletin of the Anthropological Survey of India* 21, nos. 1–2, January–June 1972: pp. 1–68.

Mṛgāvati, Sādhvī, 1989, 'Sādhvi Sangh — ek vinati' [Based on left papers]: *Ātma Vallabh Smārikā,* Delhi: p. 51.

Orr, Leslie C., 1998, 'Jain and Hindu "Religious Women" in Early Medieval Tamilnadu', *Open Boundaries*, Jain Communities and Cultures in Indian History. Ed. by John E. Cort. New York: SUNY: pp. 187–212.

Padmāvāti Upāsanā, 1980, Ahmedabad: Sarabhai Manilal Nawab.

The Peaceful Liberators, Jain Art from India. Ed. by Pratapaditya Pal et al. Los Angeles County Museum of Art, 1995.

Qvarnstrom, Olle, 1998, 'Stability and Adaptability: A Jain Strategy for Survival and Growth': *Indo–Iranian Journal* 41.1. January, pp. 33–55.

Reynell, Josephine, 1987, 'Prestige, honour and the family: Laywomen's Religiosity amongst the Śvetāmbar Mūrtipūjak Jains in Jaipur', *Bulletin d'Etudes Indiennes* 5, pp. 313–59.

—— 1991, 'Women and the Reproduction of the Jain Community'. *The Assembly of Listeners. Jains in Society.* Eds M. Carrithers and C. Humphrey. Cambridge University Press: pp. 41–65.

Schubring, Walther, 1977, *Kleine Schriften*. Herausgegeben von K. Bruhn, Wiesbaden.

Shah, Umakant P., 1956, 'A Rare Sculpture of Mallinatha': *Ācārya Vijayavallabhasūri Commemoration Volume*. Bombay: Shri Mahavira Jaina Vidyalaya: p. 128.

—— 1987, *Jaina-rūpa-maṇḍana* (Jaina iconography). Delhi: Abhinav Publications.

Shāntā, N., 1985, *The Unknown Pilgrims: History, Spirituality, Life of the Jaina Women Ascetics*, Delhi: Shri Satguru Publications (1997). [References are to the original French publication: *La voie jaina. Histoire, spiritualité, vie des ascètes pèlerines de l'Inde*. Paris: OEIL, 1985].

Stevenson, Margaret Sinclair, 1915, *The Heart of Jainism*. Delhi: Motilal Banarsidass, 1970, reprint.

Tiwari, Maruti Nandan Prasad, 1989, *Ambika in Jaina Art and Literature*, New Delhi: Bhāratīya Jñāanpīṭha.

Tkatcheva, A.A., 1996, 'Jenchtchina I Djainizm', *Indiiskaia Jena*. Moscow: Russian Academy of Sciences, Oriental Institute, pp. 89–99 [in Russian].

Vyavāharasūtra: in *Vavahāra-und Nisīhasutta*. Herausgegeben von W. Schubring, Leipzig, 1918 (reprint Nendeln, 1966).

Williams, R., 1963, *Jaina Yoga*, London [reprint 1983]; Delhi: Motilal Banarsidass.

Yaśovijayaji, Muni, 1956, 'Jain Sādhvījīo nī bhavya pāṣāṇ-pratimāo', *Ācārya Vijayavallabhasūri Commemoration Volume*. Bombay: Shri Mahavira Jaina Vidyalaya, 172–3 [in Gujarati].

Zydenbos, Robert J., 1987, 'The Jaina nun Kavuntī': *Bulletin d'Etudes Indiennes* 5: pp. 387–417.

—— 1992, 'The Jaina Goddess Padmāvatī', *Jinamanjari* 4.1, pp. 50–67.

Notes

1. An important collection of ninety-three negative characteristics of women is thus found in the *Tandulaveyāliya* (a canonical text belonging to the Prakīrṇakas), along with semantic analyses of various designations for 'women', all interpreted in a negative way: Sections X and XI (in W. Schubring's edition: Wiesbaden, 1969); Hindi summary and good selection of other canonical passages in Jain 1990: 5ff. (introduction to Boradiyā 1991); for narrative-cum-gnomic literature, see for instance Chojnacki [1998]: p. 42; Handiqui, K. K., *Yaśastilaka and Indian Culture*, Sholapur, 1968: pp. 175–7.

2. Maheśvarasūri, *Nāṇapañcamīkahā* 3.17. This concept is also exemplified in the Śvetāmbara accounts of Mahābala's rebirth as Malli.

3. Śākaṭāyana, author of the *Strīnirvāṇaprakaraṇa*, vs. 25; Jaini 1991: p. 69.

4. See for instance Haribhadra's *Āvaśyaka* commentary, p. 581a (on *Āv.-sūtra*: *paḍikkamāmi cauhiṃ vikahāhiṃ*), *Sthānāngasūtra* 4 and the corresponding *ṭīkā*; the extract from the *Niśīthacūrṇi* (on 4.23) staging a forbidden conversation between a monk and a nun (translated in Mette 1991: pp. 168–9). The interdiction of such interactions is one of the most important rules even today.

5. Similar developments are found in the *Mahānisīhasutta*, chapter 2, sections 10 to 21 (Deleu, J. and W. Schubring, *Studien zum Mahānisīhasutta*, Hamburg, 1963: pp. 105–13; chapter 3, section 39 describes the seducive powers of women through their body and attire in a picturesque way on the occasion of explaining the concept of '*kuśīla* by looking' (Deleu–Schubring: p. 145).

6. This is how the concluding remarks in chapter 12 (*strīsvarūpa*) of Śubhacandra's *Jñānārṇava* try to be temperent.

7. Barnes, N. Schuster, 'Buddhism' in *Women in World Religions* (ed. A. Sharma). Albany: SUNY. 1987: p. 114.

8. See *Strīnirvāṇaprakaraṇa*: Jambuvijaya 1974; *Pramāṇanayatattvālokālaṃkāra* of Vādidevasūri, ed. trans. H. S. Bhattacharya 1967; Jaini 1986: p. 204; Jaini 1991: pp. 41–108.

9. See references in Jambuvijaya 1974; translations and in-depth analysis in Jaini 1991.

10. *Strīnirvāṇaprakaraṇa* vss. 27ff; Jaini 1991: 72ff; *Pramāṇanayatattvālokālaṃkāra*, ed. translaion H.S. Bhattacharya 1967: pp. 610–13.

11. *Strīnirvāṇaprakaraṇa* vss. 5–6; Jaini 1991: 51ff; *Pramāṇanayatattvālokālaṃkāra*, translaion H.S. Bhattacharya 1967: p. 607.

12. *Strīnirvāṇaprakaraṇa* vss. 2ff; Jaini 1991: p. 49; *Pramāṇanayatattvālokālaṃkāra*, translation H.S. Bhattacharya 1967: p. 603.

13. *strīvedam arjitaṃ karma, strīpuṃsāv ātmakarmakṣaye hi mucyete. ātmā hy ubhayatra samāna eveti strīmuktiḥ: Pramāṇasāra* of Munīśvarasūri (15th century), ed. in Shah, N.J., *Jaina Philosophical Tracts*. Ahmedabad, 1973 (L.D. Series 41): p. 119.

14. Compare the ambiguities coming from the phrasing of rules in the Buddhist Vinaya and the way they are solved in the commentaries: Hüsken, U., 'Rephrased Rules—The Application of Monks' Prescriptions to the Nuns' Discipline in Early Buddhist Law': *Buddhist Studies* (*Bukkyō Kenkyū*) 28 March 1999: pp. 19–29.

15. See *Sūyagaḍa-nijjutti* v. 63 (*ete ceva ya dosā purisasamāe vi itthiyāṇaṃ pi*) and the corresponding prose commentary.

16. Āśādhara, *Sāgāradharmāmṛta* 2.73: *āryikāḥ, śrāvikāś cāpi satkuryād guṇabhūṣaṇāḥ/caturvidhe 'pi saṅghe yat phalaty uptam analpaśaḥ*. (The adopted translation of *satkaroti* is deliberately not literal). To what extent the rather dull adjective *guṇabhūṣaṇāḥ* should be understood as a restriction is uncertain.

17. Hemacandra, *Yogaśāstra* commentary on *Yogaśāstra* 3.119 (ed. Muni Jambuvijaya, p. 573). The quotations inserted in the passage are from the *Strīnirvāṇaprakaraṇa* vss. 29–31 and vs.4, translation in Jaini 1991: pp. 73 and 50.

18. Text as quoted in Ratnaśekhara's *Śrāddhavidhiprakaraṇa* [14th century], fifth section, p. 21. This is almost a word for word repetition of Hemacandra's discussion in the *Yogaśāstra* (ed. Muni Jambuvijaya, p. 575).

19. See *Nāyādhammakahāo* I.8 (*Malli-Jñāta*: 68–69); Hemacandra, *Triṣaṣtiśalākāpuruṣacaritra* VI.6.18–21; IV.5.298: 'Mallinātha will be born as a woman, because she practised very slight deceit in a former birth, as she had not removed the arrow of deceit' (translation H. M. Johnson, vol. 3, p. 156; at the end of a sermon about deceit).

20. Black stone image from Unnav (Uttar Pradesh) ascribed to the 10th–11th

centuries, kept in the State Museum Lucknow. The position is one of a nude meditating female, which, as such, is rather exceptional in Indian sculpture, but the identification is not perfectly sure because the cognizance is unfortunately hardly distinguishable: see *Peaceful Liberators* No. 26, p. 139. The late U.P. Shah was the first to analyse this sculpture in an article published in 1956 (see bibliography).

21. See, for instance, Caillat 1997: p. 112 referring to the mothers of the two Pratyekabuddhas Karakaṇḍu and Nami; other examples are found in Desai 1998: p. 188.

22. *Uttarādhyayana* chap. 24 (vs. 1). Prakrit *māyā* has probably here a double meaning (compare Pali *mātikā* used in the Abhidhamma texts: 'register, condensed contents').

23. See *Padmāvatī Upāsanā* (in the bibliography); Jhavery, M. B., *Comparative and Critical Study of Mantrashastra*, Ahmedabad, 1944; Mishra 1974: pp. 5–9; Zydenbos 1992.

24. Mishra 1974: pp. 13–16.

25. See Meister, Michael W., 'Sweetmeats or Corpses? Community, Conversion and Sacred Places' in *Open Boundaries* (ed. J. Cort, New York: SUNY 1998): pp. 111–38; Mishra 1974: pp. 16–19.

26. Today these stories are also often retold in various magazines in Hindi, Gujarati, etc., meant for the Jain layfollowers, or collected in books: see Desai, Kumarpal, *Glory of Jainism*. Ahmedabad: Shri Jayabhikkhu Sahitya Trust, 1998 (with pictures; there is also a Gujarati version of the book). About women, the following extract from the foreword is worth quoting: 'Into the lives chronicled here are woven a few popular stories which reflect an element of miracle or trials faced by women to prove their spotless character. Kalavati, Sushila, Prabhavati, Pushpchula, Narmadasundari, Malaysundari and Chelana are there to emphasize the importance of spotless character and piety and are to be seen in that light only. [...] I hope this will help a modern reader to trace self-assertion in a sati's willingness to be subject herself to a test to prove her spotless character' (p. 2).

27. Earlier version in the Canon (*Viyāhapannatti* 15); Balbir, 1982: p. 43.

28. For other instances of the same motif, see Upadhye, A. N., General Editorial (p. 11ff.) in *Sugandhadaśamī Kathā* [In Apabhraṃśa, Sanskrit, Gujarati, Marathi and Hindi). Delhi: Bhāratīya Jñānapīṭha Publication, 1966.

29. This is the story of Mṛgasundarī, known by several versions (Balbir, Nalini, 1982: p. 46): Ratnaśekhara's commentary on the *Śraddhapratikramaṇa-sūtra*, Jinalābhasūri's *Ātmaprabodha* (section on the *anarthadaṇḍavrata*), Vijayalakṣmīsūri's *Upadeśaprāsāda* (chap. 9); *Mṛgasundarī rās* (in Gujarati), etc.

30. Jinamati, wife of Rudhradatta and Padmalatā in Hariṣeṇa's *Bṛhatkathākośa* No. 54 and 68 (Granoff 1998: 240, 243ff.).

31. See for instance Mette 1991: pp. 155–7; Kulkarni 1994: pp. 260–1; Kelting: forthcoming.

32. For other instances, see the various narrative anthologies called *Śīlopadeśamālā*, where female lives are much more numerous and significant than their male counterparts, or any Jain *Kathākośa*.

33. See respectively Kelting (forthcoming); Granoff 1998: 177ff.; Kulkarni 1994: 74ff.

34. See *Saṃkhitta–Tarangavaī–Kahā* of Pādaliptasūri, ed. with Gujarati translation by H. C. Bhayani. Ahmedabad, 1979: L.D. Series 75; Leumann 1921.

35. See Zydenbos 1987.

36. On this question, which is more complicated than it may seem, see Hüsken, U., 'Enrichtung des buddhistischen Nonnenordens': *Studien zur Indologie und Buddhismuskunde* (Prof. H. Bechert Felicitation vol.). Bonn, 1993 (*Indica et Tibetica* 22): pp. 151–70. [English translation in *Journal of the Pali Text Society* 26 (2000), pp. 43–69.]

37. See, for instance, Vardhamānasūri's *Ācāradinakara*. Ahmedabad, 1981, p. 123b (*vratinīvratadānavidhi*).

38. See, for instance, the Prakrit stanza ascribed to the (canonical) tradition (āgama) quoted in Vardhamānasūri's *Ācāradinakara*, p. 123b (*vratinīvratadānavidhi*): ... *purisāṇaṃ na paratantattaṃ / itthī puṇa paratantā* ...

39. Vardhamānasūri's *Ācāradinakara*, pp. 123b–126a (*vratinīvratadānavidhi, pravartinīpadasthāpanavidhi, mahattarāpadasthāpanavidhi*).

40. See for instance *Jaina Pustaka Praśast Saṃgraha*. Bombay, 1943 (Singhi Jain Series 18), index: 163ff.

41. Shivaprasad, 'Śve Kharataragacchīya sādhvī paramparā aur samakālīna sādhviyāṃ' in Boradiyā 1991: 237ff. (Collection of historical data from *praśastis* and inscriptions); Babb 1996: pp. 105, 116.

42. For 1986 the statistics are not fully accurate, as data is not available for three sections of the Tapāgaccha (totalling about 552 mendicants in 1998).

43. Such motivations are equally adduced in former times: see the fictitious dialogue between a monk and a nun from the *Niśīthacūrṇi* (on 4.23) translated in Mette 1991: p. 168: 'Why did you leave the world? — Because of my husband's death / because he did not love me. This is why I left the world.'

44. Data taken from the *Samagra Jain Cāturmās Sūcī* 1998.

45. See also the contributions containing life-sketches of nuns from the Digambara *sampradāya*, the Kharataragaccha and the Sthānakvāsins collected in Boradiyā 1991: Appendix 1.

46. Vardhamānasūri's Ācāradinakara, chapter 33 (*śāntikarma*): No. 13 of the *pratiṣṭhāvidhi*-section pp. 225b–226a.

47. Thus in an article entitled 'Jain Sādhvījīo nī bhavya pāṣāṇ-pratimāo' (see bibliography under Muni Yaśovijayaji), the author considers only three such instances dating back to the 12th century, one from the Aṣṭāpada temple in Patan, one from a temple in Matar (Gujarat) and one from his own private collection.

48. A commemoration volume in her honour was also published. The first persons to pay their homage to the deceased nun are the present ācārya of the section of the Tapāgaccha where she belonged and two prominent monks belonging to his fold: see the bibliography under Mahattarā.

49. From *Jain Digest. Quarterly News Magazine of the Federation of Jain Associations in North America*, volume 20, number 4, November 1993, p. 17.

50. Kelting 1996.

51. See above (literary representations; famous female figures).

52. For common story-patterns about this theme, see above (literary representations; famous female figures).

53. Reynell 1987: p. 322; 1991: 56ff.; Laidlaw 1995: p. 224.

54. This point is contended by Kelting 1996: 'My research suggests that the centrality of fasting in the rhetoric of women has more to do with what the public—especially the male public—wishes to display as Jain piety. While most women saw fasting as a good thing to do for a variety of reasons and they acknowledged that men did far less fasting than women, they did not ever suggest to me that it was the area of female religious expertise.'

55. See above (famous female figures) for the story of Śrīpāla and Mainasundarī, whose power came from the fast known as navpad *oḷī*; several instances in Maheśvarasūri's *Nāṇapancamīkahā* (10th century): Chojnacki [1998]; etc.

56. Laidlaw 1995: p. 224 and Mahias 1985: p. 116.

57. Kiśansimha, *Kriyākośa* (18th century) vs. 1457.

58. This stress is reflected in Shah, Natubhai, *Jainism: The World of Conquerors*. Sussex Academic Press, 1998, vol. 1: p. 147 where more than half of the unique page devoted to 'Jain nuns' concerns this topic.

59. For information about the biographies of two 'Jain Women Saints in the 20th Century' see Bhatt 1997: p. 1. Panditratna Tarabai Mahasatiji (1920–1980) became a widow at 17, came into contact with some monks and nuns and took *dīkṣā* at the age of 30. She was active in Cutch, where she established a *Vyasan mukti* in order to help people to get rid of their bad habits (alcoholism, etc.); Brahmacarini Pandit Chandabai (1880–1977) became a widow at 12, and went on with her studies. Convinced that education is one of the important means for women to improve their situation, she opened a girls' school in Arrah, which gradually gained importance, and wrote many books.

60. A summary such as the following seems a little too optimistic: 'Thus, the role of women in Jain religion has been very progressive and ennobling on the whole. As mothers they have given birth to *Tīrthaṅkaras*, as wives they have provided inspiration to their husbands; as individuals they have managed large trade and commerce independently. In the Jaina way of life, woman has always been bold enough to protect her chastity and defeat the enemy. Her learning has for ever been honoured everywhere. *Sādhvīs* have set an example for the society in matters relating to the ultimate achievement of spiritual progress. The liberation of women, the freedom of women and the advancement of women are integrated in Jaina religion. These principles are sure to guide and lead the people in the ensuing decades towards the new path of attainment of the liberty of women' (Desai 1998: p. 191).

Women in Sikhism

Rajkumari Shanker

This investigation of women in Sikhism begins by indicating some of the limitations which fetter the scope of the present research, mainly due to lack of available literature on the subject, overlapping of religious categories in the subcontinent, and the various competing interpretations of Sikhism within its community. It then provides a brief overview of women in Hinduism, based on the article by Katherine Young, and also discusses how the *bhakti* (devotional) movement emerged to give hope to women's religiosity. A short presentation of the life of Guru Nanak, the founder of Sikhism in the fifteenth century follows, and prepares the ground for a discussion of Sikh beliefs.

The second section analyses the attitudes toward women and ideals of femininity in the primary and secondary Sikh scriptures. Beginning with the portrayal of women in the *Adi Granth* (c.1600–1700), the primary Sikh Scripture, the discussion moves on to shed light on women from the perspective of the Sikh gurus and models of femininity in the secondary sources of Sikh religion—that is, the *Janam Sakhis* (1580), the traditional narratives of the life of Guru Nanak and the *Rahat Maryada* (finalized in 1945), the *Khalsa* code of discipline.

After the textual passages of the Sikh scriptures have been examined, the third section surveys some of the chronicles of the Sikhs in the eighteenth and nineteenth centuries, and then goes on to assess the fortunes of women in this historical period, with reference to sati and polygamy amongst the Sikh elite. The fourth section examines the aftermath of Operation Blue Star in 1984, and the involvement, extent, quality, and limits of *Akali*-led women's movement in the Punjab.

LIMITATIONS OF THE ANALYSIS

Paucity of Research

Although the contemporary period has witnessed a surge of publications on the Sikhs and Sikhism, to date there is little scholarly research available on the subject of women in Sikhism. Apart from references, which are few and far apart, no significant or systematic work has been undertaken on the position of women in the Sikh religion. The ensuing analysis is per force primarily based on the *Adi Granth* and the secondary Sikh scriptures. The various sources of Sikh history, religion, culture and literature reflect not only androcentric biases but also ambivalant attitudes toward women, making it difficult to retrieve the images of the feminine. This is compounded by the fact that little is known of the ordinary Sikh women, and the limited material that we do possess is at times glossed over and perfunctory.

Fusion of Traditions

This analysis becomes even more complex, because until recently Sikhs had displayed little collective concern in distinguishing themselves from the predominant Hindu culture and religion. Consequently, the fortunes of Sikh women have been inextricably associated with that of Hindu women:

> Sikh notions of time, space, corporeality, holiness, kinship, societal distinctions, purity and pollution, and commensality were hardly different from those of the Hindus. Also the two shared the same territory, language, rites of passage, dietary taboos, festivals, ritual and key theological concepts. The construction of personhood within the two traditions and their solutions for existential problems were quite alike. Despite having specified their religious orientation, the semeiotic, cultural, affective and territorial universe of the Sikhs and the Hindus virtually remained the same (Oberoi, 1987, pp. 136–7).

These subjective and objective affinities were so striking that the colonial authorities until the end of the nineteenth century found it very hard to differentiate between their Hindu and Sikh subjects. In the 1855 census in Punjab, the Sikhs and the Hindus were often confused in many districts of the province. Denzil lbbetson, the Census Commissioner for Punjab, registered in his report:

> But on the border land where these great faiths meet, and especially among the

peasantry whose creed, by whatever name it may be known, is seldom more than a superstition and a ritual, the various observances and beliefs which distinguish the followers of the several faiths in their purity are so strangely blended and intermingled that it is often impossible to say that one prevails rather than the other, or to decide in what category the people shall be classed (Ibbeston 1883, p. 101).

This excerpt sums up the colonial understanding of the subcontinent's religious realities. As the religions of India grew and evolved from a variety of cults and beliefs, the citizenry did not perceive of themselves as belonging to any 'one' religion; the categories of the religions extended, intermingled and coexisted in the region, and most people continued their daily lives without bothering to label their religious beliefs. The following extracts, drawn from diverse sources, illustrate this point:

In the Indian religious tradition, unlike the Judeo-Christian, there was notion of a well demarcated religious community possessing a centralized ecclesiastical hierarchy. People did not conceive of themselves as 'Hindus' or 'Sikhs'. These categories overlapped and it is historically more precise to speak in terms of a continuum or simultaneity of religious identities rather than of distinct religious collectivities. An 'either-or' dichotomy is often of very little value in conceptualizing Indian religious traditions (Oberoi 1988, p. 140).

Religion was primarily a localized affair, often a matter of individual conduct and individual salvation. For much of their history, the people of the subcontinent went on with their rituals, pilgrimages and acts of religious piety without objectifying religion into an exclusive entity. Religious traditions were based on local traditions and not on pan-regional organization of communities. Islam may have been the only exception to this, but then, Indian Islam, heavily coloured by Sufism, is of a radically different genre from its counterpart elsewhere (Kinsley 1986, pp. 197–211).

Pluralistic Framework

Another component that complicates this study considerably is the pluralistic framework within which Sikhism has operated. Initially, there were at least eleven known traditions,[1] of which very little historical literature is available, except for the Khalsa, Udasis and Kukas. Much of the Sikh history is chronicled and comprehended exclusively as the history of the Khalsa, which was only one of the several competing cultural codes within the polyphonic complex of Sikhism. The question as to how the Khalsa came to establish its predominance over other traditions remains unresolved till date.

In the absence of a centralized church and an attendant religious hierarchy, heterogeneity in religious beliefs, plurality of rituals, and diversity of life styles were freely acknowledged. For from being a single 'Sikh' identity, most Sikhs moved in and out of multiple identities .... The boundaries between what could be seen as the centre of the Sikh tradition and its periphery were highly blurred. There simply was no single source of authority within the Sikh tradition and thus several competing definitions of what constituted a 'Sikh' were possible (Oberoi 1988, p. 137).

It is important to recognize these limitations at the very outset of the analysis for, collectively, they make it difficult to understand gender roles and project a pattern on the lives of women in the Sikh tradition. However, before we examine the textual materials at hand, it is important to examine the images of Hindu women, which remain the basis for understanding women in Sikhism.

Women in Hindu Religious Tradition

The early Hindu tradition was patriarchal, life-affirming, and demonstrated, to a certain degree, respect and appreciation of women. The complementarity of male and female roles for the well-being of the family, society, and cosmos was perceived and reflected in the religious symbols such as the concept of a divine couple. However, by the classical time (c 500–1500 AD), disparity between men and women intensified. Women were prohibited to move about in public alone, were considered ignorant and were denied inheritance. Chastity and purity became a substitute for knowledge. Since scriptural knowledge was deemed essential for enlightenment, most women were excluded from the possibility of attaining salvation, and as a result they were oriented towards rebirth (Young 1987, p. 75). The following extracts from Katherine Young's account of Hindu women are relevant in the present context:

For the ascetic, the Hindu women represented sexuality, reproduction and the family, the very obstacles to liberation (1987, p. 70).

If a woman became a widow, theoretically she had the extreme option either to perform sati, self immolation, on the funeral pyre of her husband, or more commonly to undergo the rites of passage to widowhood (1987, p. 83).

The segregation of sexes became more severe after the 12th century, specially in the areas of the subcontinent that were under the Muslim rule. ... Hindu women, already carefully controlled by or segregated from men, imitated the purdah of the Muslim women. The consequence was that many upper caste Hindu women, already bound to the home, were further restricted so that they rarely left their residence (1987, p. 87).

The Hindu woman was to focus on her husband, he was to be her 'god' ... the apotheosis of the husband ... was no simple exaggeration of androcentrism, but part of Hinduism. The Brahmins considered themselves as gods and so did the gurus and kings upon occasion ... Hindu theism became increasingly monotheistic in the sense of involving a primary if not exclusive devotion to either Vishnu or Shiva as supreme deities, a similar tendency may have developed in the domestic sphere so that the husband too became the 'supreme and only' one. This tendency helps us account for the ideal woman's 'exclusive' devotion to her husband (1987, pp. 73–4).

The patriarchal organization of the family and a woman's rebirth orientation led her to desire to be with her husband for lives to come ... a woman's appreciation of her husband as pati or god was central to her daily life (1987, p. 75).

The most explicit form of feminine self-sacrifice was in the form of a *vrata* (vow) ... in which a woman voluntarily denied something to herself; for example, she fasted in exchange for a favour for her husband (such as good health or a son). Despite the focus on her husband and limitation to the domestic sphere, the Hindu woman took pride in her powerful religious role (1987, p. 75).

In the late fifteenth century, when Guru Nanak started preaching his message, both Hindus and Muslims considered women to be inferior to men, an impediment in the way of spiritual progress, and the cause of man's normal degradation. Polygamy was rampant, widows were denied remarriage and social recognition. Sati, child marriage and female infanticide were widespread. Women were economically, socially and psychologically dependent on men. Redemption surfaced in the form of the Bhakti (devotional) movement.

It is in the context of bhakti that the women's private and public religion intersected ... and gave a universal soteriology to Hinduism just at the moment when Brahmanical sacerdotalism and asceticism encouraged extreme androcentrism. ... Popularity of Bhakti resulted in no small measure from its inclusion of such marginal groups as women and Sudras ... being female was generally no bar to Bhakti. Marriage mysticism was common in Bhakti literature. The lady (bhakta) was none other than the woman in love who lamented any separation from her beloved and ecstatically rejoiced in union with him ... concentration on the pati for a female saint meant exclusive devotion to the deity understood as supreme husband, whereas for an ordinary woman devotion was expressed both to her human husband as pati and deity as pati (assuming the chosen deity was a male) (Young, 1987, pp. 76–7).

Bhakti

The bhaktas (devotees) believed that God, though known by many names and beyond human comprehension, is the one and only reality; all else in *maya* (illusion). Singing hymns of praise, meditation under the guidance of a guru, and repetition of the name of God was deemed by the bhaktas as the means par excellence to achieve salvation. The Bhakti movement opposed monopoly of the Hindu priests and the caste system. It succeeded in inspiring a group of women and men who have left a profound influence on the religious traditions of the subcontinent. Foremost of these were two near contemporaries: Kabir (1440–1518) and Nanak (1469–1539), the founder of Sikhism. Kabir was the link between Hindu Bhakti and Muslim Sufism, which had gained considerable following among Indian Muslims. Kabir and Nanak preached that the conflict between Hindus and Muslims was wrong, because God was one.

By the time Sikhism arrived on the Indian scene, the Hindu tradition had seen at least twenty-five centuries of religious, philosophical and social beliefs and practices, along with a substantial corpus of literature, various modes of attaining salvation and all conceivable concepts of God. The Sikhs inherited not only some of the theological concept of the Hindus but also the established social and cultural norms of the society within which it took birth.

Since the fundamental religious concepts of Sikhism may not be familiar to many, and since a cursory knowledge at the very least is essential to the understanding of the role of women in the religious tradition of the Sikhs, we begin our study with a brief overview of Sikhism.

Sikhism: An Overview

The Sikhs are disciples of their ten gurus (teachers) beginning with Guru Nanak (1469–1539) and ending with Gobind Singh (1666–1708). Nanak may have founded a new religious community or path within the larger Hindu fold, but he neither violated nor abandoned the Hindu tradition. Born a Hindu, he remained one until the day he died, and so too did his successors. The doctrines that he preached were already popular in north India, and accepted by many of his Hindu audience (McLeod 1989, p. 16).

Sikhism is the evolved product of subsequent centuries, a complex system of beliefs and practices. Nanak had preached a vision, the organizations and institutions came later (Smith 1962, p. 67). A monotheistic tradition, Sikhism believes that God can be known only through personal experience of mystical union. Repudiating ritualism, Sikhs aspire to realize the experience of God through bhakti (devotion) under the guidance of a guru. They reject the Hindu caste system and the religious authority of the Brahmins.

The religious beliefs of the Sikhs, greatly influenced by the contemporary Bhakti movement, are contained in the *Adi Granth*.[2] Emphasis is given to the unity of God, complete devotion of the worshipper, and the paramount role of the guru (teacher). Sikhism believes that liberation can be achieved by devotion directed to *Akal Purukh*, the 'timeless being', or *Sat-Kartar*, the 'true creator'. In addition, and of vital importance, is the fact that the followers are given specific tenets which could be converted into daily practice: *nam* (the word), *dan* (charity), *ishnan* (cleanliness), *seva* (service), and *simran* (worship).

The nine successors of Nanak[3] continued to preach the message of the founder. They molded the followers of the emerging group into a significant religious and political community. The last guru, Gobind Singh externalized the religion by providing it with a definite form and creating the *Khalsa* (the pure) community. The Khalsas both men and women, were henceforth identified by five marks: *kes* (uncut hair), *kangha* (comb), *kachha* (shorts), *kara* (steel bracelet), and *kirpan* (sabre), which all men and women belonging to the community would carry. In addition, they were to follow the Khalsa code of conduct (rahat maryada), abstain from intoxicants and narcotics, respect women, follow the teachings of the *guru*, reject caste differences and take up arms, if necessary, for a just cause.

The Sikh religion, like most religion of the world, constructed its identity around a male mentor and his teachings. Both men and women were among the earliest followers of the emerging religion. Initially, identification with the new religion was based on choice rather than birth; access to soteriology was individual. Women could belong to the new organization and were granted the possibility of attaining salvation. Despite this universalism, in subsequent Sikh history there was not a single woman guru, and no woman held a significant position in the religious community. Moreover, very few are mentioned in the chronicles of the Sikhs.

Women in the Sikh Sacred Literature

The Adi Granth: Composition and Beliefs

The Adi Granth (or the *Guru Granth Sahib*), sacred scripture of the Sikhs, is a collection of nearly six thousand hymns of the Sikh gurus and various medieval saints of different religious denominations. The book was first compiled in 1604 by the fifth guru (Arjun Singh). In 1704, the tenth and last guru, Gobind Singh, added the hymns of his predecessors, and enjoined that after his own death the Granth would take the place of the guru. The Adi Granth is the basis, not the object of worship in the *gurudwaras* (Sikh temples), and is looked upon as the inspired word of

God, which none may question. It contains neither history nor mythology, nor incantations. The hymns are exhortations to spiritual life, arranged according to the ragas (musical modes) in which they are meant to be sung, and not in any logical sequence. The Adi Granth, in its original form is written without separating words. As a result, words may often become incomprehensible upon erroneous reading.

The Sikh doctrines, as laid down in the Adi Granth, combine elements from Muslim, Hindu and the Bhakti tradition. Importance is given to personal awareness of God. The divine-human relationship is that of the lover and the beloved, the anguish and ecstasy that ensues with separation and union of the two. Though the imagery and symbols are not to be taken literally, language of a tradition is symptomatic of the psyche of that culture. In the light of this statement, we can anticipate stereotypical portraits emerging from the Adi Granth that could prove to be important to our study. Cultural stereotypes about women often confirm what may be primarily part of the men's religion, and sometimes they may be part of a general religious outlook (Gross 1987, p. 40).

Women in the Adi Granth

Most Sikhs believe Sikhism is an egalitarian religion, more supportive of women than Hinduism, Islam, or other religions.[4] However, contrary to the opinion of the majority, the Sikh canonical text does not always endorse the idea. The Adi Granth reveals a wide spectrum of views on women, most of which reflect male attitude of the enlightened religious gentry whose attitudes seldom, if ever, reflect sexual equality.

Analogous to other religions, the Sikh religious tradition has been dominated by a patriarchal power structure. The Sikh gurus authenticated a normative *modus vivendi* for women by formulating ideals of femininity and by including them in the Adi Granth. There is a range of views—positive, negative, and ambivalent—suggesting a tension between an inward psychological struggle and outward social decorum.

Consistent with the Bhakti tradition, the Adi Granth is replete with mystical imagery in which the devotee assumes the role of the female lover, whereas God is the male beloved. The following texts, a small sampling of hymns from the Adi Granth, offer a survey of gender role patterns in Sikhism and reveal men's perception of women, and stereotypes about women's ideal behaviour. Effort has been made to compile first the positive representation of the feminine; this is followed by the negative images in the Adi Granth. However, before we proceed with the analysis of women in the Adi Granth, certain methodological assumptions must be noted. The fundamental assumption is that religious phenomenon is best comprehended on its own measure or reference. This is necessary as every religious phenomenon is irrevocably social, historical, psychological and existential. Consequently, for a better appreciation of a religious tradition, understanding of the milieu and cultural perspicacity is crucial. This often means going beyond and behind the manifest phenomenon to grasp the sacred; the sacred thus perceived, epitomizes fundamental religious and philosophical truths. The excerpts from the Adi Granth are quoted extensively[5] to substantiate and refute prevalent arguments and conclusions.

The Sikh claim to equal worth of the two sexes, and their share in human dignity surfaces in the frequently quoted verse:

> Women and men, all by God Himself are created
> All this is His own play
> Saith Nanak: All thy creation is good, holy (AG: 304).

The importance of women as procreators of new generations and those responsible for the preservation of norms is expressed in the following verse by Nanak:

> From woman is man born, inside her is he conceived;
> To woman is man engaged, and woman he marries,
> With woman is man's companionship,
> From woman originate new generations.
> Should woman die, is another sought;
> By woman's help is man kept in restraint,
> Why revile her of whom are born great ones of the earth?
> From man is born woman, no human being without woman is born.
> Saith Nanak: The holy Eternal alone with woman can dispense,
> The tongue by which is the Lord praised (AG: 473).

Maternal love remains a significant metaphor in the subcontinent's literature, both sacred and profane. On the religious plane, the Adi Granth sanctifies motherhood, especially procreation of sons. On the temporal level, the status of a woman is enhanced when she becomes a mother of sons. The mother-son relationship manifests reciprocity of love and dependency; it is a model for the devotee's love for God:

> As does the mother cherish her pregnancy, in her son pinning her hope;
> That grown up, would he give her wherewithal,
> And bring joy and pleasure,
> Even such is the love of God's devotee to the Lord ... (AG: 165).

God, in the Adi Granth, is coerced to assume the role of an indulgent mother:

> Any misbehaviour by the child made
> The mother remembers not.
> Lord, thy child am I
> Why my faults dost Thou not annul?
> Should the child in extreme anger even run off,
> The mother still in mind bears not that (AG: 478).

The concept of mother is hallowed and held in high esteem: 'Make holy thinking thy mother, thy very life' (AG: 172).

The apotheosis of the husband, a legacy of the Hindu Brahmanic and Bhakti traditions (in which the devotee enters into 'marriage mysticism' with a male deity and assumes the psychology of a woman in love [Young, 1987, p. 77] forms an integral part of the Adi Granth. In the following passages, the devotee appropriates the role of an exemplary wife:

> The devotee is like the wife enjoying wedded bliss,
> With her lord ever in her heart;
> Ever sweet-spoken and modest,
> Blessed in her lord's arms:
> Of noble repute and wedded bliss,
> Is she whose love for the Lord knows no bounds (AG: 31).

And

> The wife that wins her Lord's pleasure, is in His eyes truly beautiful.
> Saith Nanak: Those united by the holy Word never again are parted (AG: 56).

However, in order to win the Master's grace, an ideal woman must possess 'perfection of conduct', which suggests subservience to male domination:

> Possessed of thirty-two merits, holy truth is her progeny,
> Obedient, of noble mien
> To her husband's wishes compliant (AG: 371).

> What is the mark of a blessed wife?
> Pure of heart, radiant her face, in her Lord absorbed (AG: 785).

> Discarding pride, in joy she disports.
> Dedicating body and mind, no distance from him she keeps,
> Neither casting eyes on strangers nor listening to them, nor discoursing with them (AG: 793).

> The female that effaces lust, wrath, avarice and attachment,
> And self-acquired foul thinking casts off
> And in humility serves the holy,
> The Beloved's favour shall win (AG: 377).

The seeker-female, decking herself with the Master's Word
Of her egoism is rid (AG: 61).

The divine-human relationship in the Adi Granth is occasionally portrayed as that between master and servant, and sometimes as that between husband and wife. The nature of devotion is generally solemn, channelled through discipline and sacrifice. Passages indicating women's subservient status are not wanting. Although the language of the Adi Granth is considered to be allegorical, it no doubt reflects social reality:

The Lord is my husband, I his wife
The Lord is immensely great, I so small, (AG: 483).

A wife faithful to her Lord must devote
herself body and soul to him
And must behave in all respects as the faithful wedded-wives
(AG: 31).

The wife at the sight of her spouse is in bloom of joy
Thus does God's devotees live by contemplation of His name
(AG: 198).

As at the sight of the calf is the cow pleased;
As is the woman pleased at the husband's return home
God's devotees are pleased, as is sung the Lord's praise (AG: 164).

From her very childhood, the career of a woman is oriented towards securing a spouse on whom she would depend and around whom her life will revolve:

The wife in the husband's absence decking herself,
Only makes waste of her charm in ignominy.
Never shall she enjoy the couch of bliss—
Without her husband is all her decking wasted (AG: 58).

The wife without her Lord cannot live,
In the dark night, terribly long.
In love for the Lord finds she no rest ...
Without the Beloved, has she none to care (AG: 243).

The mark of a good woman is
She surrenders herself body and soul to her Lord (AG: 89).

One that surrenders to her Lord her self, mind, home and body,
Saith Kabir, is truly the blessed wife (AG: 328).

Now is my home my own, and this woman turned my wife,
She the servant:
I the exalted Master to be one of the nobles (AG: 371).

> Blessed is the happily-wedded wife whom her Lord venerates,
> His command obeys and casts-off pride (AG: 737).

The feminine is perceived to represent attachment, the profane, an obstacle to salvation and the material possession of a man:

> Attachment to progeny, wife is poison
> None of these at the end is of any avail (AG: 41).

> Maya afflicts one who by egoistic thinking is intoxicated;
> It afflicts one involved with progeny and wife,
> It afflicts too one attached to elephants,
> horses and material objects (AG: 182).

> This wealth, beauty, progeny and wife which for test to man
> have been granted,
> Man in these remains entangled, by his senses attracted (AG: 336).

> Progeny, wife, home, all objects—false is attachment to them
> (AG: 401).

> The female that effaces lust, wrath, avarice and attachment,
> And self-acquired foul thinking casts-off
> And in humility serves the holy,
> The beloved's favour shall win (AG: 377).

But

> The unlucky wife, who to the Lord has not offered constant
> devotion,
> Both worlds loses (AG: 793).

> The female of cursed matrimony cast-off from His love ...
> Devoid of the Lord's glance, in sighing she suffers
> Deluded by her great pride (AG: 928).

> Cursed is the life of the woman abandoned, by duality deluded:
> Like a wall of alkaline sand, day and night is she crumbling
> to fall ...
> Deluded woman! What good decking thyself without thy Lord
> (AG: 18).

And again

> A woman full of unapproved qualities shall be cast-off
> from the sight of the spouse (AG: 37).

> A woman not having bliss with her Lord,
> Her youth has wasted
> Thou ignorant woman without merit! what joy for thee?

> With beloved gone to strange lands, the lonely wife pines
> Like a fish in shallow water she wails ...
> The woman of false mind, of bad ways is found of little merit;
> In her father's home and in the husband's
> With her false and bad ways is she ever in torment (AG: 54).
>
> The egoist is like a woman, doing make-up
> with her husband gone to strange lands (AG: 127).

Whereas subservience, obedience, docility and dedication by women were cherished and rewarded, such attributes by men are not:

> Men obedient to their womenfolk
> Are impure, filthy, stupid,
> Man lustful, impure, their womenfolk counsel follow (AG: 304).

Negative images of women are also found throughout the Adi Granth:

> The egoist is like a woman foul of mind (AG: 639).
>
> From door to door with evil minds they wander
> Like a woman of ill repute (AG: 651).
>
> The ten sources of senses which are to be controlled are like ten females (AG: 693).
>
> Maya attachment is like a loose woman,
> A bad woman, given to casting spells (AG: 796).

And

> Whoever worships the Great Mother
> Shall though man, be incarnate as woman (AG: 874).

Repudiation of goddess worship can be explained in part by the fact that Sikhism is a strict monotheism. Acceptance of one God (male figure) is assumed to be an essential factor in the quest of liberation. This is perhaps incidental, as men held virtual monopoly over all the intellectual, cultural and religious functions of the society. The worship of a goddess is not only rejected ideally, but being born as a woman is perceived as a catastrophe of cosmic dimension, to be feared like a plague. The very birth as a woman is said to be the result of bad *karma* and a curse. One might thus deduce that women by nature were considered to be inferior and subservient to men.

The present investigation displays conflicting images of the feminine: from the hallowed image of the mother, to the harlot, a woman without a husband. These images were sanctioned in the popular literature of the subcontinent and were instrumental in influencing the preachers and proletariat alike.

Women: From the Gurus' Perspective

In the formative years of Sikhism, the gurus pronounced the doctrines for the new social and religious order, and subscribed equal religious status for both men and women. The same teachings were dispensed, the same spiritual path was open to all, the same goal pointed out. The gurus (from Guru Nanak to Guru Gobind Singh) even succeeded in giving the same conceptual message. The gurus, in other words, advanced the same

d practical responses as the circum-

nd Guru Ramdas (1534–1581) encour-
mardas condemned the practice of pur-
) the *sangat* (assembly) without veiling
omen to go forth and preach the new
, from the Punjabi word for chair. Guru
ations, advocated monogamy, encour-
riage of widows, and strictly forbade

the practice of sati. Guru Hargobind (1595–1644), called women the conscience of man, gave importance to household life, condemned asceticism and the belief that marriage was a barrier to achievement of self-realization. Guru Gobind Singh (1666–1708) made the Sikh Khalsa baptism compulsory for both men and women.

The precepts of the gurus, concerning the amelioration of the situation of women, remained just that: precepts. The reason for this shortcoming might be attributed to historical and cultural circumstances. The Sikhs and Muslims during the time of the gurus were too embroiled fighting wars, which were a combination of guile, regional ambitions, feudalism, and later on survival. Another justification for not implementing the professed reforms could be attributed to the deep-rooted traditional and cultural attitudes towards women, which proved to be too powerful for the Sikh leaders to eradicate. Or, it could have been that some gurus themselves accepted the status quo and endorsed the male-dominated religious system, which relegated women to oblivion. In other words, there existed, a tremendous gap between Sikh precepts and practices.

Images of Sikh Women in Later Centuries

History books contain little information about women; and the few glimpses that are provided are for the most part about those who rose to prominence or fell to disgrace. Portraits of these women, certainly cannot be said to be typical of women in Sikhism. However, the excerpts that follow do give us a fragmentary picture of the attitudes towards women in Sikhism, acknowledging the fact that stereotypes do incorporate an element of authenticity.

On the military front, Sikh women demonstrated exceptional determination and valour. During the period of persecution of Sikhs from 1748 to 1763 by Mir Manoo, the Governor of Lahore, Sikh women reportedly stood by the side of their men. Thousands of women were tortured and imprisoned, but not a single one is said to have relinquished her faith despite atrocities. George Thomas states in his memoirs:

> Instances have not infrequently occurred in which Sikh women have actually taken up arms to defend their habitation from the desultory attacks of the enemy, and throughout the contest behaved themselves with an intrepidity of spirit that was highly praiseworthy (Singh, 1965: p. 15).

These were exceptional women; the routine behaviour for women revolved around the house, husband and children.

Sati and Polygamy

The gurus had consistently condemned ills that plagued society, such as polygamy, sati, and female infanticide. As often the case, the elites of the society did not concede to the reforms of the new religion. Polygamy, sati, and female infanticide remained rampant.

Ranjit Singh (1780–1839), the only *maharaja* of the Sikh kingdom, which lasted for no more than fifty years, is said to have had twenty-two wives. When the Maharaja died on 21 June 1839, Rani Guddun (Singh 1966; 1–140) is said to have 'placed the head of the deceased on her lap, while the other ranis with seven slave girls seated themselves around, with every mark of satisfaction on their countenances' (*Lahore Akhbar*, June 1839).

Dr Honigberger (1852) takes up the tale: 'The *Brahmins* performed their prayers from the *Sastras*, the priests of the Sikhs did the same from their holy scriptures called *Granth Sahib* ... . Along with the ruler of Punjab, four of his wives and seven slave girls were reduced to ashes'.[6]

This was not an isolated instance of sati among the Sikhs. When Maharaja Kharak Singh died on 5 November 1840, two of his wives are also said to have committed sati. However, when Chand Kaur, one of Kharak Singh's widow proclaimed herself as *Maharanee*,

> The Punjabis were unable to reconcile themselves to being ruled by a woman who could not leave the veiled seclusion of the zenana. And Chand Kaur proved to be singularly inept in the art of diplomacy; she was vain, ill-tempered and given to using language that became a bazaar woman more than a Maharanee.

Bedi Bikram Singh of Una, who had come to Lahore to carry out the investiture ceremony, stated categorically that he had come to give the *Tikka* (saffron mark) to Kanwar Sher Singh and not to a woman, for no woman had or could ever reign at Lahore (Singh, 1966: II–14–15).

The short reign of a month and a half ended, and she was obliged to relinquish her claim to the throne.

L. J. Trotter (1880: I–197, 206) in his *Life of Lord Lawrence* records:

> Female infanticide was not only practised by the Rajputs, but was universal among Sikhs ... they had never allowed a single female child to live. John Lawrence, when renewing the leases on the land holders made them repeat, 'Beva mat jalao' (do not burn widows), 'Beti mat maro' (do not kill daughters).

This occurred despite the fact the Guru Gobind Singh had prohibited female infanticide, and said he would excommunicate those who killed female children. Guru Gobind Singh's prohibition can still be seen printed in large characters at the entry of the Akal Takht alongside the Golden Temple. Sati was legally outlawed in 1829 in British India; remarriage of widows was authorized under the Government Act of 1856. In 1853, the code of rules limiting the extent of dowries, one of the primary reasons for not wanting female children, was drawn up. And yet,

> By the turn of the century, one of the places in Punjab where you might fancy buying pornographic literature, or bedding a prostitute, or perhaps gambling, was the Sikh temple, the gurudwara. This was not an isolated scourge. And this astonishing decadence had touched even the noblest of places, the Golden Temple at Amritsar. Innocent women coming to pray in the temples were not safe: the mahants or priests used to boast about this, rather than feel embarrassed, announced to those who felt too concerned about the morality of their women should avoid sending them to the gurudwaras. Women from the 'best' families often got pregnant after a bout of 'worship'. The Mahant at Guru ka Bag, for instances, used to keep two mistresses ... in addition to a regular harem of prostitutes (Akbar 1985, p. 134).

Beginning of a New Sikh Identity

The Sikh had lost their independence, their symbols, their temples, their fortune by the end of the nineteenth century. 'Notwithstanding the Sikh Gurus' powerful denunciation of Brahmans, secular Sikhs now rarely do anything without their assistance. Brahmans help them to be born, help them to wed, help them to die, and help their souls after death to obtain a state of bliss' (Macauliffe 1909, 1 vii).

Hinduism seemed to be assimilating Sikhism. The gurudwaras were becoming either Hindu temples or haunts of depravity or both. If Sikhs were to exist as an independent religious community, they had to understand their religion. Day-to-day life was influenced by a network of kinship and caste relations. Consequently, the religious groupings of Hindu and Sikh remained fluid and frail. There was hardly any difference between the way Hindus and Sikhs received a child into this world, contracted marriage alliances, or performed funeral rites. These commonalties tied them together into a common symbolic universe. The result of all this was that the two were integrated into a common cultural universe. They shared the same grammar of social relations based on vertical ties of kinship and caste rather than the horizontal solidarity of religion and community.

However, the Khalsa sub-tradition did not blend very well with the amorphous state of the Sikh faith. The Khalsa Sikhs had their own notion of what constituted the Sikh past and more importantly they possessed a distinct life-cycle ritual in the form of 'Khande da pahul' or baptism rites. Those who maintained this rite had to maintain the well known symbols of the Khalsa and in addition strictly observe the injunctions laid down in the Rahat Maryada (Oberoi 1988, p. 147).

Identity formation is inevitably a dual process. It is not sufficient for a group of people to think that they constitute a separate entity; those among whom they interact must also recognize this claim. Therefore, the Khalsa's self-perception of being distinct from the rest of the civil population in the province did not automatically mean that they were accepted as such by others who belonged to the Sikh tradition or by the Hindus. The Khalsa urge to strike a separate identity was further diluted by the fact that it was not mandatory for all Sikhs to undergo *khande da pahul* (rite of sword-baptism as initiation to the Khalsa). Secondly, the different sub-traditions constituting the Sikh movement had their own distinct rites of initiation:[7] 'Of all the competing entities, symbols and norms that went into constituting Sikh movement, it was the Khalsa sub-tradition that came to imprint its image on the 'new' community' (Oberoi 1988, p. 150).

The Khalsa's condemnation of existing rites was based on three major factors : they were Hindu in origin, intent, and purpose. Sikh Gurus were opposed to these practices and had developed separate rites for their followers. Finally, many elements within the prevalent rites were considered to be unprogressive.

The pre-natal and post-natal practices, described as Hindu rites, were simply discarded. All Sikhs—Jats, Khatris, Mazhibs—were required to perform the same rituals without any reference to their caste or *biradari* traditions. A comparable change was effected in marriage arrangements.[8] How and why this happened has been discussed by Oberoi (1988). What initially were changes introduced by only a minority, imperceptibly came to be accepted by the Sikh public at large. The Khalsa transformation of these rituals, however, turned them into powerful bearers of the 'new' Sikh consciousness. They came to dramatize the distinction between 'us' (Sikhs) and 'them' (Hindus).

In sum, the Khalsa gave an identity, a particular vision of history, an exclusive communal solidarity to the Sikhs. While the roots of the drive for this cultural autonomy may be traced back to Guru Nanak, the reasons for its consolidation certainly lie entangled in the social history of the late nineteenth-century Punjab. The oft-repeated rhetorical statement *hum Hindu nahin*, 'we are not Hindus', now had a real basis. Innovations in the sphere of language, history, theology, sacred places, religious calendar and territory enhanced the sense of a separate identity.

The Khalsas not only defined a distinct identity for the Sikhs, they also incorporated changes for women in the Rahat Maryada.

Women in the Rahat Maryada.

The Rahat Maryada, in its present form did not come into existence until as recently as 1945. It had a long period of development and years of intense deliberations and discussions. The Rahat Maryada, guide to the Sikh way of life, spells out the basic beliefs, principles and practices of an ideal Sikh existence. The passages that follow demonstrate a certain deference towards women indicating an improvement:

Sikhism condemns infanticide outright, particularly female infanticide, and Sikhs should have no dealings with any who condone it;
Sikhs must not commit adultery;
A Sikh should respect another man's wife as his own mother, and another man's daughter as his own daughter;
A man should enjoy his wife's company and women should be loyal to their husbands;
It is contrary to Sikhism for women to veil themselves;
A Sikh daughter should marry a Sikh;
Child marriages are not permitted. A girl should marry only when she has attained physical and mental maturity;
Neither a girl nor a boy should be married for money;
There is no prohibition against widows or widowers remarrying if they wish. The ceremony should be the same as that of the first marriage.[9]

MODERN AGE

The Sikhs, however, were unable to bring about any significant change in the community, mainly because their primary concern was to consolidate Sikh authority rather than engender change for women.

Nevertheless, change did surface after the tragedy of Jallianwala Bagh in 1919 when R.E.H. Dyer ordered the massacre of a primarily Sikh congregation of unarmed men, women and children. Punjab rose against the British after this incident. The members of the Akali (political party, created to reform the Sikh temple) formally committed themselves to the cause of freedom by passing a resolution supporting Gandhi's call for non-cooperation with the British :

> The British Raj went so far as to add the reason of social concern for Hindu (Indian?) women to its rationale for ruling India. Hindu leaders appropriated this criticism of Hindu women on political and domestic fronts and sought reforms. Hence, it is no surprise to find the cause of Indian Independence was simultaneously the cause for women's liberation from more oppressive aspects of the domestic situation. Significantly, it was a cause that both Hindu men and women joined (Young 1987, p. 93).

Mahatma Gandhi had been the source of inspiration to the women of India. He realized how women could become the leaders in the national movement of satyagraha (struggle for truth) 'which does not require the learning that books give but does require the stout heart that comes from suffering and faith' (Harijan, 24 February 1940).

Women knew well the language of self-denial, suffering, self-control and patience. They could redirect that orientation from the domestic arena to the national front. When their traditional religious psychology became a tool for changing a situation rather than coping with it, they experienced a new freedom. Gandhi helped women break out of their domestic prisons by redirecting their traditional self-sacrifice and service from the husband to the nation (Young 1987, pp. 96–7).

With India's independence, women were granted social, political, and economic rights along with men. Fifty years later, despite making giant strides to improve the general situation of women, problems such as bride burning, dowry, abortion of female foetus remain.

Participation of Women in the Akali Movement

The fate of the Sikhs centred primarily around the Akalis who believed that it was inconceivable to defend the faith without the control of political power. The Akali-led movement in Punjab was dramatically enhanced during the Emergency in the late 1970s and in the 1980s. The participation of women was striking; they began to come out in large numbers in response to the call of Longowal, their leader, for help.

The women dedicated themselves to the cause, even though the movement had nothing to offer women as women. The repression unleashed by the Indian government on their men was a more important causal factor for their participation than any of the political demands. They repeatedly said that they had joined the movement to do sewa or service, to give rather than to take. 'You take whatever sewa you want from me' was their general attitude. An unquestioning obedience to leadership in a do-or-die spirit was conspicuous during the agitations.

> The Akali women were able to become a significant presence in the movement despite the fact that in normal times the political participation of women in rural Punjab is particularly low. Women normally live extremely secluded and restricted lives and are not allowed political participation even at the gurudwara or village level. The participation of this movement became possible because the men of the community were willing to release them from domestic responsibilities so that they could strengthen the movement (Kishwar 1988, 2755).

In fact, the bravery and steadfastness of these simple, illiterate women, had been the main strength of the whole movement (*Manushi*, No, 40, 1987, p. 6). Often, it has been noted that women are deliberately put in the front line to face repression. This has been justified on the grounds that police would show restraint in the presence of women protesters, and even if they do not, women would face the attacks more valiantly than men. In many instances, women were exploited by their men. When villages were raided, men would flee to the woods, abandoning women, children and the elderly. Some men openly admitted that they had to hold off the police by putting women in the front. The reasons they offered were: 'Women do not lose their cool as easily as men do, and are able to resist without unnecessary violence; if the police start using force, women do not run away as men tend to do; they often fight to the last to protect their men and children' (*Manushi,* 1986: p. 6).

While female victims of aggression were often projected as heroines and martyrs, their own husbands and communities often rejected and ostracized them, particularly if they had suffered sexual assault while defending the community. They were routinely denied family protection and not allowed to participate in any rituals.

Since women, by and large, participated in movements more out of desire to support their men in a crisis than out of determination to acquire any clout as women, there are hardly any instances of women pressurizing the leadership to improve the lives of women. Women's fronts remained auxiliaries. They seldom became involved in power struggles. While women competed with each other, they did not offer any competition to male leadership.

The impetus to organize *Stree Akali Dal* (the Women's Akali wing), came at the initiative of male leadership. Most of the activists confirm that the few women who were able to take an active part in movements were wives of men already involved in such activities. Women who came against the wishes of the male members of the family were seldom able to sustain their involvement over a long period of time.

Linked to the crucial need for family permission is the age factor. In most movements, while a number of male activists are unmarried youth, young unmarried girls are seldom allowed to participate. An important reason is that parents fear a girl's reputation would be ruined if she associated with men in a public domain, and her chances of marriage would be reduced. For older women, this is a lesser problem, but they face the double disadvantage of being heavily weighed by work and often being illiterate. However, young married women may more easily get permission from their families to join in movement activities if respected older women of the village are already involved and can act as escorts.

Women did not determine the agenda. The Stree Akali Dal did not raise the question of oppression of women because this was not on the agenda of Akali leadership. Sant Longowal's message to women as reported by Harwant Kaur was: Do not harm anyone. Live in peace and love with all. When you go to your in-laws' house, love everyone there. Serve your husband. Have no relationship with any man other than your husband.

The Akali leadership even proposed to curtail women's rights by introducing a personal law for Sikhs which would have deprived women of whatever legal inheritance rights they had, and legally legitimized the practice of levirate. Despite rural women's militant contribution to the movement, no protest against this move emerged from the Stree Akali Dal. Whatever protest was voiced came from urban women's groups in Chandigarh and Delhi, even though the question of land inheritance primarily affects rural women.

> On the whole, men were more interested in women participating in large numbers in action programmes, but were less interested in their developing an independent identity. As a result, while women came and participated in a big way in demonstrations, and were often in the forefront, they did not have any decision making or leadership roles (*Manushi*, no. 14, 11).

There is no doubt that despite the auxiliary role they play, women who are mobilized for different actions gain significantly in terms of self-confidence, mobility, and a chance to see the world outside the village and to interact with other women.

The knowledge that they played an indispensable role in the movement's success helps women build a more positive self-image. Women's heroic actions become part of the movement lore and some individual women may emerge as role models different from the more normal model of woman as server and giver within the family. Even if they get pushed back into the domestic sphere once the crisis is over, each phase of participation represents an irrevocable step of some kind, and does change somewhat the collective consciousness of women. They become at least conscious of their ability to emerge and act in the public and political domain.

A necessary precondition for women's mobilization is the general and usually prior mobilization of men in the community. Movement leaders have seldom, almost never, begun by mobilizing women as an integral part of their organizations. In almost all cases, their organizing efforts have initially focused primarily on men—whether the organization is of peasantry or of the landless poor. However, as soon as the organization undertakes mass action and gets into a state of confrontation for getting its demands met, women often come out spontaneously to lend support to the movement, specially at moments of crisis. This is true of the Akali Dal, besides other movements in India.

Even though women tend spontaneously to join rural and urban movements during the phases of militant action, it has been found that, in most cases, the leadership begins to make a special appeal to women to join when the movement is facing a crisis like government and police repression or a backlash from oppressive forces. At such times, the leaders call on women more easily because the community is compelled to suspend social norms in order to cope with the emergency, and the men become more willing to encourage women's participation. At such times of crisis, women too tend to perceive their participation as a duty to family and community.

Conclusion

The present investigation of portraits of women demonstrate the extreme views of misogynist attitudes, on the one hand, and the religious ideals of wisdom and universal salvation, on the other. These views were upheld in varying degrees throughout a wide range of Sikh literature and history. The traditional attitudes towards women tended to relegate the feminine to the sensual realm as opposed to the spiritual realm. The imminent seductive powers of the feminine suggest that men perceived women as potential threats to their spiritual welfare. The evil power of sexuality were associated with women and household life. Possible notions of pollution or contamination through any interaction with women remained implicit. Women were viewed as the cause of mental anguish and pain, and as threats to familial stability because of their perceived adulterous behaviour.

Woman as mother was also tied to the sensual realm, to a state of attachment to home and children. Although woman as mother does not threaten the family structure, being almost synonymous with the household life, she cannot move out of the domestic sphere to the religious. She [illegible] a paragon of womanhood through her procreative func[illegible]dren, but she is also inextricably entwined wit[illegible]amely, a world of children and attachment to [illegible]on represents the compromising efforts of rec[illegible]een ingrained prejudices and religious goals to [illegible]ich the gurus imposed on the women, were pri[illegible]ng their own spiritual position; recognition th[illegible]ed by society, particularly by their close asso[illegible]nsibilities, which were more demanding for w[illegible]sociation of seductive powers to the feminine, g[illegible]s inherently sensual and destructive beings. [illegible] the Guru Granth reflect the concern for the disintegration o[illegible] structure, if women were to leave their homes. Accounts of the happily wedded wives and other women also implied, in some instances, dependence and subordination. The happily wedded wives were capable of teaching and respecting the *gurumat* through their daily activities. The familiar associations with a husband, father, or child is constantly mentioned, suggesting that it was through her familial responsibilities that she could attain God. God is exemplified as all loving, spiritually perfect and omniscient, frequently described as both the mother and father of all living beings. Certain texts go on to suggest that the female sex was weaker both physically and mentally, more vulnerable to ignorance, and perhaps even somewhat defective, in terms of spiritual weakness and physical handicaps.

The Sikh scriptures affirm that women ought to take an active part in the social, cultural and religious pursuits. The idea that woman is evil, unclean, or an impediment is not rejected, as often made to think, but endorsed in the Guru Granth. The episodes from the Janam Sakhis (stories about the birth and life of the gurus)[10] often suggest that Guru Nanak was a reformer speaking and acting against the caste system and working to improve the situation of women.

However, we do see conflicting images in the Guru Granth, one affirming equivalence and the other defining women as subordinate to men, socially and even ontologically.

Granted the subordinate status she inherited from the Hindus, the Sikh woman did not fare horribly. If she were a good wife and mother, specially of sons, she could expect praise. Marriage continues to be the norm for both men and women. The goal and purpose is to bring under control all the unruly potentialities of sexuality. Overall, the female domain of home and family was considered material. The spiritual and religious domains belonged to men. It is, however, fair to say the women were usually cherished in private and treated with respect in public, but considered inferior to men.

The prevailing societal restrictions on women also undoubtedly influenced descriptions of women and the feminine. Portraits of women frequently focused on the woman's important functions within the household life. Women were expected to bear the majority of familial responsibilities. If women were to leave the domestic sphere of activities, social institutions would collapse with the expected breakdown of the family. However, there are sympathetic portraits of women and the feminine.

BIBLIOGRAPHY

Akbar, M.J., 1985, *Indian: The Seige Within*. New Delhi: Penguin.

Gross, Rita M., 1987, 'Tribal Religions: Aboriginal Australia', Arvind Sharma (ed.), *Women in World Religions*. Albany, N.Y.: SUNY Press.

Honigberger, J.M., 1952, *Fifty-Five Years in the Past*. London, H. Bailliere.

Ibbetson, D.C., 1883, *The Religion of the Punjab*. Calcutta: Government Printing Press.

Kinsley, David, 1986, *Hindu Goddesses*. Berkley: University of California Press.

Kishwar, Madhu, 1988, 'Nature of Women's Mobilization', *Economic and Political Weekly*, Dec. 24–31.

Macauliffe, M.A., 1909, *The Sikh Religion*. Oxford: Oxford University Press, vol. 1.

Manushi, 1987, no. 40.

McLeod, W.H., 1989, *The Sikhs: History, Religion and Society*. New York: Columbia University Press.

—— 1984, *Textual Sources for the Study of Sikhism*. Manchester: Manchester University Press.

—— 1980, *Early Sikh Tradition: A Study of the Janamsakhis*. Oxford: Clarendon Press.

Oberoi, Harjot Singh, 1988, 'From Ritual to Counter Ritual', J.T. O'Connell, M. Israel and W.G. Oxtoby (eds), *Sikh History and Religion in the Twentieth Century*. Toronto: Centre for South Asian Studies, University of Toronto.

—— 1987, 'A World Reconstructed: Religion, Ritual and Community among the Sikhs', Ph.D. dissertation, Canberra, Australia, Faculty of Asian Studies, Australian National University.

Singh, Khuswant, 1966, *A History of the Sikhs*. Delhi: Oxford University Press, vols. 1 and 2.
Singh, Ranbin, 1965, *Glimpses of the Divine Masters*. New Delhi: International Trade Corporation.
Smith, W.C., 1962, *The Meaning and End of Religion*. New York: Macmillan.
Trotter, L.J., 1880, *Life of Lord Lawrence*. Oxford: Oxford University Press, vol. 1.
Young, Katherine K., 1987, 'Hinduism', Arvind Sharma (ed.), *Women in World Religions*. Albany, N.Y.: SUNY Press.

NOTES

1. The eleven traditions being Udasi, Nirmala, Suthreshahi, Khalsa, Sangatshahi, Jitmali, Bakkatmali, Mihanshahi, Sahajdhari, Kuka, and Sarwaria.

2. The Adi Granth or Guru Granth Sahib, the primary scripture of the Sikhs, contains hymns attributed to Guru Nanak, followed by those of the third, fourth, fifth, and ninth gurus, and the verse of Kabir, Farid, Namdev and Ravidas. The book is a collection of nearly six thousand hymns of the Sikh gurus (religious leaders) and various early and medieval saints of different religious castes. The book was first compiled by the fifth Sikh guru, Arjun, at Amritsar in 1604 AD. He included his own hymns and those of his predecessors, the gurus Nanak, Angad, Amardas and Ramdas, and a selection of devotional songs of both Hindu and Muslim saints (notably Kabir). In 1704 AD, the tenth and last guru, Gobind Singh, added the hymns of his predecessor, Guru Tej Bahdur (the sixth, seventh and eighth gurus did not write hymns), and enjoined that after his own death the Granth would take place of the gurus. The book opens with the Mul Mantra (basic prayer), which is a declaration of the nature of God, followed by the Japji (recital), the most important Sikh scripture, written by the founder of the Sikh religion, Guru Nanak. The hymns are arranged according to the musical modes (ragas) in which they are meant to be sung. The language is mostly Punjabi or Hindi, interspersed with Marathi, Persian and Arabic words. After the death of Guru Gobind Singh, his own hymns and other writings were compiled into a book known as the *Dasam Granth*.

3. The nine successors of Guru Nanak being: Angad, Amardas, Ramdas, Arjun, Hargobind, Har Rai, Har Krishan, Tej Bahdur, and Gobind Singh.

4. The literature (see Bibliography) used, and people of the community (friends and total strangers) from across Canada and overseas, endorse the idea of equality between sexes.

5. The number indicates the page of the standard 1430-page printed original text of the Adi Granth. It is to be noted that the quotations used in this study are from the English rendition of the Adi Granth by Gurubachan Singh Talib more for reasons of convenience than choice. In fact, there is no adequate translation available in English. Much is lost in the process of translation mainly because certain concepts, words, and expressions remain unique to a given culture and,

regardless of the quality of the translation, there are invariable portions that remain irreclaimable or misplaced. The task of translating the Adi Granth continues to be demanding, as the hymns are arranged according to the Indian classical mode of music—that is to say, the sound as well as the significance of the hymns are equally important. See *Sri Guru Granth Sahib* (4 vols.) translated by Gurubachan Singh Talib, Punjabi University, Patiala, 1987.

6. Honigberger, *Thirty Five Years in the East*, p. 16.

7. For a comprehensive description of the rites and procedure to be followed for the ceremonial initiation, see Avtar Singh Vahira, *Khalsa Dharm Shastar*, Amritsar, Sodhi Ram Narain Singh, 1914.

8. For extensive background on the ritual procedure, see Taihal Singh, 1903, *Gurmat Riti Vivah Anusar Bidhi*, Lahore.

9. For a detailed description on Rahat Maryada, see the chapter in S.N. Mukerjee, ed., *Indian History and Thought: Essays in Honour of A.L. Basham* (Calcutta: Subarnarekha, 1982).

10. There are four groups of Janam Sakhis: the Puratan Janam Sakhi. Miharban Sakhi, Bala Janam Sakhi and Gyan Ratnavali. For further details, see *Early Sikh Tradition: A Study of the Janamsakhis* (Oxford: Clarendon Press, 1980).

Zarathushti, Zoroastrian, Parsi: Women in Zarathushti Din, Zoroastrianism*

Ketayun H. Gould

What's in a name, especially since all of these terms refer to the followers of the Prophet Zarathushtra and the religion that he propagated? The answer is simple. There are historical as well as ethnic factors that need to be analysed in order to understand why communities in various parts of the world came to be associated with one of these names. Furthermore, the differentiations are not a simple matter of categorization. The scriptural interpretations and traditions of the different sub-groups have had a significant impact on the status of women in the religious and societal domains in their respective countries.

Zoroastrianism has been the most widely used term in the West to denote the religion since the Prophet Zarathushtra was known to the ancient Greeks as Zoroaster. The names Zoroaster and Zoroastrianism as a religious category are also used by the Indian government as well as the community in India as the standard, official designations in all their

* I have drawn on my earlier work in writing this present chapter. See Gould, Ketayun H., 'Outside the Discipline, Inside the Experience: Women in Zoroastrianism' in *Religion and Women*, ed. by Arvind Sharma (Albany, N.Y.: State University of New York Press, 1994), pp. 139–82, 253–6.

publications. But in the vernacular (Gujarati) writings, the traditional terms—Zarathushtra, Zarathushti (follower of Zarathushtra) and Zarathushti Din (religion)—are more commonly used than the more widely known Western nomenclatures that are favoured by authors who publish in the English language. Generally, however, in India and Pakistan, the followers of Zoroaster are distinguished as Parsis—persons from Pars, the province in the south-west of Iran which was originally called Persia or Persis by the Greeks. 'In Iran they are called Zartushti by non-Zoroastrians, and Beh-Din among themselves.'[1] In the North American continent, there is a move towards ethnicization by gradually standardizing the usages of the terms *Zarathushtra*, *Zarathushti* and *Zarathushti Din* in order to abnegate the Greek 'corruption' of the prophet's name and religion: Zoroaster and Zoroastrianism. In addition to these specific titles, 'a neutral and all-embracing nomenclature' that has been used for the followers of the religion is *Mazdayasni*, the worshipper of *Mazda*, the Sublime Wisdom.[2] Accordingly, the religion is called *Mazdaism*. In what follows, all of these terms will be used to discuss the status of women in the religious texts, the beliefs and practices of the living faith, plus ethnographic inquiry into the actual lives, attitudes and behaviour of women.

Despite their diversity, the Indian and the diaspora communities share the assumption (to a greater or lesser degree) that the ultimate authority for a wide range of practices of the living faith, including personal and public conduct, lies in the scriptures. The general problem with this orientation is the fact that the Zarathushti theology as well as the religious tradition encompasses a very complex history—a period from about 1500 BCE to the present. Moreover, the transmission of Zarathushtra's message must have acquired new meaning through the retelling involved in oral traditions, philological questions arising in recasting the original languages into the respective vernacular texts and the resultant issues about interpreting the religious, political and social contexts in which the translations are located. Often, these problems must have been exacerbated by the cultural and linguistic distance between the original and the vernacular texts of the day, although efforts were made to reduce the gap by several layers of intervening commentary. It is no surprise, then, that there is a bitter controversy about what portion of the extant scriptural texts are Zoroastrian as against simply reflecting an Iranian heritage. In other words, the argument is based on the premise that if the entire collection is ascribed to the prophet, they represent his 'Divine Message', and thus, any changes in the 'basic laws' are considered to be heresies. On the other hand, if there is an understanding that certain traditions might have been promulgated at specific points to suit the societal conditions or the predilections of the dominant classes, that these traditions might have been subsequently elevated to the status of religious injunctions, and that the possibility exists that some of these principles might be untenable in the present circumstances, then changes in the laws might seem to be a normal state of development and adaptation.

From the author's perspective, the 'women and religion' domain requires an analysis of *all* of the 'divinatory' documents (whatever they are labelled) in order to grasp the individual and societal prescriptions that both religion and tradition impose on women. In suggesting this approach, excluding any arena from scrutiny glosses over the adverse effects of certain religious precepts on women. Moreover, it results in a tendency to defend these positions in the name of religious/cultural solidarity or superiority of insiders' knowledge and sensitivity to their worldviews. Having grown up as a member of the Parsi community in India, the author can bear witness to these tendencies which are clearly reflected in the limited literature on women in Mazdaism: the totality of the experience that an ethnic-minority religious community imposes on its followers. Understanding of its vulnerable position as a minority religion, however, had never persuaded the author that there was a necessity for absolute compliance on all counts; nor did the extremes of a relativist position succeed in convincing that a feminist critique across cultures is completely unjustifiable. As Duara has stated so clearly

> ... there is a significant tension between transcendent and humanist claims within the culture ... it is possible to justify a moral claim across cultures provided the claim is couched in negative terms: that is, while we may not prescribe an ethical code for another society, we have a right to speak out on behalf of ... minority voices.[3]

Needless to say, feminist analysis across religious boundaries needs to be blended with a cultural sensitivity in order to avoid a chauvinistic interpretation of data where one's religious/feminist framework becomes a model for the others.

This chapter, however, is not simply concerned with what Simmons has rightly described as an over-reliance on texts that tend to emphasize the most orthodox/conservative viewpoints within the religious tradition. Simmons is on the right track in asking scholars to examine the practices of the living faith—the worldview that translates these beliefs and practices into everyday experiences.[4] The author has done research on the Parsi community in India that might help to present more than the author's personal views on the contributions of women in social and economic spheres. The indepth, demographic studies of Parsi households reveal information on the actual lives, attitudes and behaviour of women. Although there is no necessary correlation between the status of women in the religious tradition and their participation in the societal domain, the latter information is helpful in providing a reality base to test if the gender differentiation embodied in the written word is part of daily practice.

On the other hand, a relatively egalitarian ideal that might govern societal sex role behaviour is no defence in downplaying the significance of possible negative images of women in the texts and traditions. In other words, it is important to disentangle these various sets of information and recognize the fact that societal changes in sex roles is not a precursor of *automatic* changes in old sex role models that are endorsed by patriarchal religions. To construct a new social order that also seeks religious validation for the transformation of female and male roles, one has to deal with the politics of both religious and societal institutions. This argument does not deny the fact that, at certain historical junctures, some religious leaders might have played a determining role in bringing about radical changes in societal views of appropriate sex roles. However, as Tong has pointed out:

> Society has shaped religion much more than religion has shaped society. As soon as a religion adapts to its social *environ*, its critical or counter-cultural impact is weakened. Gradually, it loses any ability it may have had to transform society; and ultimately it becomes a mirror for the culture which has overpowered it.[5]

In this chapter, it is proposed to survey the major periods in the history of Zoroastrianism from the perspective of the theology and the practice of female-male relations within the context of the religious tradition as well as society. This is a very complex history, which encompasses a period from about 1500 BCE to the present. It also involves the study of diverse cultural contexts. Zoroastrianism was a major religion in ancient and medieval Iran. After the Arab conquest of Iran by 651 CE, it became a minority religion, and many Zarathushtis migrated to India. Today the Parsis of India are considered the most influential segment of this religious community. Zarathushtis continue to dwell in Iran although the exact number of adherents is uncertain. Besides these two major centres, Zoroastrians have settled in Pakistan Britain, Canada, United States, Australia, Singapore and Hong Kong, among other places. Thus, to talk about women in Zoroastrianism, particularly as it relates to the modern period, is to make over-generalizations that cannot possibly apply to the total religious community. In addition, the experiential base in the Parsi community limits any familiarity with the topics as it applies to women in other Zoroastrian concentrations to available literary sources. The only other exception is a limited familiarity with some Zarathushtis and their social and religious concerns as they are manifested in the North American context.

ANCIENT PERIOD

The religious culture of Zarathushti Iran originated perhaps three thousand five hundred years ago, but clearly many of the traditions associated with the Prophet Zarathushtra must reach back much further. Because of its antiquity, the chain of evidence that can be used to trace the history of the Zoroastrians to Indo-European times is a mixture of 'fact, legend and myth'.[6]

In all probability, the Iranians and Indo-Aryans originally formed one complex of people who were a branch of the Indo-European family of nations. The linguistic evidence suggests that these people lived on the south Russian steppes, to the east of Volga. They lived as pastoralists, tending their cattle on foot. It is generally believed that sometime during the third millennium BCE one group of these people, the Indo-Aryans, moved across north-east Iran and settled in north-west India, taking over the Indus Valley civilization. A further wave moved into Iran later in the second millennium BCE. Before these two groups drifted apart, they forged a religious tradition whose elements are preserved to this day in the ancient scriptures of the two countries—the Hindu *Vedas* and the Zoroastrian *Avesta*.

Indo-Iranian Heritage

The fragmentary evidence regarding the Indo-Iranian society in this nomadic stage points in the direction of a kingship system that concentrated power in the hands of high kings. The division of society into two main groups—priests and warrior herdsmen—reflects an orientation that stressed wars and conquest, pastoralism and hope of the salvation for those who had the means to win the favour of the gods. The patriarchal hierarchy, mounting up to a position of great power for its head, was based on a kingship system that supported the extreme male dominance through a four-fold grouping: house, clan, tribe and country.

Boyce supports the *traditional* explanations for this social structure on the grounds that it was a necessary stage in the establishment of kingdoms since the 'uncertain conditions of a wandering life' and a societal pattern of conquests required 'good leadership'.[7] Interestingly, 'this pattern of society appears to have become reflected in that of the gods'.[8] Boyce comments on the kingship imagery in the *Mihr Yast* (one of the oldest of the Avestan hymns) as mirroring the societal patterns of the day. She also believes that the aristocratic and priestly traditions of the times might have been responsible for denying ascent to paradise to the humblest members of the community, 'with women and slaves', and consigning them to the kingdom of shadows beneath the earth.[9] A feminist perspective, however, suggests that the aristocratic and priestly frameworks are not sufficient to explain the consignment of all women, even those of noble class, to the subterranean kingdom of the dead. A conscious application of the feminist framework might provide the missing perspective to understand why women as a *class* of people were excluded from full participation in the religious experience.

The ancient Iranians did relate feminine imagery to the divine level. The links with traditional feminine attributes are obvious. For example, there is an old coupling between Father Sky and Mother Earth—the god *Asman* and the goddess *Zam*. The goddess is viewed positively with her name interpreted as 'bounteous beneficent earth' or 'bounteous devoted earth', referring very probably to the nurturing qualities attributed to a female deity as well as earth. Another divinity is the pagan goddess of fortune—*Asi*—who is described as 'great gifted' or 'treasure laden'. Her yast—scripture devoted to the worship of divine beings—(verses 6–14) describes what she is able to bestow: 'values of the good things of this world ... frank pleasure in ... earthly riches ... in a world of which man is the centre and wherein the woman, like the cattle, the gold, and the silver, minister to man's enjoyment'. Indeed, this is a perfect depiction of patriarchal heaven.

It is also interesting that while mortal women were thought unworthy of attaining paradise, the soul of a dead man on its departure from earth at the end of the third day after death is seen as meeting a female figure on its upward journey—the maiden of the bridge. Those souls who had acquired merit in the eyes of the gods could hope to ascend to heaven by crossing safely over the 'bridge of the separator'. The undeserving fell from this bridge to live in the dark shadows of the underworld under the rule of the lord of the dead. If the pleasures of paradise were visualized as being reserved solely for the delights of men, the apparition of the welcoming maiden makes sense since woman's role was perceived as ministering to men's needs. The sustaining power of feminine energy as a source for *others* rather than *self* is a common theme in patriarchal religions as well as society.

The Indo-Iranian views about the world also included beliefs in spirits, some kindly and some malevolent. Some of these spirits were conceived as female beings. The benevolent *fravartis*, the guiding spirits of the dead, are winged creatures who inhabit the air and could be persuaded through offerings to come to the aid of humans. The evil supernatural beings, *parikas* (Yast I.10), could beguile men to their harm by taking on human form of extraordinary beauty. They were capable of harming humans physically by undermining their moral character or damaging the material world around them. The recognition of feminine power as a symbol for good or evil has been mythically expressed in many religious beliefs.[10] It often goes hand in hand with a deep ambivalence regarding women—a natural consequence of the general misogyny of patriarchal societies that spawned these religious traditions.

Zarathushti Religious Inheritance

Boyce summarizes the speculations regarding Zarathushtra's homeland by discussing the 'tangle of legends, false claims and fanciful speculations' that have surrounded this topic.[11] A large number of scholars, however, have concurred that the northern region of eastern Iran was the realm of Zarathustra's birth. On the other hand, the date of the prophet's birth is still a matter of dispute, with such widely varying dates as 6000 BCE to 600 BCE being proposed by various authors.[12] After reviewing the evidence, Boyce concludes that the 'possible chronological limits thus appear to be c. 1500 – c. 1200; and a date at the lower limit, i.e. around 1200, seems the most reasonable one to postulate since it is reconcilable with all the known data ...'[13]

The revelations of the Prophet Zarathushtra relating to the religious status of women contain some of the Indo-Iranian elements mentioned previously that became blended with the prophet's own teachings. But it is safe to say that despite the fact that the religion retained the patriarchal characteristics that were part of its pagan past and its male-dominated society, it also challenged the status quo by introducing a more gender-inclusive philosophy—even if it still reflected a male worldview. The most significant departure from the pagan tradition was that Zoroaster promised the hope of salvation to both women and men. Paradise was no longer the exclusive domain of men who had the means to achieve it. From the *gathas* (hymns or songs believed to be composed by the prophet himself), it is clear that Zoroaster's conception of the morally good life went beyond a design for ethical human behaviour; it implied an eschatology. Paradise was now attainable by all those who had chosen to live the righteous life—whose good thoughts, words, and deeds outnumbered the bad. Thus, the prophet proclaimed: 'Man or woman ... whomever I shall impel to your invocation, with all these shall I cross the Bridge of the Separator' (Yasna 46.10). In fact, the prophet's handling of the belief in the maiden of the bridge illustrates how some pagan ideas were accepted and harmonized with his own teachings.

The stress on righteous living as the passport to paradise is emphasized by the fact that the maiden is now seen as personification of an individual's conscience (*daena*). If the person has led a good moral life, then the soul is guided over the bridge to paradise by its own daena in the form of a lovely young damsel. But if the soul is that of a wicked person, it is met by its conscience, a hideous hag, who plunges with it off the bridge down into hell. The break from past traditions is evident in the prophet's attempt to provide an ethical connotation to a previously amoral figure of the welcoming maiden. The imagery, however, of a damsel and a hag to personify goodness and wickedness seems to be an acceptable vehicle to introduce radical ideas in traditionally understood sex-linked stereotypes.

The *Avestan* texts provide further elaboration of the fact that on some counts the prophet did provide a vision of equality between women and men in the religious experience. Even when the transcendent was imaged as a supreme male being (the wise lord—Ahura Mazda—often referred to in the texts as the 'father'), his first creative act of bringing into being six lesser beneficent divinities in the struggle against evil (the Amesa Spentas) included three female yazatas. The scripture (Yasna 39.3) talk about worshipping the 'bounteous immortals' (Amesa Spentas), both females and males. Each of them protects one part of the total creation in the material world against the onslaught of evil from the evil spirit (Angra Mainyu). The assignment of female yazatas to guard over earth, water and plants can be explained easily as a reference to the females' capacity for nurturing and growth.

What is more interesting, however, is that in the later, more conservative era, the Pahlavi literature fully sets out the association of Spendarmad—the Amesa Spenta who protects the 'lowly submissive, and fecund' earth with that of protector of 'virtuous woman'. And Ohrmazd (wise lord) is said to preside over 'just man', which seems to divide up the protection of women and men between female and male immortals.[14]

It is also worth noting that the sex-linked attributes—virtuous and just—might be the appropriate role models that the religious world considered worthy to be singled out for attention. Moreover, Spendarmad, the guardian of earth (and by association, peasants) and a virtuous woman is known by her characteristic—devotion—that must have been prized among those who are low in the social gradation since 'women and peasants were expected to be devoted and submissive'.[15] Again, the degree of correspondence between the societal arrangements of the day and religious imagery gives us a chance to understand how far the prophet went in presenting new ideas, to what extent these beliefs retained the patriarchal structure, and how the combination might have helped the followers to accept his message.

The sacred liturgy reveals another area where the prophet included women in the religious tradition. Veneration is offered to the *fravasis* (the Indo-Iranian fravartis referred to earlier) of the just women as well as men (Yasna 37.3). The inclusion of the former seems to be a specifically Zoroastrian conception. Fravardin Yast (Yast 13), which preserves the names of those who upheld the faith at its inception, lists the names of '261 persons, sixteen of whom are married women and eleven are maidens'.[16] In fact, Ahura Mazda is said to have created women to aid him in vanquishing the corporeal and spiritual evil through following the path of righteousness. In this sense, Ahura Mazda needs the women along with men to be his allies in seeking salvation for the world—to defeat Angra Mainyu and the onslaught of evil—and restore the world to its pristine state. Thus, in the initial stages of the spread of Zoroastrianism, women and men were ideally considered to be equal partners in the struggle against evil. According to the Avestan texts, both women and men were entitled to be initiated into the religion by investiture of the sacred shirt and girdle. Women as well as men were asked to fulfil their duty to proclaim and teach what is true and good (Yasna 35.6). In fact, there is some evidence that besides taking part in the holy ceremonies and solemn offerings, women were considered fit, under certain circumstances, to officiate for the minor priestly duties.[17]

At the same time, it is true that the duty to marry and procreate is thought to be not only desirable, but a holy pursuit for both women and men. The Zoroastrian strong ethnic self-consciousness made the begetting of children for the propagation of the race and spreading of the faith a religious function—to further the kingdom of Ahura Mazda and cripple the power of Angra Mainyu. But to fulfil her religious destiny, the Zarathushti wife was not only to bear children, but *specifically* bear 'male children', 'a troop of male children' (Yast 8.15). Having a son is a blessing bestowed by the benevolent spirits upon the righteous (Yast 10.65), and again, the gift is denied to a woman who does not follow the proper rituals (Yasna 10.15). Moreover, sons were necessary to have the proper ceremonies performed after death to aid the departed family members' souls on the upward journey to paradise. In fact, the importance of the cult of ancestral dead required that provision be made for the adoption of a son in case a man had none born to him. Interestingly, although the texts are silent on the issue of praying for female children, or receiving the blessings of female children from the good spirits, some authors seem to display the defensive cultural attitude discussed earlier by interpreting the *omission* as a 'lack of displeasure' at the birth of daughters.[18] The ethnic self-consciousness of the Zoroastrian community about their past accomplishments, plus the protective tendencies of scholars who might be over-identified with their subjects, tend at times to present a somewhat idealized picture of the laudable manner in which women were treated in this religious tradition.

Perhaps, a more accurate description of the status of women in the religion and everyday life might be that the Zoroastrian religion represented a significant step in the recognition and appreciation of the *traditional* roles of women—an improvement on patriarchy in the Indo-Iranian context. Furthermore, the religion emphasized the *mutual* responsibilities of husband and wife, albeit within a particular structure. This is illustrated by the language used to denote the status of the wife (*nmano-pathni*, the mistress of the house), while the husband is addressed as *nmano-pati* (the master of the house). Zoroaster's advice to the bride and bridegroom sets forth the injunction to 'let each one cherish the other in righteousness; thus alone unto each shall the home life be happy' (Yasna 53.5). Thus, marriage and the family unit become part of the divine order of the world and the begetting of children contributes more hands to do battle against the evil spirit and achieve the renovation promised to humanity.

In this context, the traditional duties of woman as wife and mother become an important instrument to achieve religious objectives. Moreover, her involvement in the family and the rituals plays a pivotal role in the cosmic battle against evil. The co-participation of husband and wife in the daily prayers to the wise lord and her co-presence in the domestic and public rituals lends credence to the importance of housewife's role in the total religious experience. Besides, in certain aspects, the housewife's contribution must have been paramount in the preservation of the religion such as the religious instruction to children and fulfilling the requirements of the performance of rituals. Because the religion, which catered to the well-being of the family, was centred in the home, it must have provided a degree of recognition plus sustenance for many women's faith that their home-centred work was part of the larger cosmic picture. In fact, the texts specifically mention the fact that although the housewife is encouraged to pray with her husband, her work in the home is so valuable that it may itself serve as prayer if her duties preclude her reciting the required *Nyayases*.[19] Furthermore, in the daily cleaning of the home, the housewife is thought to sweep away the dirt and decay that are the weapons the evil spirit uses to spoil Ahura Mazda's good creation.[20]

The reinforcement of women's traditional roles and the emphasis on the 'cult of domesticity' is understandable in the historical context of a male-dominated society. But even in the home environment, there is enough evidence illustrating that the woman might have been the 'minor partner of man in the religious life of the family'. This is because, as the head of the family, the man was the 'chief of all family worship'.[21] Other evidence about the ideal role of a woman can be gleaned from the development highlights that are singled out for attention in the sacred liturgy. The Avesta contains direct allusions to the status of a maiden in the *father's* house (the patrilineal and patrilocal family). She was given training in the religious schools after the age of seven so she could be initiated into her faith. Other than that, education consisted of preparation for the housewifely role.

This concern for building a stable family life and begetting children led to the early marriage of girls at about the age of fifteen. Obviously, chastity is considered to be the most essential quality in the bride, although no mention is made about the value of the same quality in a groom. The other characteristics that are praised besides a 'mind absorbed in piety' (Yast 11.4) are 'receiving her instruction well, having her husband as her lord' (Ga 4.9).

The texts also provide an instructive view of the ideal images of the maiden and her phantasies of the prospective bridegroom. These passages display not only an interest in physical beauty, but also a connection between youthfulness and virility, and the childbearing capacity of the maiden. In her daily prayers, the maiden is said to ask for a boon of 'a husband, young and beautiful of body, who will treat us well, all life long, and give us offspring; a wise, learned ready tongued husband' (Yast 15.40). And what is the ideal of female beauty? The ideal is personified in the description of the maiden of the bridge discussed earlier: 'beautiful maiden, brilliant, white armed, strong, well-grown, erect, tall, high-bosomed, graceful, noble, with a dazzling fall, of fifteen years'.[22]

The parents or guardians arranged the marriage, although the girl was consulted in the choice of the husband. The ideal union was considered to be based on mutual affection. There is some evidence, however, that under certain circumstances, there was some room for love marriages. Moreover, in this context, women were described as being capable of stepping outside the societal constraints of role definition and display the 'force of character' to 'go straight to (their) objective without hesitation'.[23] Thus, we read in the Shahnama, book of kings (the Persian epic), that women like Manijheh, Rudabeh, and Tahmina were 'transported by love into making active advances', while at the same time protecting themselves and soothing their beloved's male ego by disclaimers about their 'immodesty': 'No one has ever seen me outside the purdah nor has any man ever heard my voice'.[24]

The fact that there were at least a few Zoroastrian women who gave themselves permission to act in an unconventional manner through using conventional excuses (transported by love) cannot be seriously doubted. Nor can it be denied that the stories display a certain amount of grudging respect for women who are the responsible parties in consummating the union. There is no reason, however, to believe, as some authors have done, that these scattered instances of alliances between aristocratic lovers can be generalized as proof of the 'high' status of women in the Zoroastrian tradition.[25]

The general Zoroastrian view of sexual love is that, within marriage, sex and procreation are virtuous acts, since begetting of children brings more people into the world to do battle against the evil spirit. Every new birth is seen as sending a thrill through the whole creation of Ahura Mazda and casting a shadow of gloom over the wicked world of Angra Mainyu. In this sense, sexuality is viewed in the context of a religious duty and, as such, it is a pious act only within the confines of marriage. However, within this narrow definition, there is no downgrading of the physical needs of the human body compared to the higher status of the spiritual sphere. Hence, the celibate state is discouraged. In fact, the Avesta recognizes the joy that the sexual encounter can bring to both husband and wife, although the language and imagery reflect a male world view: 'The men whom thou dost attend ... have their ladies that sit on the beds, waiting for them: they lie on the cushions adorning themselves ... "When will our lord come? When shall we enjoy in our bodies the joys of love"?' (Yast 17.10).

The patriarchal nature of the family and society during the ancient period is evident from the fact that conjugal infidelity as a sin and an offence is spelled out very carefully in the case of a woman, but the texts are silent on how adultery is perceived among men. The infringement of chastity on the part of woman grieves Asi (feminine personification of piety), who is pictured as fleeing to the heavens or sinking into the earth at the sight of an unchaste female: 'the courtezan who destroys her fruit' and the 'courtezan who brings forth a child conceived of a stranger and presents it to her husband'. Such a woman is unfit to offer any prayers

(Yast 17.54). The yazata Haoma is entreated to hurl her mace 'against the body of the harlot, with her magic minds o'erthrowing with (intoxicating) pleasures' (Yasna 9.32).

Other taboos on sexual intercourse are centred on the Zoroastrian belief that menstruation results in a woman losing her ritual purity and becoming capable of spreading the impurity to all who have contact with her. Thus, husband and wife are strictly forbidden to have intercourse during this period, and for three days after the wife has performed her post-menstrual ablutions. Obviously, the Zoroastrian conception of menstruation and its relationship with the status of women is a far broader subject than the taboos associated with marital relations. The notion that menstrual blood is dangerous is widespread among many cultures and religions. In the Zarathushti Din, all substances leaving the body are considered ritually impure and polluting. Such substances include hair, nails, skin, faeces, saliva, breath, semen, and menstrual blood.

These substances are open to grave pollution by the corpse demoness since any flow of blood out of the body is a breach of the ideal physical state of human beings. Boyce attributes this phenomenon to the fact that these substances are 'associated with change and mortality rather than with the static state of perfection'.[26] Douglas, in analysing the concept of pollution, states that any matter that traverses the boundaries of the body tends to be considered 'marginal stuff'.[27] Thus, it is understandable that the Zoroastrian doctrine linked the origin of menstruation to a blight caused by the evil spirit. The flow of blood from the body is perceived as an attack by the demons on the perfect creation of Ahura Mazda. As Choksy has noted, this conception allowed the primitive beliefs and fears surrounding blood and its power to be reinforced by demonology, and elaborate rules then had to be evolved to combat the ritual impurity resulting from this dreaded pollution.[28]

Thus, at the onset of menstruation, very rigid precautions were called for to prevent contamination of the good creation of Ahura Mazda. During menstruation, the woman is supposed to withdraw from the family, sitting apart in a designated place. Boyce describes the original practice of having the woman pass these days in a tiny windowless hut that had only one entrance. She had to wear old clothes that were set apart for this purpose. Any Zarathushti who had physical contact with her was required to purify himself or herself with unconsecrated bull's urine and water. The menstruant was supposed to abstain from performing any household duties, since everything she touched became polluted.[29]

After the end of menstruation, a woman had to purify her entire body three times with unconsecrated bull's urine and water while saying the required prayers. Other prayers that specifically ask for expiation from sins were also recited. At menopause a woman was required to have priests perform a solemn purification ceremony, which marked her rejoicing in 'being wholly and perpetually clean at last, and able thus to prepare herself for eternity'.[30]

Although pregnancy gave a woman respite from the restrictions attendant on menstruation, the texts specify that childbirth also results in ritual impurity to both the mother and the child. All taboos that apply to the menstruant are to be enforced during this period. It would seem logical to assume that childbirth might have been conceived as an act of purity, since it increased the ranks of the faithful who could do battle against the evil spirit and his pandemonium. In fact, all Zoroastrians are thought to be polluted by impurities associated with the birth process and their mother's milk, which is believed to be derived from blood.[31] Moreover, birth had no place in the perfect world created by Ahura Mazda, and will have no place in the universe after the final renovation. Birth belongs, therefore, only to this world of mixture—to fight the evil spirit—and so can logically be considered as partly a result of demonic forces.[32]

Zoroastrians considered miscarriage and stillbirth as even greater sources of contamination, since these meant that the woman had borne a carrion within her womb. Abortion was prohibited since the Zoroastrians regarded it as murder and prosecuted people for this crime.[33] If the woman received help in getting an abortion from the 'man' or another person in the form of drugs, all three were considered equally guilty. The man is exhorted to take care of the woman and child, and bring up the child until the age of seven.

The Zoroastrian beliefs regarding menstruation, childbirth, and miscarriage probably represent elaborations of ancient restrictions inherited from the Indo-Iranian period. Most authors seem to view the phenomenon within the general context of the Zarathushti emphasis on fighting the spread of impurity (the creation of the evil spirit), and prescribing the required purification rituals in order to reintegrate the person into ordinary life.[34] Here, it is worth noting though that the literature on women in Zoroastrianism is remarkably lacking in presenting a feminist-cultural perspective which recognizes that cosmic claims—however logical they may seem within the confines of the faith—reflect the views of the dominant class and religious institutions. Viewed thus, it is obvious that the belief systems would function to preserve male hegemony rather than worry about representing the female voice in religious doctrines.

The texts present *indirect* evidence on some other subjects that are very relevant in terms of their impact on women. No literature (sacred or secular), however, is available that deals with these important topics —monogamy/polygyny and consanguineous marriages—in terms of recording the effects on women. After all, women had no voice in establishing the religious or societal decrees that governed the most intimate aspects of their lives. What is more pertinent from the methodological point of view is that none of the authors writing about women in Zoroastrianism has covered these topics from a feminist perspective. The concern seems to be highly focused on either the existence or morality of these practices, with the writings reflecting a lot of cultural defensiveness that adds to the complications of sorting out facts from fiction.

Regarding the question whether polygyny prevailed in Iran during the ancient period, there is no passage in the texts that provides direct evidence on this subject. Buch points to a stanza in the Vendidad (3.3)—'in the house of the righteous, women and children are present in rich abundance'—as the one that has given rise to speculation that polygyny prevailed in Zoroastrian Iran.[35] Sanjana and Katrak concur with Buch on this point and agree with his interpretation that the stanza might not imply the practices of polygyny. All three authors seem to believe that in a joint family situation that prevailed in ancient Iran, the plural 'women' may also refer to sons' wives.[36]

However, there is contradictory evidence on this subject, which seems to stress the testimony of Greek writers that 'every Persian marries many lawful wives'.[37] The disagreement on this subject seems to hinge on the point whether some kings or noblemen flaunted custom and practised polygyny, or whether the sacred texts endorsed the practice and it was the customary marriage pattern in ancient Iran. Both Sanjana and Katrak take great pains to go through the Avesta and point out every passage that refers to the wife in the singular form, which leads them to conclude that monogamy was the preferred system of marital union.[38]

Similarly, there is even more of a debate whether the original meaning of the Avestan word *xyaetvadatha* referred to consanguineous marriage as defined by incestuous relationships or as marriage between first cousins—a practice that is still very prevalent among Zoroastrians in Iran[39] and in India.[40] Choksy cites the work of Richard N. Frye on Zoroastrian incest to demonstrate that there is no evidence for the widespread practice of incestuous marriages among Zoroastrians in the ancient period.[41] Boyce is a little more tentative. She does refer to the testimony of Greek writers to raise the possibility that the practice might have prevailed among certain Achamenian kings and their subjects.[42] Again, Sanjana and Katrak question the credibility of the evidence presented by Greek writers. They claim that the foreign writers misunderstood the cultural practices; that among many traditional communities, the designation 'sister', 'daughter' or 'mother' is a honorific term that is applied to other close relatives. Therefore, the marriages that were assumed to be incestuous (within the close family circle) were in fact unions between first cousins.[43] Whatever the practices may have been, one thing is perfectly clear: in the debate over the existence of polygyny and consanguineous marriages, women are non-existent.

Before concluding the discussion on the ancient period, it is important to note that although Zoroastrian women were far from equal to men in the sphere of religious activities, they did enjoy some independence. Dhalla provides evidence to demonstrate that Zoroastrian women did not veil themselves, and attended social and religious gatherings in the company of men. They owned and managed property. They could act as the guardian of a son who was disinherited by his father. They could legally conduct a plea on the husband's behalf, and manage his affairs in his name. If they were being mistreated, they could seek redress in a court of law against a cruel husband and secure his punishment. They could give evidence in cases involving litigation and they could serve as judges.[44] Therefore, when it was a question of social, economic, and legal rights, women seemed to enjoy some degree of benefits, even though it might have occurred within the boundaries of a patriarchal society.

MEDIEVAL PERIOD

What has been said above has demonstrated that the Zoroastrian religion represented a significant step in the recognition of the traditional roles of women as compared to the patriarchy in the Indo-Iranian context. At the same time, it is quite evident that the growing elaboration of beliefs and practices that regulated ritual purity and pollution must have affected women more disproportionately than men because of the impurity associated with menstruation, parturition, and abortion. Choksy believes that this elaboration occurred between the tenth to the third centuries BCE and was codified in the *Vendidad* (the law against the demons).[45]

However, it is very clear that it was the medieval period, which encompasses the Sasanian and Islamic centuries (third to sixteenth century CE), that witnessed the most dramatic change in the perceptions of women's religious and secular roles. In reaching this conclusion, it has to be acknowledged, as Simmons has charged, that there is a tendency to place an over-reliance on texts, most of which are concerned with matters of ritual purity.[46] Undoubtedly, the scriptures during this period reflect the most conservative viewpoints since the Sasanians institutionalized the Zoroastrian faith as the official religion of the kingdom. The establishing of temple worship created a powerful elite of chief priests who wielded considerable power—hereditary offices that were an exclusive male domain.[47] Furthermore, Dhalla maintains that under the Sasanians, the priesthood spent an inordinate amount of time dealing with cultic and theological issues, which 'descended to rigid formalism, stifled independent inquiry, stigmatized honest doubts as Ahrimanian, and sought to overrule original thinking by dogmatic assertions'.[48]

The post-Sasanian period, with the stress involved in change of status of Zoroastrianism from state to minority religion (under the dominance of Islam) must have played its part in driving the religion to adopt a very patriarchal worldview. Zoroastrian fear of an alien religion and culture, especially when it was tied to their status of being the subjugated sect (Boyce refers to many 'stories' of rape and abduction of Zoroastrian women—a common fate suffered by many conquered populations)[49] must have encouraged the surfacing of extremely punitive attitudes towards women. In addition, Dhalla demonstrates that religious dissensions, especially the growth of sects 'had racked the Zoroastrian world' during this period.[50]

In examining this era, it is instructive to note some similarities between different world religions in their treatment of women. Swidler hypothesizes that one of the attractive forces of certain world religions (e.g. Christianity, Islam) is the fact that the 'initial burst of human liberation extended to women as well as men in a very high degree ... To the degree women later do not participate in full measure ... that religion is unfaithful to its initial insight.'[51] The author would tend to modify Swidler's thesis slightly and state that the ambivalence towards women's full religious participation is present in all patriarchal religions, although it is true that the initial vision does provide a sense of possibilities for women. If the societal forces change in the direction of conservatism, these forces usually dictate the course of religious response. The ambivalence towards women then gains religious validation, plus endorsement from all the dominant structures in society. Therefore, as stated before, transcending this phase requires ability on the part of women to have enough of a power base to deal with the politics of both the religious and societal institutions. This thesis can be easily supported by Choksy's observation that the 'medieval images and functions of women ... underwent little change within the Zoroastrian religious tradition until the modern period. The socio-economic independence of women increased during the nineteenth and twentieth centuries',[52] providing the necessary critical mass to force society and religion to re-evaluate their official stance on women's full partnership in these institutions.

Parsi Settlements in India

Zarathushti contact with India did not begin with the Arab invasion of Iran. The emigration can be traced over many centuries, involving economic, political and religious reasons. The Parsis, however, have looked to a legendary account—*the Kissah-i-Sanjan*—to trace the history of the Zarathushti refugees' flight to India (due to religious presecution) in 936 CE. The story itself makes some references to women that are instructive. The *Kissah-i-Sanjan* was written in 1600 CE by a learned priest whose sources were old books plus oral history. It claims that when the refugees came ashore, the local ruler was afraid of the large body of armed strangers, and asked the priest who had come as the group spokesperson to explain their religion and customs. The priest answered in sixteen Sanskrit *shlokas* (stanzas). Interestingly, the references in these stanzas to women stress their traditional roles—'(a community) whose married females are not (looked upon as) pure if devoid of husband'—or the fact that females observed the menstrual taboos: 'Pure-hearted men, whose females in menstrual period, become pure on the seventh night,(and when) delivered of child pure in body after a month from the day of delivery; (whose females) are noble on account of their graceful conduct ... are powerful and strong and have always laughing faces.'[53]

Scattered references to topics pertaining to Parsi women are also available in other sources such as foreign travellers' accounts of what they observed in India. The Rev. Edward Terry, chaplain in the service of the East India Company, 1616–19, noted about his visit to Surat that the 'Parsis had only one wife'. Thus, the practice of polygyny must have been on the decline, although Zoroastrian men were still permitted to take a second wife if the first was infertile. Another priest, Rev. Henry Lord, who was in Surat between 1615 and 1623, described the five forms of marriage that were prevalent among the Parsis, and the types match the medieval period marriages among the Zoroastrians in Iran.[54]

Modern Period

The patriarchal structure of society was gradually eroded by the fact that by the middle of the seventeenth century the Parsis had made the transition from villages to towns, and had branched out from agriculture to become artisans, merchants, traders and bankers. By the end of the eighteenth century, there was an exodus from the hinterlands to the port of Bombay, where the Parsis assumed the mercantile role, which became a source of their wealth and power. They established a mutually beneficial relationship with the British as 'mediators and pace-setters of social change'[55]—a role that would expose them to what must have seemed like a very liberal Western system of sex-role relations. The introduction of Christian mission school education, especially female education, played its part in providing an avenue of social mobility, although it brought its share of turmoil over community identity.[56]

The 1880s saw the beginning of yet another radical trend that was not so obvious in terms of its consequences for the future of the community. Visaria has demonstrated that as early as 1881 the marital fertility of the Parsis was only 46 per cent of the maximum potential.[57] Obviously, the finding indicates that even before the introduction of modern contraception, resort was sought to some form of control of fertility within marriage. The continuing demographic decline of the Parsi community during the twentieth century with its pattern of late marriage, non-marriage, and low fertility has led to a few studies (some sponsored by the Bombay Panchayat) to understand and possibly deal with this critical phenomenon.[58] The 1991 census reveals that the Parsi population of India was 76,382, with 60,051 or 79 per cent of them living in greater Bombay. The increase in numbers—4,752—over the 1981 census figures is the first growth in population that has been recorded since 1951. However, without a careful analysis, it is impossible to gauge if the increase is real or the result of some statistical problems.[59]

Although an involved discussion of the above subject is beyond the scope of this study, the topic itself has great significance for understanding the bitter religious controversy regarding conversion and intermarriage, and the ambivalent attitude toward the status of women in Zoroastrianism.

The issue of how the Parsi community should respond to intermarriages of Parsi females was complicated by the passage of the Special Marriage Act of 1954 which nullified the necessity of renouncing one's faith in the case of a civil marriage (required by the Civil Marriage Act of 1872). The 1954 law strengthened the argument that a Parsi woman does not leave the community automatically when she marries a non-Parsi as long as she continues to profess the Zoroastrian religion. The roadblocks, however, to establishing and maintaining the religious rights of these Parsi women are numerous. The main problem are some orthodox priests who exert their authority in their own 'territories' and influence their *anjumans* to support their decisions to prevent such women from entering fire-temples, attending religious ceremonies, and having their remains disposed of in the customary Zoroastrian traditions of the community. Thus, there is a checkered pattern of compliance with the

Special Marriage Act of 1954 and the decision in Saklat v. Bella 1925, which stated that trustees are not 'bound' to treat converts as trespassers.[60]

Recently, the question of conversion has assumed a new urgency due to certain well-publicized incidents. In 1981, during a concerted effort to reform the antiquated Bombay Parsi Panchayat (BPP) electoral system, six Parsi women married to non-Parsis took their case to the Bombay High Court. They were barred from registering on the BPP electoral rolls unless they filed affidavits that they were married under the Special Marriage Act and had continued to practice the Zoroastrian faith. The Court ruled that Parsi women married to non-Parsis under the Special Marriage Act do not cease to be Parsis. Therefore, no such affidavit was required to register them on the Panchayat electoral rolls. This decision was a step forward in recognizing the women's legal status, if not their religious status, as Parsi Zoroastrians.

This development was marred by an uproar over the case of a Parsi woman married to a non-Parsi who had died in a car accident on 27 July 1990. Roxan Shah had expressed a wish that upon her death, her body should be consigned to the towers of silence in accordance with Zoroastrian practices. The chairman of BPP refused permission. The resulting bitterness was exacerbated by the pronouncement of a Bombay High Priest (opinion was requested by BPP) that a Zoroastrian woman married to a non-Zoroastrian ceases to be a member of the religious community, even though she had married under the Special Marriage Act and had not renounced her religion. 'To marry outside the fold is next to adultery since the marriage is not solemnized according to the rights and customs of the Zoroastrian religion.' Furthermore, 'a child born in such a situation is considered to be illegitimate in the Zoroastrian religion though, in view of the Special Marriage Act, the child does acquire all the rights as, legally, the marriage is recognized.'[61] Thus, Shah's family was refused permission to have her body consigned to the towers of silence although she had married under the Special Marriage Act and had continued to practise the Zoroastrian faith.

In the aftermath of the heated debate, the BPP trustees decided to solicit various views that were prevalent in a cross-section of the Parsi community. On the basis of the consultation, the trustees decided to 'conditionally permit' Parsi women married to non-Parsis the right to the use of the towers of silence. By a five-to-two vote, BPP agreed to permit consignment of these bodies to a tower of silence 'specifically earmarked for the purpose'. In addition, the BPP made this decision contingent on the family submitting an affidavit that the woman had been married under the Special Marriage Act and had 'continued to follow the Zoroastrian religion till her demise'. The BPP also decreed that it would not be obliged to make arrangements for priests to perform the necessary funeral ceremonies; the relatives of the deceased would have to be responsible for making these arrangements.[62]

The discriminatory nature of these rulings were not lost on the liberal sectors of the community, specially the women who were most affected by the rulings. Several prominent Parsi women expressed critical opinions that are worth noting: (1) a separate tower of silence is kept 'only for criminals and those who commit suicide. These ladies are practising Zoroastrian Parsis ...'; (2) the ruling reflected gender based discrimination since Parsi males married to non-Parsis were not required to submit an affidavit regarding their marriage or religious practices nor were their bodies consigned to a separate tower of silence; (3) a Parsi male who had married a non-Parsi was not automatically considered to have renounced his religion by taking such a step while a Parsi female married to a non-Parsi was deemed to have renounced her religion; and (4) children of Parsi women married to non-Parsis were not permitted to attend their obsequies—a rule that did not apply to the children of Parsi men married to non-Parsis.[63]

Nevertheless, thirty-two Parsi women married to non-Parsis wrote to BPP requesting an assurance that at their demise, their bodies would be interred at the towers of silence since they had married under the Special Marriage Act and had continued to profess the Zoroastrian faith.[64] The ruling also impelled Parsis married to non-Parsis to organize themselves to establish the Association of Inter-Married Zoroastrians. The orthodox section of the community also mobilized themselves by doing the following: (1) 130 priests signed a memorandum denying any religious rights to Parsi women married to non-Parsis; (2) public meetings were organized to protest against the BPP decision to conditionally permit Parsi women married to non-Parsis the right to the use of the towers of silence; and (3) a monthly publication titled *Deen Parast* was started to air their views.[65]

In the light of this uproar, it is interesting that the Bombay High Priest involved in the Shah controversy (along with other priests) was also involved in another incident that took place in 1994 which illustrates the patriarchal nature of the Zoroastrian religion and societal structure. The 81 year old scion of the prominent industrial family—the Wadias—who was raised in the Church of England (his father had converted from Zoroastrianism to Christianity before his birth) had expressed a wish to become 'a Zoroastrian again', and resume the religion of his ancestors. He consulted the high priests in India. After some initial reluctance due to scriptural injunctions, five of the seven high priests whose permission was sought consented to have his *navjote* performed. The ceremony took place on 24 September 1994. His initiation, and subsequently the initiation of his son, was justified by the priests on the grounds that some Zoroastrians might have formally adopted an alien faith 'only a generation ago'. Such Zoroastrians may be called 'Zoroastrians who have gone astray. If such Zoroastrians realize their ancestral religion ... then they are allowed after ceremonial repentance'.[66]

The public debate on this issue was interestingly muted compared to the Roxan Shah controversy, especially since the Wadias are a prominent family whose fortunes have benefited the Parsi community. There were some questions raised, however, about the following points (1) How was the definition of conversion handled since Zoroastrianism does not sanction this practice? Does the 'one generation' rule establish the principle of 'reverting to the ancestral faith' and nullify the issue of conversion?; (2) How was the navjote performed on an 81 year old when the age limit for the initiation is supposed to be 15?; and (3) Most important, for the topic under discussion, how will the ruling apply to Parsi women who are automatically considered to have renounced their religion by marrying non-Parsis although they continue to profess the Zoroastrian faith? Furthermore, could the women induct their children into the Zoroastrian faith by having their navjote performed?

The question of conversion has assumed such urgency for another reason. There is sentiment in some liberal quarters that part of the solution of the demographic decline might be to accept the children of Parsi women married to non-Parsis as Zoroastrians—an issue that has not been dealt with at all since the prior question of the Parsi woman remaining a Parsi Zoroastrian has not been established in practice. The supporters of the idea of initiating the children of Parsi women married to non Parsi men into the Zoroastrian faith point out the fact that the 1908 judgement in the Parsi Panchayat case was clearly discriminatory against females, that Parsi males married to non-Parsi women were provided an option that was never even considered for females—the right to decide whether their children could be initiated into their religion. They argue that a new legal precedent needs to be established, which gives equal religious standing to both females and males.

A related concern regarding conversion was sparked in the 1980s with the passage of the Adoption Bill. The community opposed the bill since they feared that it would be a 'covert way of permitting non-Parsis entry to the community'. However, an appellate order by the division bench of the Small Causes Court held that adoption is recognized among the

Parsis. Aggrieved by the decision, the BPP filed an intervening application in the High Court in 1994. On 12 February 1998, the High Court ruled in their favour that adoption is not recognized among the Parsis.[67]

The ambivalent attitude towards women is also evident in some other laws. Although the Hindu code puts the daughter on the same footing as the widow and the son in the matter of inheritance, Parsi women did not enjoy the same privileges till the Indian Succession Act amendments were passed in 1991. The 1991 amendments, however, have not completely eliminated the distinctions along sex lines.[68]

The Parsi Marriage Law is spelt out in the Parsi Marriage and Divorce Act, 1936, as amended in 1988. The amendments have decreed that the required ages for a valid marriage now are 21 years for a male, and 18 years for a female. Two other important conditions are also specified in the amendments. 'The parties must not be related to each other in any of 33 ways, called prohibited degrees of consanguinity and affinity, laid out in a schedule to the Act.' Secondly, the marriage must be performed according to the Parsi form of ceremony with the priests consecrating the marriage by *ashirvad* (blessings) in the presence of two Parsi witnesses. As discussed previously, this condition has been evoked consistently in denying Parsi women married to non-Parsis all the rights and privileges attendant upon continuing to be a member of the Zoroastrian faith, with the related privilege of initiating their children into the Zarathushti Din.

A Parsi marriage can be terminated in two ways. First, if the marriage is not consummated due to natural causes, either party may seek a decree of nullity. Secondly, divorce can be obtained on several grounds: husband being ignorant of pregnancy at the time of marriage, adultery, cruelty, causing 'grievous hurt', desertion, and ceasing to be a Parsi. Since 1988, a divorce may also be obtained by mutual consent after a separation of one year. The courts that have been set up to hear such cases are presided over by a High Court Judge, who is required to submit the facts of the case to five Parsi delegates, who act as a jury. The delegates are appointed by the government (on the recommendation of the local communities) for a term of ten years. Decisions in these cases have to be reached by a majority of the delegates. The delegate system, however, has been criticized by both the judiciary and the community as giving rise to 'perverse decisions'.[69]

The legal rulings on the status of Parsi women married to non-Parsis and its consequent effects on the demographic decline in community numbers have generated an emotional rather than an enlightened debate. There are no reliable data to judge whether statistically this is a significant problem.[70] Hinnells found that 15 per cent of his population of 'overseas'

Zoroastrians had married non-Zoroastrians.[71] Khullar reports that out of a small Parsi population of 219 families in Delhi in 1978, sixty-nine families (approximately one-third) were 'mixed'. Moreover, the number of Parsi females marrying out of the community was more than double the number of males (forty-nine versus twenty). However, a 1980 update of the survey found that out of a total of forty-nine more such marriages since 1978, the ratio of males marrying outside had increased considerably: out of forty-nine 'mixed' marriages, twenty were males.[72] A more recent study by Kharas showed that inter-community marriages accounted for barely one-tenth of the factors that contributed to declining numbers.[73]

These scattered statistics are only representative of a very specialized universe—hardly the basis for deciding the extent of the 'problem'. Unfortunately, the orthodox sentiments of the community prevent it from recognizing the benefits of keeping or collecting reliable data on intermarriages that would help in making rational decisions regarding this sensitive issue.

Aside from examining the various laws and regulations affecting women in Zoroastrianism and the Zoroastrian communities, it is also instructive to examine some demographic data to see if the stereotypes regarding the socio-economic independence of Parsi women are correct. For example, the high proportion of never-married Parsi females has been blamed on the fact that these women do not think that Parsi males measure up to their standards because of their own achievements—high education, employment and personal income. The author's demographic studies of 551 households in the rural and urban areas of Gujarat, revealed that these factors were not significant in differentiating between never-married women who rated themselves 'likely' and 'unlikely' to get married. Moreover, in complete contrast to the theory that education is a 'sterilizing factor' for women,[74] it was the females who considered themselves 'likely' to get married who happened to be the most educated group rather than those who rated themselves 'unlikely' to get married. Furthermore, contrary to the author's expectations, an utterly traditional resource, household income, turned out to be the most significant factor in differentiating 'likely' from 'unlikely' females in terms of their prospects for marriage—which indicates how slowly old customs die.[75]

Since the educational achievements of Parsi women have generated so much discussion (especially in comparison to Parsi males), it is worthwhile to examine data from the previous demographic study to check the following: (1) if there were sex differences among school-age persons in enrolment at different levels of age and education; and (2) if families of current students provided equal educational opportunities to their daughters and sons.

The respondents' definition of 'educational opportunity' was based on two factors: receiving education in schools that had the English medium of instruction and, for best results, being sent to elite English medium boarding schools, since these tracks were the accepted avenues for upward mobility. The results of this study indicated that in the rural areas, 26.9 per cent of women who studied in the Gujarati medium (the vernacular language) dropped out of school after four to seven years, compared with 8 per cent of the males—a sex differential that did not show up statistically for any other group. When parental characteristics were considered, it was revealed that even in a patriarchal framework, the mothers' medium of instruction was the *strongest* variable in the rural areas in predicting whether the daughter went to English medium schools: 60 per cent of the female children in families where the mother was educated in the English language received that extra boost to be sent to English medium schools. Moreover, when these female children received the opportunity of studying in the English medium, they also got the added advantage (even more than the boys) to attend the elite boarding schools—63.6 per cent of them were sent outside the rural areas, as compared to 46.2 per cent of the boys to attend these prestigious schools.

The urban picture was more encouraging in closing disparities between the education of girls and boys. Yet it is worth noticing that only 10 per cent of the urban females who had completed their education in the Gujarati medium had had some college education compared to 30.2 per cent of the males. In general, the comparison of all of the subgroups revealed that conditions had to be perfect before females received equal educational opportunities as males, while men received these opportunities regardless of external factors.[76]

Finally, the discussion about the status of women in Zoroastrianism during the modern period has to consider Choksy's point for claiming religious equality between women and men: the decline in observance of beliefs and practices relating to purity and pollution. Undoubtedly, the elaborate, scripturally prescribed *rituals* connected with women's status —menstruation and parturition—are not adhered to as strictly today, and the practice of *complete* seclusion of women during these periods is definitely on the decline. But Choksy is mistaken when he asserts that 'only a few orthodox *elderly* women still maintain the practice of staying at home'.[77] Here he is underestimating the strength and numbers of orthodox Parsis—both among priests and laity—who believe in the power of menstruation in endangering the purity of all beings. Thus, sitting separately during menstruation, albeit not in a dark secluded corner, is a phenomenon that involves more than *elderly* women in orthodox households, as found in the author's demographic studies.[78] Moreover, even the educated urban working women from orthodox families might leave the house during menstrual periods to conduct their 'public' working lives, but will come home and observe the practice in 'private' of sitting separately from other family members.

Rudolph and Rudolph and others have commented on many of these traditional practices in the Indian setting that are adapted to modern circumstances, which they have labelled the 'modernity of tradition'.[79] In addition, Choksy is wrong in claiming that 'strict abstinence from sexual intercourse during menses was practised by the Parsis up to the 1930s'.[80] Statistical data from the author's demographic studies of urban and rural Parsis demonstrate that the beliefs about menstruation are so deeply and so unconsciously ingrained that, even today, none of the respondents had sexual intercourse during menstruation.[81] Here it might be suggested that Choksy's idea that only 'a few devotees abstain from intercourse during menses' might be based on a non-probability sample study that dealt with qualitative, rather than quantitative, data. In Iran, Boyce and Simmons found the same pattern that was observed in India —that segregation of women during menstruation is still practised, and abstinence during menstruation is a common pattern.[82]

The question then arises whether any of these beliefs and practices regarding purity and pollution have consequences for the status of women in Zoroastrianism. Unfortunately, it prevents the consideration of women to be ordained as priests since they are afflicted by the 'pollution' of menstruation, which manifests itself regularly. Thus, even if there is an effort to remove the restriction that priests have to belong to the hereditary, priestly caste (in Iran they accept the young *laymen* as assistant priests),[83] women would not qualify because of the misogynistic beliefs about menstruation. Boyce does report that in Iran women who had passed menopause and had undergone the proper ritual ceremonies to purify themselves could be 'appointed the guardians of lesser shrines' and play an active part in the religious life of the community.[84]

The remaining question has to deal with the effects of such patriarchal religious attitudes on the personal and spiritual identity of women in Zoroastrianism. Boyce has maintained all along that although Zoroastrian women have suffered under these menstruation taboos (more so in past generations), the orthodox observe them voluntarily. 'The rules are stern, to observe them is often a struggle, but they are part of the fight against evil, and so to be strictly kept'.[85] Boyce believes that Zoroastrian women are not 'warped by a sense of physical degradation' because of these scriptural definitions of women's being and are 'stoic' about the rigours involved in following the rituals.[86] Culpepper, on the other hand, asserts that 'to feel one's self so primordially unclean ... is severely damaging to one's self concept'. It must have left Zoroastrian women feeling 'vaguely in league with evil'.[87]

In fact, Boyce goes a step further and puts forth the arguments used by many priests and orthodox laity—that the enforced rest involved in seclusion during menstruation is beneficial to health. Moreover, she argues, if women suffer a 'monthly eclipse', they also re-emerge every month to enjoy the freedom that was taken away from them for a few days.[88] As a Parsi Zoroastrian who has an experiential understanding of the problem, the author can only reiterate that both Boyce and Culpepper present an unidimensional view. On the one hand, the notion that the women *actively* feel that by suffering passively they are helping positively to restrict the infection of evil is a projection on the part of a scholar who is very strongly identified with the religious tradition and the living faith.

On the other hand, Culpepper's *theoretical* interpretation of the dire effects of menstruation taboos on women's self-concept comes from a complete unfamiliarity with the experiential base of the living faith. This is an equal and opposite problem from Boyce, since Zoroastrian women are not so naive that they would suffer severe damage to their self-concept by buying some priestly assertion that women are carriers of the 'sin' of menstruation. Ultimately, however, important as it is to consider the *personal* beliefs or practices of Zarathushti women, the religious quest for true sexual equality and partnership cannot be based on individual opinions. The focus in Zoroastrianism has to be the same as in all patriarchal religions: to examine and analyse *systemic* problems in religious thinking and practice, and deal with the *structural* problems and politics that have allowed generations to victimize women. Zoroastrianism, like all religions, needs to write a new script whereby the religious and societal lives of *all* individuals can take on meaning.

In what has been said above, the author has tried to demonstrate that the status of women in the Zarathushti Din cannot be understood without examining the inevitable politicization of the knowledge that is embodied in the scriptures, as well as the 'customary usages' arguments that are utilized to justify religious practices. These tenets are 'born of and engaged in society'.[89] Quoting chapter and verse of various scriptures to justify the 'religious' laws might be defensible as long as there is an awareness that this *self-selective* methodology may be tied to the interests of particular groups; that the oft-quoted passages are not necessarily representative of the universe of the prophet's message. In other words, a biased selection should not be mistaken for objective proof, especially if the effort is an exercise in silencing the minority voices, such as women.

If women in the Zarathushti Din remember the prophet's admonition that 'of all the virtues, righteousness is the most desirable', there would be no hesitation in subjecting all *official* pronouncements of women's status in the living faith to the following simple test: commonsense notions of justice. If these criteria are applied, there would at least be a way to make the system defend its absolutist beliefs that justify women's domination in the name of time-honoured traditions. Unfortunately, what Patel has said in the Indian context—separating the concept of an ethno-religious group from the religious teachings—is generally true in all Zarathushti diasporas: '... there are many Parsis in our community but very few Zoroastrians.'[90]

NOTES

1. Mehr, Farhang, *The Zoroastrian Tradition: An Introduction to the Ancient Wisdom of Zarathustra* (Rockport, MA: Element, 1991), p. 2.
2. Ibid.
3. Duara, Prasenjit, 'Knowledge and Power in the Discourse of Modernity: The Campaigns Against Popular Religion in Early Twentieth-Century China', *The Journal of Asian Studies*, 50, no. 1, 1991, pp. 72–3.
4. Simmons, H. Michael, 'The Spandarmad/Jeh Syzygy'. Paper Presented at the Annual Meeting of the Middle East Studies Association, Baltimore, Maryland, 1987, 7 pages.
5. Tong, Paul K.K., 'A Cross-Cultural Approach to Women's Liberation Theology' in *Beyond Androcentrism: New Essays on Women and Religion*, ed. by Rita M. Gross (Missoula, MT: Scholars Press, 1977), p. 339.
6. Pangborn, Cyrus R., *Zoroastrianism: A Beleaguered Faith* (New Delhi: Vikas Publishing House, 1982), p. 1.
7. Boyce, Mary, *A History of Zoroastrianism, vol. 1. Handbuch der Orientalistik*, ed. by B. Spuler (Leiden: E.J. Brill, 1975), p. 5.
8. Ibid., p. 4.
9. Ibid., p. 251.
10. O'Flaherty, Wendy Doniger, *The Origins of Evil in Hindu Mythology* (Berkeley: University of California Press, 1976).
11. Boyce, Mary, *Zoroastrianism: Its Antiquity and Constant Vigour* (Costa Mesa, CA: Mazda Publishers, 1992), p. 1.
12. See, for example, 'The Date and Place of Zarathushtra: A Historical Review', *FEZANA Journal*, 10, no. 3, 1997.
13. Boyce, 1992, op. cit., p. 45.

14. Boyce, 1975, op. cit., p. 204.

15. Ibid., p. 207.

16. Jafarey, Ali A., 'Women: Venerated and Victimized', *Parsiana*, 13, no. 10, 1991, p. 31.

17. Dhalla, Maneckji Nusserwanji, *Zoroastrian Civilization: From the Earliest Times to the Downfall of the Last Zoroastrian Empire 651 AD* (New York: Oxford University Press, 1922), p. 74.

18. Sanjana, Dastur Darab Peshotan, *The Position of Zoroastrian Women in Remote Antiquity* (Bombay: Education Society Steam Press, 1892), p. 16.

19. Simmons, op. cit., p. 1.

20. Hinnells, John R., *Zoroastrianism and the Parsis* (London: Ward Lock Educational, 1981), p. 37.

21. Dhalla, op. cit., p. 75.

22. Haug, Martin, *The Parsis: Essays on their Sacred Language, Writings and Religions*, Revised by K.W. West (New Delhi: Cosmo Publications, reprint, 1978), p. 220.

23. Vacha, P.B., *Firdosi and the Shahnama* (Bombay: New Book Company, 1950), p. 169.

24. Ibid., pp. 169–70.

25. Sanjana, op. cit.

26. Boyce, 1975, op. cit., p. 306.

27. Douglas, Mary, *Purity and Danger: An Analysis of the Concepts of Pollution and Taboo* (London: Routledge and Kegan Paul, 1966), p. 121.

28. Choksy, Jamsheed K., *Purity and Pollution in Zoroastrianism: Triumph Over Evil* (Austin: University of Texas Press, 1989), p. 94.

29. Boyce, Mary, 'The Zoroastrian House of Yazd' in *Iran and Islam: In Memory of the Late Vladimir Minorsky*, ed. by C.E. Bosworth (Edinburgh: University Press, 1971), pp. 125–47.

30. Boyce, 1975, op. cit., p. 308.

31. Choksy, op. cit., p. 100.

32. Boyce, 1975, op. cit., p. 308.

33. Sanjana, op. cit., p. 46.

34. See, for example, Boyce, Mary, *A Persian Stronghold of Zoroastrianism* (Oxford: Clarendon Press, 1977); *Zoroastrians: Their Religious Beliefs and Practices* (London: Routledge and Kegan Paul, 1979); *A History of Zoroastrianism, vol. 2, Handbuch der Orientalistik*, ed. by B. Spuler (Leiden: E.J. Brill, 1982); Choksy, Jamsheed K., 'Women in the Zoroastrian Book of Primal Creation: Images and Functions Within a Religious Tradition', *Mankind Quaterly*, 29, nos 1–2, 1988, pp. 78–83; and Choksy, 1989, op. cit.

35. Buch, Maganlal A., *Zoroastrian Ethics: The Gaekwad Studies in Religion and Philosophy, IV* (Baroda: A.G. Widgery, 1919), pp. 128–9.

36. Sanjana, op. cit.; and Katrak, Jamshid Cawasji, *Marriage in Ancient Iran* (Bombay: Published by the Author, 1965).

37. Choksy, 1989, op. cit., p. 89.

38. Sanjana, op. cit., and Katrak, op. cit.

39. Fischer, Michael M.J., 'On Changing the Conceptual Position of Persian Women' in *Women in the Muslim World*, ed. by Louis Beck and Nikki Keddie (Cambridge: Harvard University Press, 1978), pp. 189–215.

40. Karkal, Malini, *Survey of Parsi Population of Greater Bombay* (Bombay: International Institute for Population Sciences and Trustees of the Parsi Panchayat Funds and Properties, 1984); Gould, Ketayun H., 'An Aging, Dwindling Community', *Parsiana*, 9, no. 9, 1987, pp. 44–51; and Gould, Ketayun H., 'Parsi Demography: Biological or Sociocultural?', Paper presented at the South Asia Seminar, University of Texas at Austin, 14 April 1988.

41. Choksy, 1989, op. cit., p. 153

42. Boyce, 1975, op. cit., pp. 53–4; Boyce, 1982, op. cit., pp. 75–7.

43. Sanjana, op. cit., and Katrak, op. cit.

44. Dhalla, op. cit.

45. Choksy, 1988, op. cit.

46. Simmons, op. cit.

47. Boyce, 1982, op. cit., pp. 229–30.

48. Dhalla, Maneckji Nusserwanji, *History of Zoroastrianism* (New York: Oxford University Press, 1938), p. 324.

49. Boyce, 1977, op. cit., p. 12.

50. Dhalla, 1938, op. cit., pp. 442–3.

51. Swidler, Leonard, 'Is Sexism a Sign of Decadence in Religion?' in *Women and Religion*, ed. by Judith Plaskow and Joan Arnold (Missoula, MT: Scholars Press, 1974), pp. 167–8.

52. Choksy, 1988, op. cit., p. 81.

53. Paymaster, Rustom Burjorji, *Early History of the Parsees in India: From their Landing in Sanjan to 1700 AD* (Bombay: Zartoshti Dharam Sambhandhi Kelavni Apnari Ane Dnyan Felavnari Mandli, 1954), pp. 10–13.

54. Firby, Nora Kathleen, *European Travellers and their Perceptions of Zoroastrians in the 17th and 18th Centuries* (Berlin: Verlag Von Dietrich Rimer, 1988) pp. 107–9.

55. Kulke, Eckehard, *The Parsees in India: A Minority as Agent of Social Change* (Delhi: Vikas Publishing House, 1974), p. 9.

56. Hinnells, John R., 'Parsis and British', *Journal of the K.R. Cama Oriental Institute*, no. 46, 1978, pp. 2–92.

57. Visaria, Leela, 'Religious and Regional Differences in Mortality and Fertility in the Indian Subcontinent', Unpublished Doctoral Dissertation, Princeton University, 1972.

58. See for example, Visaria, Leela, Ibid.; Visaria, Leela, 'Demographic Transition among Parsis: 1881–1971, III - Fertility Trends', *Economic and Political Weekly*, 9. No. 43, 1974, pp. 1828–32; Gould, Ketayun H., 'Parsis and Urban Demography: Some Research Possibilities', *Journal of Marriage and the Family*, 34, no. 2, 1972, pp. 345–52; Gould, Ketayun H., 'Singling Out a Demographic Problem: The Never-Married Parsis', *Journal of Mithraic Studies*, 3,

nos 1–2, 1980, pp. 166–84; Gould, Ketayun H., 'The Never-Married Parsis: A Demographic Dilemma', *Economic and Political Weekly*, 17, no. 26, 1982, pp. 1063–72; Gould, 1987, op. cit.; Gould, 1988, op. cit.: and Karkal, op. cit.

59. *Census of India 1991 Series I, India, Paper 1 of 1995, 'Religion'* (New Delhi: Controller of Publications, 1995), pp. 55–7.

60. 'The Privy Council Judgement: Saklat vs. Bella 1', *Parsiana*, 12, no. 10, 1990, pp. 28–30.

61. Kotwal, Dastur Firoze M., 'The Divine Laws of God Must Prevail', *Parsiana*, 13, no. 3, 1990, pp. 27–8.

62. 'In the Matter of the Late M. Roxan Darshan Shah', *Parsiana*, 13, no. 9, 1991, pp. 25–6.

63. Mama, Arnavaz S., 'The Reaction to the Resolution', *Parsiana*, 13, no. 12, 1991, pp. 33–6.

64. Mama, Arnavaz S., 'The Controversy Continues', *Parsiana*, 13, no. 4, 1990, pp. 27–30.

65. Patel, Jehangir R., 'To Think Anew', Editorial Viewpoint, *Parsiana*, 17, no. 4, 1994, pp. 3–8; Arnavaz S. Mama, 'We the Devout Priests', *Parsiana*, 13, no. 6, 1990, pp. 26–8; and Parinaz Gandhi, 'A Stab in the Back ...', *Parsiana*, 13, no. 12, 1991, pp. 37–40.

66. 'A Zoroastrian Again', *Parsiana*, 17, no. 3, 1994, pp. 31–4, 48; and Mirza Dasturs Hormazdyar K., Kaikhusroo M. Jamasp Asa, Firoze M. Kotwal and Hormazdiar N. Dastur, 'The Priests' Rebuttal', *Parsiana*, 18, no. 4, 1995, p. 29.

67. Gandhi, Parinaz M., 'Parsi Adoption Not Legal', *Parsiana*, 20, no. 9, 1998, p. 29.

68. Gould, Ketayun H., 'Status of Women: Sacred and Secular, Part 6, Women's Singular Status', *Parsiana*, 18, no. 9, 1996, p. 37.

69. Shroff, Kersi B., 'Parsi Marriage Law in India', *FEZANA Journal*, 13, no. 1, 1995, pp. 42–3.

70. Gould, 1987, op. cit.

71. Hinnells, John R., 'An Ancient Religion in Modern Exile: Contemporary Zoroastrianism Outside Iran', Paper presented at the 76th Annual Meeting of the American Academy of Religion, Annaheim, California, 23–26 November 1985, 19 pages.

72. Khullar, Ava, 'Demographic Despair', *Parsiana*, 12, no. 7, 1990, pp. 34–44.

73. Gandhi, Parinaz, 'Outmarriages: Fact and Fiction', *Parsiana*, 16, no. 8, 1994, pp. 22–4.

74. Desai, Sapur Faredun, *A Community at the Cross-Road* (Bombay: New Book Company, 1948), p. 65.

75. Gould, 1980, op. cit.; and Gould, 1982, op. cit.

76. Gould, Ketayun H., 'Sex Inequalities in the Dual System of Education: Parsis of Gujarat', *Economic and Political Weekly*, 18, no. 39, 1983, pp. 1668–76.

77. Choksy, 1989, op. cit., p. 99, italics added.

78. Gould, 1988, op. cit.

79. Rudolph, Lloyd and Susanne Hoeber Rudolph, *The Modernity of Tradition* (Berkeley: University of California Press, 1967).

80. Choksy, 1989, op. cit., p. 92.

81. Gould, 1988, op. cit.

82. Boyce, 1977, op. cit.; and Simmons, personal communication.

83. Shahzadi, Ervad Rustam, 'Adopting to Future Possibilities', *Parsiana*, 12, no. 9, 1990, pp. 37–40.

84. Boyce, 1977, op. cit., p. 106.

85. Boyce, 1975, op. cit., p. 308.

86. Boyce, 1977, op. cit., pp. 106–7.

87. Culpepper, Emily E., 'Zoroastrian Menstruation Taboos: A Women's Studies Perspective' in *Women and Religion* ed. by Judith Plaskow and Joan Arnold (Missoula, MT: Scholars Press, 1974), p. 207.

88. Boyce, 1977, op. cit., p. 107.

89. Duara, 1991, op. cit., p. 81.

90. Patel, Jehangir R., 'Whither Good Thoughts, Words and Deeds?', Editorial Viewpoint, *Parsiana*, 13, no. 3, 1990, p. 3.

Muslim Women in India

Sheila McDonough

The situation of Muslim women in India is best understood as part of an ongoing process of what Marshall Hodgson has called *The Venture of Islam*, namely, a process begun within history by the Prophet Muhammad's experience of receiving revelation, and carried on by the subsequent long and complex efforts of members of the Muslim community to work out how, within the constraints of particular historical contexts, to implement what they have discerned to be the imperatives imposed on them by the revelation.[1] The phrase 'venture of Islam' implies an ongoing effort by Muslims to discover how to realise the imperatives of justice and compassion, which they believe have been imposed on them as obligations to be made in response to their recognition of gratitude to their Creator. Hodgson's subtitle *Conscience and History within a World Civilisation* indicates that Muslims are persons whose conscience is shaped by the teaching and rituals of their cumulative tradition, and that they struggle, within specific historical contexts, to discern and do what their conscience dictates. The imperatives of the conscience vary, as do the contexts.

Thus, most twentieth century Muslim thinkers would agree that in past history the constraints of economic, social and political characteristics of medieval society made the acceptance of slavery unquestioned, whereas in the twentieth century it is generally accepted that slavery is wrong. Twentieth century Muslim thinkers acknowledge that imperatives can be found in the *Qur'an* and in traditional Muslim religious and legal thinking to justify abolishing slavery, but only in the twentieth century has this been generally acknowledged as the right way to understand the Qur'anic imperatives of social justice. The imperatives were latent, as it were, in the core discourses of the tradition, but only the changes resulting from economic and political developments in this century have brought these latent ideals to the forefront of the community's awareness. The phrase 'The venture of Islam' is meant to suggest that, as the community moves through time, the believers will continue to discover new ways to implement the basic principles of the Qur'an and the *Sunnah* in the light of changing possibilities emerging from changes in the way people live.

Thus Muslims believe that justice is an extremely important attribute of God which should also be implemented among humans on earth. But what such implementation would actually mean differs from century to century according to the constraints and possibilities of the prevailing situations. Further, in any actual historical context, Muslims often disagree with each other as to what the correct implementation of justice should be in a particular situation.

In twentieth-century India, the issues relating to Muslim women are best understood as a contemporary expression of this ongoing process of the venture of Islam. What gives coherence to the lives of individual Muslims, in India as elsewhere, is the continuity of Muslim practice, learning the Qur'an, hearing sermons, taking part in prayer, fasting, alms-giving and pilgrimage, and attempting to internalize the virtues of the tradition. The venture takes place in the efforts made by individual believers to discover and implement what they discern to be the core values that have been handed down to them.

There are a number of contemporary Muslim women scholars who are urging that the conditions of life in modern, industrialized societies make it possible to affirm new visions of what the ideals of the core discourses of Islam should mean for women. Just as justice is now understood to mean the abolition of slavery, although Muslim legal and theological thinkers for centuries accepted slavery, so, these women argue, the medieval thinking about gender should be transcended by new ways of understanding what justice should mean for Muslim women. The abolition of slavery and the changing of ideals about gender are understood as analogous issues. One such contemporary Muslim woman scholar, Leila Ahmed, argues in her book *Gender and Women in Islam* that Muslim women need to think differently about Muslim history.[2] She maintains that there has always been a tension within Islamic history between the ethical demands, such as the demand for social justice, of the core discourses, the Qur'an and the Sunnah, and the later interpretations of those discourses.

The first Muslims arrived in Sind in the seventh century not very long after the death of the Prophet Muhammad in the year 630 CE, and after the subsequent rapid expansion which had sent Muslims out of the Arabian Peninsula to found new Muslim communities across vast territories from Spain to the Indus valley. No one, including the Muslims, could have predicted or expected such a rapid expansion of the new community founded on the revelation which had come through the Qur'an. Muslims in the seventh century were just beginning to work out how to administer these many new territories, and develop effective institutions to establish and maintain social, political, religious and economic order and prosperity.

The Ummayad dynasty, which dominated Muslim life from 660 to 750 CE, was characterized by practices which aimed to keep control in the hands of the members of the various Arab tribes which had implemented the expansion. They were largely motivated by the impulse to develop the trading capacities which were their main sources of income. The leaders of this dynasty were known not to be interested in facilitating conversion as such, nor in welcoming participation in their trading and military leadership from anyone who did not belong to one of the Arab tribes. They did take wives from the many different peoples they were now ruling over, from the conquered Goths of Spain to the Hindus and Buddhists of Sind.[3] At this point, the cultural practices of the Arabs would have been largely the same wherever in the world they had chosen to settle.

In *Gender and Women in Islam*, Leila Ahmed has argued that the practices relating to gender among the Muslims of these early communities were shaped by several factors.[4] One was what she calls the ethical voice of the Qur'an: the imperatives from the scripture to treat women and men as equal before God, called to the same ritual practices, and responsible directly to God as individuals. She notes that many of the first women believers, including Khadija and Aisha, were persons characterized by strong characters, active religious commitment, and the status of exemplars for the rest of the struggling new community. With the passage of time, however, the participation of Muslim women in the life of the community declined as they came to lead more secluded lives in the large cities of the new Muslim empires.

The establishment of the new family model, which came from the Qur'an, was effective as a substitute for the tribal morality which was disappearing as the Arabs increasingly became urban traders rather than desert nomads. The family laws of the new Muslim community were comparable in many respects to the family laws of the other religious communities of the Mediterranean world. At a basic level, the family had become the unit to protect children and women in the new form of society in which tribal protection no longer functioned well.

Leila Ahmed says that in many respects the family structures of the new Muslim community were similar to the family structures of the older Mediterranean civilizations such as the Byzantine Christian Empire and the Zoroastrian Empire. This tended to mean an increase in the patriarchal authority of the father as the one providing protection and requiring obedience. She thinks much of this emphasis on paternal authority came more from the adoption of previous cultural practices from the Mediterranean cultures rather than from the Qur'an itself. In Leila Ahmed's view, these patriarchal attitudes were not the same as what she calls the ethical imperatives of the Qur'an. However, she thinks that the patriarchal attitudes rather than the ethical imperatives tended to dominate in the earlier centuries.[5]

The Muslim community which was established in Sind would thus be very similar in attitudes and practices towards gender to the other new Muslim communities in the Mediterranean societies and in Iran. The Ummayads were interested in developing trading activities with the local people wherever they settled, and they often adopted local practices in many respects. This is why the Muslims of Sind would, over time, be influenced by the practice of the local Hindus and Buddhists, as the Muslims of Spain were influenced by the Goths and those of Iran by the Iranians, and so forth. The interests of professional traders tended to be in the direction of coexistence and good relations with the local people as incentives to business. At the time of these original settlements in Sind, the members of the Muslim community were still in the process of working out how to live in the light of the *revelation* they had recently received. They were still adaptable in many respects. Over the centuries, Muslim traders settled along the southern and eastern coasts of India as well as in the western Indian territories.[6] In most of these cases, the patterns followed were like the original ones in Sind, developing contacts for trade, intermarrying with local women, and adapting to some degree to local customs. The relatively easygoing nature of these trading contacts meant that, over time, certain types of synthesis in music, food, and even mystical practices developed among the Muslims and their neighbours.

The most notorious of the Muslims coming into India, Mahmud of Ghazna, came in the eleventh century.[7] His background, aims, policies and customs were different from those of the earlier Arab traders. The warrior tribes of Central Asia had become Muslim centuries after the original Islamic expansion. Their cultural background was shaped by the harsh living conditions of Central Asia. The warrior tribes tended to live by war and conquest. Women under those conditions of war were generally treated as potential captives, often captured in war, and some times kept in rigid seclusion.

Although the soldiers of the first Islamic expansion to Sind and elsewhere had been controlled by the Caliphs of Medina, such as Umar, and had been ordered to treat churches and other religious buildings with respect, it is also true that, by the time of Mahmud of Ghazna, 'these earlier imperatives had been neglected. Mahmud came into India as a warrior looking for loot, and he found it in the rich Hindu temples. The practice of Muslim looting of Hindu temples dates from this era. In the following centuries, Muslim rulers from this background established dynasties which ruled over most of northern India. In the thirteenth century, a Muslim woman ruled briefly. Raziya, the daughter of the ruler Iltutmish, was considered by her father more able than her brothers. When her father died, she appeared before the people and asked for a chance to prove her worth. The people of Delhi accepted her as ruler. But the powerful nobles were opposed to her, and caused her to be attacked and subsequently murdered.[8]

By the time the second wave of Muslim began coming in large numbers into India, the Muslim scholars of the Abbasid dynasty centred in Bagdad had elaborated written codes of religious law, the *Shariah*, based in parts on the reports about the Prophet Muhammad and his companions, and *Hadith*, which had also been collected and written in the mid-ninth century. The principles of Islamic jurisprudence had now been formally articulated and written down, and the major schools of Islamic religious law, Sunni and Shia, had been codified.

This codification of Islamic law under the Abbasids meant that gender relations among Muslims had become more systematized and formal. Leila Ahmed argues that the scholars who collected the Hadith reports and who formalized the Shariah codes were influenced, consciously and unconsciously, by the assumptions about gender characteristic of the ninth-century Bagdad culture. This was a culture dominated by the absolute power of one ruler who was backed up and protected from the people by the army. Much of the cultural life of the Abbasid rulers was modelled on the style of the earlier centuries of absolute monarchs, Zoroastrian and others, who had preceded them in the many empires that had come and gone in the Tigris-Euphrates area.

Abbasid civilization was an empire, like the earlier ones in that part of the world, in which the rulers had great numbers of slave women as concubines, and in which the purchase of female slaves, taken from those conquered in war, was a normal part of the life of the wealthier classes in the big cities. When women can easily be bought and sold, the men who buy and sell them readily fall victim to the assumption that women are inferior, irrational beings, and that men must control them. These attitudes to women can be seen as characteristic of any society which permits the buying and selling of female slaves. Under these circumstances, women tend to lose dignity and to be considered by men as little more than instruments for casual pleasure. The legitimate wives under these circumstances live secluded lives, and are sometimes not awarded much more respect than the slave women.[9]

Leila Ahmed maintains that this widespread use of female slaves in the Abbasid era meant that the Muslim scholars who collected the Hadith and formulated the Shariah tended to be influenced by the cultural assumptions of the time in relation to the widespread ideas that women were fragile, incompetent, and unreliable. The general thrust of the legislation formulated in this way on gender issues tends to be towards controlling and protecting women in the family. In the legal codes formulated at this time, there is relatively little about the ethical imperatives to equality which Leila Ahmed argues had been a part of the original Qur'anic message.

The dynasties that dominated Muslim India after Mahmud of Ghazna were influenced by these perspectives from the Abbasid period. The life styles of the rulers were similar to those of the Abbasid rulers. After the codification of the principles of Islamic jurisprudence, *madrassas* were established for training *ulema* to become the guardians of the religious law. At times such as the thirteenth century, when the other parts of the Muslim world were suffering external invasion and internal collapse, many Muslim religious scholars emigrated to India and became spiritual guides of the community there. Madrassas were established in many parts of India, and the Abbasid perspectives came to dominate thought and practice about gender issues.

In practice, this usually meant that anyone consulting the ulema on gender questions would tend to get answers emphasizing the need to protect women and establish male authority. But these were, of course, not the only factors at work in medieval Islamic society in India. Among the upper classes in particular, several women became known as distinguished poets. The Sufi orders spread throughout India from the twelfth century onwards. Relatively little is known about the impact of Sufi practices on Muslim women, but it is clear that Sufi practices, and religious poetry made their impact on the spiritual lives of women. The great Sufi writer of Spain, Ibn ul Arabi, said that two of his teachers in spiritual wisdom were women.[10] Ibn ul Arabi's writings were, and still are, widely read among Indian Sufis. Sufism sometimes gives spiritual guidance to women, not the least because the first famous and influential Sufi poet was a woman, Rabia.

The influence of Sufism on women in India needs much more study. Richard Eaton shows that the village women of the Deccan in the seventeenth century and later used Sufi poetry as part of the traditional forms of folk singing. This meant that women sung these Sufi songs as they went about their household duties. The Sufis used this popular literature as a way of transmitting values and practices.[11] Throughout the medieval period, therefore, Muslim women in India tended to live by following the patterns of behaviour coming from the early Islamic societies. Family life and childbearing were their central concerns. Those with mystical tendencies may have become involved with the practices of the local Sufi orders, and in some cases become Sufi poets themselves. Muslim society has generally considered drawing attention to women's lives to be improper, and, therefore, relatively little is available to be used as written source material from this period.

The impact of British dominance, as exemplified by the destruction of the court life of the Mughals in Delhi in 1857, precipitated Indian Muslims into various new reactions. Those who followed Sayyid Ahmed Khan in advocating the acquisition of modern education, as expressed first through the establishment of the Muslim University at Aligarh, did not originally concern themselves with the education of Muslim women. Sir Sayyid himself is reputed to have said that the education of the Muslim men was the first priority, and that the educated men would later think about what was appropriate for Muslim women. The first Muslim woman to go away from home to attend boarding school at the end of the nineteenth century, and later to become an independent professional woman, a dentist in Bombay, was Fatima Jinnah.

A different reaction to the British was illustrated by the founding of the new madrassa at Deoband which was intended to give strength to the insecure Muslim community at the local level by training religious leaders. One of the leaders of Deoband, Maulana Thanavi, published a small book intended to strengthen the moral well-being of Muslim women. This book, *Behishti Zewar*, was very widely read over the last century and is still highly regarded. The theme of this book is the importance of the welfare of the family, the society in general, and of the moral integrity of the woman who serves as wife and mother. Her virtues of nurture and wisdom are shown as essential for the moral well-being of the children and the courage of the husband. The Muslim woman is portrayed as essentially a strong person who keeps the integrity of the family alive through her courage and support for all the members.[12] This might be seen as a significant response to the debilitating effects of colonial domination on the Indian Muslims' self-respect. The moral strength of the mother and wife is shown as an answer to the threats of moral and social disintegration caused by the domination of the imperialists.

As the impact of British rule became more dominant over India, various movements of national liberation came into being. Women gradually entered into the struggle for national independence. In 1903, a Muslim woman spoke to the Mohammedan Educational Congress in Bombay. The woman was Chand Begum from Madras. Her paper was read to the meeting. In it, she praised 'the Reform Party, a group of Muslim supporters of female education, and [she] hurled bitter invectives on reactionary *maulvis*. She called upon the Muslim women to follow fervently the female reform movement which was advocating modern education amongst Muslim women, and to say goodbye to immovable *maulvis*'.[13]

These Muslim supporters of reform supported the idea of a normal school for training women teachers. Eventually, such an institution was opened at Aligarh in 1913. The first Urdu journal for women was launched by Shiek Abdullah the following year. The poet Altaf Husain Hali supported the cause of women and inspired a couple, Maulvi Sayyid Mumtaz Ali and Muhammadi Begum, to devote their lives to promoting women's education. This team and their newsletter came to be known as the 'beacon for all women'.

The first Muslim Ladies' Conference was held in 1915. They were particularly interested in promoting education for women. In 1917, a group of leading Muslim women activists passed a resolution against polygamy which caused controversy in Lahore. Begum Jehan Ara Shahnawaz from Lahore was one of the leading Muslim women activists in the period after World War I. At the first Round Table Conference in London in 1930, she and Mrs Subbaranyan from Madras submitted a memorandum demanding rights for all people, regardless of religion, caste, creed or sex. Begum Shahnawaz has written an autobiography which tells us something of the excitement and enthusiasm of women who entered into political life during this time.[14] Another Muslim woman from Bengal, Shaista Ikramullah, tells us in her autobiography about how, as a young teenage girl, she began organizing other women to join the independence movement. She did this while she and friends still lived within the *purdah* system. Later, with her husband's support, after partition she became a member of Parliament and eventually part of the Pakistan delegation to the United Nations.[15]

Most independence movements in the modern period, among Muslims as among other groups have encouraged the participation of women. Bi Ammi, the mother of the Ali brothers, broke with tradition when she publicly addressed the Muslim League in 1917. She spoke while wearing her veil, but her public appearance was a new event. In 1921, she addressed another meeting without her veil. She did so not so much as a symbolic gesture, but because she found it a hindrance to the work she was trying to do. The Muslim League had a women's section which encouraged women in the years between the World Wars to participate in the independence struggle. Some Muslim women also worked for the Congress Party, and some were communists.

After the partition of the subcontinent, many of the Muslim women who had been leaders in the Muslim League women's section emigrated to Pakistan. The All Pakistan Women's Association was founded by them; this group has played an active role in lobbying with the government for women's rights, and for encouraging changes in the law such as the Pakistan Marriage Reform Act of 1960. Fatima Jinnah herself campaigned to be President of Pakistan in 1965 when she was in her seventies. Although she lost the election because of the rural votes, she won in Karachi and Dacca, and led a campaign which was considered a marvel of aggressive fighting for democracy by a strong-minded old lady.[16] The fact that she won the majority of votes in the big cities is a certain indication that Muslim people generally are not opposed to leadership of a woman they respect.

In India, after independence, no comparable national organization of active Muslim women developed. It is often the case that members of minority communities feel the need to speak with one corporate voice rather than as independent individuals. In her study of the Khilafat movement, Gail Minault has argued that the Khilafat movement itself was essentially an effort to create a unified voice for the political purposes of the disunited Indian Muslim community.[17] Since the independence of India, the minority status of the Muslims has tended to create a feeling of need for some kind of comparable unified voice. For this reason, the Muslim women of India have not organized to oppose the opinions of the ulema, but have rather supported the tendency of the Indian Muslims to wish to be represented by one voice. The approach of the Muslim women of India has rather been to try to influence the opinions of the ulema.

One offshoot from the Sufi tradition in India has been the development of what has become a worldwide reform and missionary movement, the Tablighi Jamaat. The movement originated from the famous shrine of the Sufi saint Nizam-ud-Din Auliya in Delhi in the 1930s. It began as a volunteer organization of persons willing to go out to villages surrounding Delhi in order to help guide semi-Islamized village people to better Islamic ritual practice.[18] The movement has been generally apolitical. As it has become worldwide and vast in scope, it has continued to stress ritual practice as a central value. The social practices of members of this group are very conservative with respect to the role of women. This transformation of certain forms of Indian Sufism into a modern form of conservative revival movement is a remarkable phenomenon. Women often do participate in their own discussion groups in this movement. Their discussions usually focus on Qur'an and Hadith, and what is perceived as correct ritual practice. The literature of the organization provides guidance for these discussions. Although these women are encouraged to live separate lives, and to be very observant about practices which emphasize the separation of the sexes and the modesty of women, nevertheless, here too, the women are asked to understand and appropriate the values for themselves. This kind of participation in discussions in many cultural situations is often a first phase of moving into more active concerns for the possibilities of changing and improving the known world. Thus, although movements of this kind have obvious conservative characteristics, nevertheless, slow processes of social change are at work.

With respect to gender issues among Indian Muslims, the ulema and leaders of the politically active revivalist movements like Jamaat Islami have tended to become the dominant spokespersons of the Muslim community. The perceived need felt for one voice for the minority community has tended to express itself in acceptance of the ulema as the agents of that voice. The famed Shah Bano case of 1985 developed when the Muslim community seems to have reacted negatively when a Hindu judge said that Muslim women should receive alimony. The Muslim negative reaction reflected a feeling of intrusion on the community's values by outsiders. Although a Muslim woman had initiated the request for alimony, once the matter became perceived as an assault on Muslim control over their own personal law, the Muslims tended to revert to speaking with one voice. This widely publicized event and the reaction to it exemplifies clearly the extent to which the ulema and the revivalist leaders have managed to get themselves accepted as a spokespersons for the Muslim community in India.[19] The fact that the same groups do not play comparable roles in either Pakistan or Bangladesh is understandable only if we recognize that it is the minority status that gives communities the feeling that they must have corporate identity. It is easier for Muslims to differ publicly among themselves in Pakistan and Bangladesh than it is in India.

The ulema and revivalist leaders are very concerned to preserve their status as spokespersons for their community. Their own attitudes to gender are not necessarily always exactly the same. Maulana Mawdudi, the founder and long-time leader of the Jamaat Islami, wrote a book when he was living in Delhi in 1939 which was entitled *Purdah and the Status of Women in Islam*. It is quite different in tone from the book written about the moral strength of Muslim women written by the Deoband scholar Maulana Thanavi. The latter stressed the importance of the strength of the moral integrity of Muslim women, whereas Mawdudi tends to focus on female weakness and need for male authority and supervision. Maududi's book is explicitly a warning of the demoralizing effects of modernization on Muslims, especially on Muslim women. Mawdudi is very critical of birth control, a relatively new attitude among Muslim jurists. Mawdudi speaks of birth control as a threat to the moral well-being of Muslim society. He uses the image of God as an Engineer with a plan for humanity as a key for his picture of the Will of God for humanity. In his words:

All things We made in pairs [Al-Qur'an, 51:49].
This verse makes a reference to the universality of the sex-law and the Master Engineer of the universe Himself divulges the secret of his Creation ... .

1. The principles according to which Allah has created this world and the way according to which he is running its great System cannot be unholy and vile. ... Though the opponents of this scheme may hold it as dirty and despicable, and so shun it, the Maker and Owner of the Factory cannot desire that His Factory should cease to function. He will naturally want that all parts of His Machine should continue working in order to fulfil the purpose for which they have been designed.
2. The existence of both the active and the passive partners is equally important for the purposes of the Factory. Neither the 'activity' of the active partner is in any way exalted nor the 'passivity' of the passive partner in any way debased. ...
3. 'Activity' in itself is naturally superior to 'passivity' and femininity. This superiority is not due to any merit in masculinity against and demerit in femininity. It is rather due to the fact of possessing natural qualities of dominance, power and authority. ... If the cloth is as hard as the needle, sewing cannot take place[20]

According to Mawdudi, the Divine Engineer has thus created a Factory which works because the male is active and the female passive. Mawdudi sees the main threat to this plan of the Divine Engineer as coming form what he calls the 'white jaundice'.[21] This white jaundice is the sexual excessiveness of the modern western world which Mawdudi thinks is influencing South Asian Muslims. The characteristics of this jaundice are the emphasis on the education of women, equality between the sexes, birth control, divorce, and so on. All these he sees as leading inevitably to disease and corruption, and the destruction of the effective working of God's Factory.

Clearly, this image of the Divine Engineer is a modern symbol, and not one of the traditional Muslim names of God. The idea that creation in pairs necessarily means one active and one passive partner is an unproved assumption by Mawdudi himself, and is by no means an obvious implication of the text. He has read his own assumptions into the text. The contemporary Muslim women scholars of the Qur'an, whom we have referred to earlier, do not read the Qur'anic creation stories in this way. They understand creation in pairs to mean equality and similarity between males and females. Mawdudi's Qur'anic exegesis is often arbitrary in this manner. His stress on human nature is also a departure from traditional Muslim thinking. The word 'naturist' in the 19th century was used by traditional Muslim thinkers to condemn what were then perceived as the radical ideas of Sir Sayyid Ahmed Khan. It is somewhat curious that the emphasis on knowable and essential human nature, which Islamic theology once considered an intellectual error, has become in Mawdudi's thought an axiom. His rhetoric is, however, powerful partly because of his effective use of metaphors like the Divine Engineer and the Factory.

The revivalist ideas of Mawdudi's followers have been a significant factor in the political life of Pakistan, India and Bangladesh since the 1950s. In Pakistan, it was during the regime of Zia ul Haq in the eighties that the ideas of this group were most influential in terms of government policy. Some efforts were made to impose flogging for adultery and other such punishments. The organized Pakistan women's movement, the Women's Action Front, became one of the leading opponents of these political practices. After the death of Zia ul Haq, the issues have become less significant and the Jamaat Islami less of a political force in Pakistan.

In both Pakistan and Bangladesh, the marriage reform laws of 1960 have continued to operate despite criticism from the revivalists. Mawdudi's followers opposed those marriage reform laws. The organised Muslim women's movements in these countries are one reason why these reforms have continued to operate. In India, however, there is a sort of stalemate. Because the Indian Constitution permits the Muslims to retain control over their personal law, there has been relatively little state interference in Muslim personal law. The Muslim women of India have not been organized in the way that their peers in Pakistan and Bangladesh have been, and they have not had comparable access to ways of influencing public policy. The situation for Indian Muslim women interested in reforms in personal law seems to be one of the Catch 22 problems. Catch 22 indicates a dilemma with no obvious solution. Because of the minority status of the Muslim community in India, the members of the community feel the need to speak with one corporate voice. This tends to mean that the ulema and the revivalists become acknowledged as the spokespersons of the community. The Indian Muslims who might disagree with the points of view of these spokespersons are sometimes perceived as disloyal.

In response to the turmoil caused among many people in India as a result of the widespread publicity given to the Shah Bano affair in 1985, an Indian Muslim woman named Safia Iqbal wrote a book entitled *Women and Islamic Law*. She says that a survey was conducted of Muslim women in Delhi in 1986 by the Social Bureau of Muslim Women. The survey report says that the greatest problem discerned by the poor Muslim women is that both men and women lack proper knowledge of their faith, and that this is why Muslim men sometimes mistreat their women. The women are wrongly denied freedom of expression, according to the report, and the men wrongly refuse to offer sufficient support to their families.[22] The author reports that upper-class and middle-class Muslim women said that economic instability was a factor causing problems, but that the poorer women rather emphasized ignorance of true Islamic values as their major problem. The author comments as follows on the report:

> The major problems of women in modern-day society are, at a glance, as follows:
>
> 1) Ignorance about and non-implementation of Islamic principles,
> 2) Illiteracy,
> 3) The joint family system and alien, un-Islamic customs,
> 4) Deprivation of woman's rightful place in the domestic order,
> 5) Exploitation and misuse of women,
> 6) Economic instability,
> 7) Communal riots,
> 8) Ignorance and non-implementation of women's rights granted by Islam.
>
> Evidently, these problems have stemmed from years of decadence. Years of set patterns of thinking of the men, influence of non-Muslim communities, a virtual famine of moral values, a wide chasm between actual Islam and the Muslims, and intolerance between the communities are the root causes of Muslim women's

afflictions. ... It is not without significance that the survey of women ... revealed among other things, a deep, emotional attachment to the Shariat among the women.[23]

As these comments indicate, the women interviewed trust that the answers to their many perceived dilemmas lie in better understanding by them of the principles of their faith. They distrust the status quo of their situation, and hope for a better future. One of the pre-eminent sociologists of religion in the world, Peter Berger, has noted that distrust of the elite by the poor is a widespread contemporary phenomenon. He writes:

I was recently a consultant on a study of 11 countries that examined what we called 'normative conflicts'—basic conflicts about philosophical and moral issues. We found in most countries a fundamental conflict between elite culture and the rest of the population. Many of the populist movements around the world are born out of resentment against that elite. Because that elite is so secular, the protests take religious forms. This is true throughout the Islamic world, it's true in India, it's true in Israel and I think it's true in the US.[24]

This survey of the Muslim women of Delhi, and the analysis of that survey by Safia Iqbal, would seem to represent a vivid example of the kind of distrust Peter Berger is talking about. Safia Iqbal's position represents an interesting blend of the approaches of Maulana Thanavi and Maulana Mawdudi, along with a distinctively firm female voice. That firm female voice indicates a readiness to accept the males in their properly defined roles as economic supporters of the family, but is profoundly critical of males who mistreat women. Safia Iqbal says the Muslim women firmly believe that the answers to the problems of life lie in the Shariah, properly understood and applied. She claims that these poor Muslim women reveal a 'strong longing for a change in the social and family order, an order which might restore to them the rightful place in the social order'.[25]

This longing seems to represent hope that the world could be better than it is, and confidence that the answer lies in the wisdom of the ancestors properly understood. Another significant historian of religion, Mircea Elliade, referred to the quest for 'In Illo Tempore', the 'original time', as the most characteristic form of all serious religious life.[26] This longing for a better world is real and serious, and should be viewed with respect. Safia Iqbal is eloquent on the subject of the need for wives and mothers for privacy within their homes so that their nurturing capacities are not interfered with by outsiders. She understands Muslim women, somewhat as Maulana Thanavi did, as strong moral persons whose nurturing capacities are essential for the well-being of their families. She also thinks these wives and mothers will be strengthened by better education in their own tradition so that they can protest more effectively when their men mistreat them.

Maulana Mawdudi is the main authority she quotes. His commentary on the Qur'an seems to have been a major source of authority for her. Her confidence that the wisdom of the Muslim past contains answers to present-day problems is expressed through her belief that the Muslim community should be guided by the ulema and by Shariah courts for personal law. She agrees that *ijtihad*, the exercise of personal judgement on religious matters, should be used with respect to new problems. She has a chapter on this subject, so she clearly knows that this is a crucial issue for Indian Muslim women as for Muslim women in other countries. Where her position would differ from that of the organized women's movement in Pakistan, and elsewhere in the Muslim world, is that she thinks that ijtihad must be done by properly qualified members of the ulema. In Pakistan, the women members of the commission that changed the marriage laws explicitly quoted the poet Iqbal to the effect that the Muslim community should always be moving.[27] They understood this movement to mean that Muslim citizens in general, through their governments, could exercise ijtihad and reform laws as they deemed appropriate. In most countries where Muslims are the majority, the issues of legal reform have been acknowledged and acted upon through parliaments.

Safia Iqbal seems to be a representative voice for the points of view of many contemporary Indian Muslim women. Unlike the representatives of organized Muslim women in Pakistan and elsewhere, the Muslim women in India generally still see the need for the ulema to be the spokesperson for the Muslim community in matters of personal law. As we have indicated, the reason for this seems related to the insecurity existing among Indian Muslims because of their minority position. However, we should also understand that Muslim women often find ways to advance their interests in whatever context they find themselves. Although Safia Iqbal quotes Mawdudi as an authority, her attitude of self-confident criticism of men who behave badly indicates a robust feminine self-confidence. She indicates respect for the ulema, but she is ready to lobby them for causes that seem just to her. She writes:

> Setting up Shariah courts in every city or state is a laudable solution to many of the legal tangles in which Muslim women find themselves enmeshed. The Indian Constitution guarantees the freedom of religion, the freedom to practice personal laws. The setting up of Shariah courts, which will dispense cases pertaining to the Personal Law of Muslims, will be totally constitutional and unquestionable. ... The religious scholars are that elite section of the Muslim community to whom

the Muslims look forward for leadership. It would only be in the fitness of things that they should set the ball rolling and shake up the social order by solving the Ummah's problems. ... Upon the activities of these religious scholars, especially those among them with a modern, western education too, hangs the future of the Muslims.[28]

Safia Iqbal's voice represents one Indian Muslim woman's response to the nationwide publicity caused by the Shah Bano affair. This is plainly a situation which requires careful decoding of the symbols, and an analysis of what the emotions are which are stirred as they have been by these symbols. We need to ask what it means to say that the Muslim women surveyed represented a deep emotional attachment to the Shariah? Clearly, it does not mean that they read Arabic and could discourse at length on the principles of Islamic jurisprudence. That is why Berger's term 'signal' is a useful interpretative tool; these Muslim women are deeply attached to something that signals something to them. Ultimately, the signal involves confidence in ancestral wisdom, loyalty to what they perceive as the best in what has been transmitted to them, and hope for a better future. The dialectic of religious life involves withdrawals from the present to commune with the past in order to move towards making the future better. In their own ways, these Muslim women seem to express all these basic religious attitudes. Safia Iqbal concludes that these women need leadership from the ulema who have been trained both in their traditional knowledge and in modern knowledge. In other words, they need guides who can help them discover how to use the best of the past and the present in order to make the future better. Symbolically, this might be understood as meaning that they are aware of the need of guidance from the traditions of both Aligarh and Deoband. These Muslim women want the ulema to guide them, but they also want the ulema to receive modern forms of education. This appears to mean that they want leadership which will be effective in indicating how to use traditional values in a constructive way in a modern context.

What are the implications of this approach for public policy in India? Sayyid Ahmed Khan was explicit about the need for a modern state which would interfere as little as possible with the daily lives of the citizens. In his words: 'No one can hold stronger views than I do, that no measure relating to the welfare of the public should be adopted by the State without due regard to the feelings of those to whom the measure relate'.[29]

He fought extremely hard to get Muslims to change and adapt their ideas and practices in many respect, but he wanted them to change of their own free will and not because the government was pushing them to do so. He agreed to support compulsory vaccination against smallpox, but even that troubled his conscience, and he said very plainly that the state should leave citizens alone as much as possible. Peter Berger has expressed a similar position. Berger says 'if the state fires you, at least you might get a job from your uncle if the business world is separate from the state'.[30] Put in another way, one might say that really creative ideas for a better society are more likely to come from the voluntary associations of concerned citizens acting of their own free will than from state-controlled bureaucrats. The Nobel Prize for Peace has just gone to an American woman who fought against landmines even though this is not the policy of her government. It is often the case that citizens can think better, and become more morally responsible and serious, when the state leaves them alone.

Non-interference by the government in religious affairs is an important element of modern India's contemporary use of traditional wisdom. It is certainly a wise approach because it implies, as Sayyid Ahmed Khan well understood, that persons accept change much more readily and sanely when they have understood for themselves the reasons for the change and have freely consented to them. It is noteworthy that Safia Ahmed has confidence that the kind of enlightened ulema she envisages would make decisions in the interests of women as she understands those interests. She is particularly exercised about the inequities of the traditional Islamic ideas about triple divorce, the idea that the male divorces his wife by repeating a formula three times. She wants this changed, and she thinks Shariah courts would help implement such changes. She does not think of the ulema as persons who might obstruct such change, although she does want the ulema who have had access to modern forms of education. One difficulty with this approach is that, symbolically, the traditions of Aligarh and Deoband with respect to education have not as yet been harmonized. Safia Iqbal's position seems to indicate the hope that this could be done. The state can support innovation in educational structures.

Safia Iqbal's understanding and use of Mawdudi's ideas is different from that of many of the Muslim extremists who were active in Pakistan under the regimes of Zia ul Haq, and are still active in Afghanistan. Mawdudi's ideas have been appropriated and used differently in different social contexts. In his two recent books on Mawdudi, Vali Nasr offers a detailed analysis of the Muslim revivalist's life, thought and influence. Mawdudi came from a family which had lost dignity and prestige because of the destruction of Delhi and its culture after the failure of the 1857 revolt against the British.[31] Mawdudi was driven by an urge to find a way back for Muslims to the lost dignity of pre-Mutiny Indian Islam. His grandfather had rejected the Aligarh answer, and he himself found the ulema not helpful in providing a clear system that would unify Indian Muslims. His many writings are shaped by this underlying concern to find a new way, an Islamic system, to recover lost dignity. Safia Iqbal, like many other Indian Muslims, thinks that the implementation of Shariah courts in India would be one way to implement what she understands to be the ideals of a new Islamic system. Persons who have responded to Mawdudi have done so in diverse ways. Safia Iqbal takes from Mawdudi the idea that there should be an Islamic system, but she thinks of the system as one which will reform Muslim men so that they will not mistreat Muslim women.

There are no simple solutions to these issues, but better training in religious thought which helps escape the illusion that any one thinker can do justice to the long and complex heritage of Islamic thought and practice may help dissipate some of the confusion. What is needed is to become aware of the difficulties of transforming a religious heritage into a fixed ideological system. The religious leadership of all traditions is more likely to be constructive if the leaders have been well educated in understanding the contexts in which they live. The state could do more to help women and men from all religious traditions acquire a better grounding in the history of the religious thought of their traditions. Better ways of studying religious traditions need to be developed so that people become aware of the fallacy of using elements of any tradition to form a contemporary ideology which justifies using violence to impose that ideology on a state.

Safia Iqbal does have confidence in education. Perhaps her hopes for a better future for Indian Muslim women could be facilitated by granting quick access to higher education facilities for those Indian women who want to become scholars of Muslim law, history and religion. She is eloquent on the need of Muslim women to enhance their status and dignity. She writes:

> Women naturally desire the right to live with honour and dignity, a healthy personal life, a rightful place in society and in the development process of the world, and the rights granted through Islam. Persons who raise generations are surely worthy of this status. The Islamic Shariah grants this and more to any woman who enters its fold. Her dignity and self-respect which, apart from her faith, are her cherished treasures, are protected and developed by Islamic laws and insulted by man-made laws.
>
> It is clear from past experience and present indifference of society that women themselves will have to rise to stem the stagnation in society and to enhance their status and intensify their role. Mass education of women and men in

It is not men only but often women too who repress other women. Hence special social and counselling work must be introduced among women by Muslim women themselves not only to acquaint them with their rights and the real spirit of Islam but also to educate them in social relations. It is high time to return to the source of Islam—the Quran. Women alone can set the ball rolling in this direction. ...

Islamic and other laws, and a deep, unbiased examination of women's rights and standing in the Islamic system ... knowledge and its implementation alone is the antidote to dispel the poisonous effects of ignorance and oppression, which is why Prophet Muhammad ... made the attainment of knowledge obligatory on every Muslim man and woman. Worldly and religious knowledge and its active operation in practical life transforms frail woman into a rock against the strong tides of exploitation and cultural invasions into her religious laws, her identity, honour and self-respect.[32]

This feeling of Muslim women that they need more education in their own tradition can be very positive. In this instance, it seems to indicate confidence that the means to reform can be found within the tradition. Although it might not yet be feasible for highly educated Muslim women to become the actual judges in the Shariah courts in India, in the long run it is not impossible. In any case, the more educated the women are, the more influence they can hope to exert on those who are the judges and authorities. The urge the Indian Muslims feel to speak with one voice is partly a matter of their perception of the situation. That urge would be less strong if they felt more secure.

There are some male Indian Muslim voices asking that Muslims themselves rethink about their attitudes to gender. One such instance is the book *The Rights of Women in Islam* by Asghar Ali Engineer. He argues that Indian Muslims, like Muslims elsewhere in the modern world, need to look more carefully at their own intellectual history, and to realize that many of their customary ideas as to gender characteristics and roles simply reflect certain facets of their community's past experience. He writes:

Thus, in the past women were thought to be weak and this was a direct outcome of a concept of male superiority which was sociological, not theological. The problem was that the sociological often became the theological and was defended as such even when the sociological conditions changed. In our own times, women are no longer described as the weaker sex and are treated at par with men. They not only move about alone unviolated but can also earn their own livelihood by working outside the home. ...

However, to argue that purdah is no longer needed is not to argue that chastity too can be dispensed with. Chastity is the norm while purdah was a contextual means to achieve it. A woman can protect her chastity without observing purdah.

Thus, if our concept of morality is sufficiently dynamic and creative, we will not resist attempts to give purdah a new form, discarding the old one and, circumstances permitting, doing so without sacrificing the essential norm. In other words, the sociological and the empirical should be as important to us as the theological. This balance should never be lost. It is a requirement of the moral dynamics of a society.[33]

Asghar Ali Engineer's approach is to call for a reopening of discussions about gender among Indian Muslims in a manner that will help the people themselves resolve the questions of social change. Sayyid Ahmed Khan's persistent arguing with his own community about the need to distinguish between the basic principles of religion as opposed to customary practices is coming alive again in this new form. Indian Muslims taking this approach are insisting on justice as a primary Qur'anic value. This perspective carries with it an obligation to work at discerning what is actually just in a particular context. It entails an effort to recover what Leila Ahmed called the ethical voice of the Qur'an, and to discern how to implement the imperatives of this voice.

A recent report in 1996 from the Women's Research and Action Group in Bombay is entitled 'Marriage and the Politics of Social Change in India's Muslim Communities'.[34] The authors indicate that, in their opinion, because of the politicized state of religious and ethnic identity in India, it is unlikely that most Indian Muslim women in the near future will be interested in civil marriage. They think it is much more realistic to work within the existing structure, namely the Muslim Personal Law Board. They think that pressure from women can influence the thinking of the religious scholar-jurists who serve on the Board. Probably Safia Iqbal's statements about the need to limit the triple-divorce formula was aimed at this Board which has been considering this matter. Indian Muslim women who accept the minority's need to have the ulema as their spokespersons are thus arguing that the women need to influence the thinking of the ulema.

The Bombay group stresses several issues which they perceive as having immediate relevance to the situation of Muslim women in India. A Women and Laws programme which they have implemented has collected data from fifteen Indian states about Muslim women. They found divergences in practice in different parts of the country. For example, in Kerala, the consent of the bride was not required for marriage, whereas in Gujarat the bride was required to sign the marriage contract. It is possible in India under the Special Marriages Act of 1954 for Muslims like other citizens to have in effect a civil marriage, but so far Muslims have rarely used this legal possibility. The research shows that 70 per cent of their respondents had married before 18. The reason for the differences with respect to the consent of the bride are because the Hanafi schools of law requires such consent, whereas the Shafi school as practised in Kerala does not. The signature of the father or male guardian is considered adequate. Practices in contemporary India relating to *mahr*, the material right granted to the wife at marriage are also problematic according to the researches of this group. They have observed a social trend requiring the bride's family to pay dowry to the groom. This is not part of traditional Muslim legal practice but it is becoming increasingly common.

A third significant issue is that of a written marriage contract, *nikahnama*. This form of contract issued at the time of marriage can be used to guarantee the wife whatever seems desirable, such as the right to divorce if the husband remarries. In some Muslim countries such contract is used to give the married woman the right to work and to pursue education. The Indian women's rights activists want the All India Muslim Personal Law Board to approve a standard form for such a contract which could then be widely used. The matter is under consideration by the senior ulema who serve on the Board.

The Bombay group concludes the report with the comment that the Indian Muslim women are not in a static situation, and that they are finding ways to work within their situation to bring about changes that seem desirable to them. The greater sophistication of Muslim women in terms of understanding their religious heritage, its diversity, and its processes of change and development tend to push matters towards what the women themselves see as reappropriating the rights which follow from the basic principles of their religion. This is one reason why greater knowledge of Islamic law and history is likely to motivate more Indian Muslim women to work for more changes. The underlying idea is that the Qur'an emphasizes justice as a significant value.

Another example of a new Muslim voice calling for the recovery of the Qur'anic imperative to social justice is coming from contemporary South Africa. Many of the Muslims who took part there in the struggles against racism have understood, and said that sexism is like racism, and that Muslims seeking justice must combat both.[35] Indian Muslim women may go about seeking greater justice for themselves in ways that differ from the Muslim women of other countries, but the underlying processes of seeking better ways to implement basic principles are the same. The Muslim conscience works within whatever contexts are given to seek ways towards a better future.

Notes

1. Hodgson, Marshall, *The Venture of Islam* (Chicago: The University of Chicago Press, 1974), 3 Volumes.

2. Ahmed, Leila, *Women and Gender in Islam* (New Haven: Yale University Press, 1992), See also Amina Wadud-Muhsin, *Qur'an and Woman* (New York: Oxford University Press, 1995); Mernissi, Fatima, *Beyond the Veil* (Cambridge: Schenkman, 1975); Abbott, Nadia, *Aisha the Beloved of Muhammad* (Chicago: University of Chicago Press, 1942).

3. MacLean, Derryl N., *Religion and Society in Arab Sind* (Leiden: Brill, 1989).

4. Ahmed, Leila, pp. 41–78.

5. Ahmed, Leila, pp. 79–100.

6. Mujeeb, M., *The Indian Muslims* (London: Allen and Unwin, 1967).

7. Ikram, S.M. *Muslim Civilisation in India* (New York: Columbia University Press, 1964), pp. 22ff.

8. Ikram, S.M., pp. 51–2.

9. Ahmed, Leila, pp. 91, 92.

10. Ahmed, Leila, p. 99.

11. Eaton, Richard, *The Sufis of Bijapur* (Princeton: Princeton University Press, 1978), pp. 157, 158.

12. Metcalf, Barbara, *Moral Conduct and Authority* (Berkeley: University of California Press, 1984), pp. 185–95.

13. Mumtaz, Khawer and Farida Shaheed, *Women of Pakistan: Two Steps Forward One Step Back* (London: Zed Books, 1987). The authors quote Sarfaraz Husain Mirza *Muslim Women's Role in the Pakistan Movement* (Lahore: University of the Punjab, 1969), p. 18.

14. Shahnavaz, Jehan Ara, *Father and Daughter: A Political Autobiography* (Lahore: Nigarishat, 1971).

15. Ikramullah, Shaista, *From Purdah to Parliament* (London: Crescent Press, 1965).

16. Mujahid, Sharif al, 'Pakistan's First Presidential Election' in *Asian Survey* (Berkeley: Institute of International Studies, University of California, vol. 6, 1965).

17. Minault, Gail, *The Khilafat Movement: Religious Symbolism and Political Mobilization in India* (New York: Columbia University Press, 1982), p. 212.

18. Haq, Anwarul, *The Faith Movement of Maulana Ilyas* (London: Allen and Unwin, 1972).

19. Embree, Ainslie T., *Utopias in Conflict* (Berkeley: University of California Press, 1990), p. 96.

20. Mawdudi, Abul Ala, *Purdah and the Status of Women in Islam* (Lahore: Islamic Publications, 1972), pp. 136–8.

21. Mawdudi, Abul Ala, op. cit., pp. 217–19.

22. Iqbal, Safia, *Women and Islamic Law* (Delhi: al Asr Publications, 1988), pp. 164, 165.

23. Iqbal, Safia, op. cit., pp. 217–19.

24. 'Epistemological Modesty: an Interview with Peter Berger' in *The Christian Century* (Chicago: The Christian Century Foundation, October 19, 1997), pp. 972–5. See also Peter Berger, *A Rumour of Angels Modern Society and the Recovery of the Supernatural* (New York: Doubleday, 1969).

25. Iqbal, Safia, p. 167.

26. Eliade, Mircea, *Myth and Reality* (New York: Harper, 1975).

27. Mumtaz, Khawer and Farida Shaheed, op. cit., pp. 124–32.

28. Iqbal, Safia, pp. 131, 132, 174.

29. Graham, Major-General G.F.I., *The Life and Work of Sir Syed Ahmed Khan* (Karachi: Oxford University Press, reprinted 1974), pp. 157–8.

30. 'Epistemological Modesty: An Interview with Peter Berger,' op. cit.

31. Nasr, Seyyed Vali Reza, *The Vanguard of the Islamic Revolution: The Jama'at Islami of Pakistan* (Berkeley: University of California Press, 1994). See also Nasr, Seyyed Vali Reza, *Mawdudi and the Making of Islamic Revivalism* (New York: Oxford University Press, 1996), pp. 11–14.

32. Iqbal, Safia, op. cit., p. 169.

33. Engineer, Asghar Ali, *The Rights of Woman in Islam* (London: C. Hurst, 1992), p. 6.

34. Women's Research and Action Group 'Marriage and the Politics of Social Change in India's Muslim Communities' in *Women and Law in the Muslim Programme Special Dossier: Shifting Boundaries in Marriage and Divorce in Muslim Communities* (Women Living Under Muslim Laws, Boîte Postale 23, 34790, Grabels, France), vol. 1 (fall 1966).

35. Esack, Farid, *Quran, Liberation and Pluralism* (London: Worldview Press, 1997).

The Status of Christian Women in Kerala

Susan Visvanathan

When I read Arundhati Roy's book *The God of Small Things*, I felt a deep sense of sadness. It mingled with my laughter. She was a good anthropologist except that her data was not out there. It was in her family, her courtyard, in her bones. It is not easy to be a hybrid—neither this nor that, or half this or half that. But rather than splicing her in two and saying 'Which half of you is Syrian Christian?' as if magical severings of beautiful women is a routine act of the sociologist, I would like to comment on her book and what it says about the status of Christian women in India, specifically Syrian Christian women in Kerala.

Firstly, Roy is very clear that rules are social constructs. People who break them receive severe punishment—ostracism, death, guilt, alienation, pain. These are felt so deeply by the subject that they know in no small measure they do not belong to the society. Every act of theirs is an underlining of the fact that they are rebels, and by that fact rendered marginal. Not surprisingly then, Roy uses adultery and incest as the two major petards with which to hoist her novel. Funnily enough, the lawyer Sabu Thomas who wanted to take Roy to court for obscenity only wished to see her punished on the court of adultery. Incest, which follows in the next couple of pages, is so subtly rendered that it probably bypassed Sabu Thomas' English completely.

I had met Mary Roy in 1981 during the course of my field-work.

My friends Markose and Susan Vellapally were very closely attached to Mrs Roy, since Markose had been a consultant lawyer while the property case and the inheritance act of the Travancore Christians were being contested by Mrs Roy. She invited me for dinner. She lived in a beautiful house built by the famed Laurie Baker, attached to the school which Mrs Roy owned—Corpus Christi. All the rich plantation owners who could not bear to send their children away from Kottayam were her clients. Mrs Roy offered a substantial education for rich children.

We had a marvellous dinner which she told me was cooked on methane gas harvested from the children's toilets. And a light and delicate souffle appeared, topped with honey collected from the school gardens. Mrs Roy told me that she had recently met Mrs Gandhi and asked for a ticket to stand in the elections but had been refused. (Most Syrian Christian, being landed merchants, never vote left, and it is nice that the late E.M.S. Namboodripad described Mary Roy as a strong woman, stronger than Ammu as portrayed in the book). I went away after meeting some other friends of the Vellapally's—all landowners who spent their holidays in America or the Greek Isles. They seemed to have no connection with the middle class, conservative and orthodox Christians whom I had chosen to study. These urbane upper-class Christians were educated in exclusive schools in the Nilgiris, and in colleges in New Delhi. They were part of India's elite who are at home everywhere and at home nowhere—cultured, intelligent people with lesions all their own. Warner had described this for the '30s in America brilliantly—the club, excesses of wealth and entertainment, adultery and divorce, some alcoholism. It was nothing very aberrant—in this circle it was normal to fall in and out of love, and to spend a lot on good books, furnishings, wine, complicated chicken recipes. Their lives never seemed painless or empty, it was just different from the conservatism of the middle-class morality of the people I was studying. The latter would just laugh and say 'Oh! the rich'. It conveyed everything.

One day I dropped in to see Mrs Roy thinking that I would follow the clue that she was descended from a Bishop's line—in fact, one of the key proponents of reformation in the Church in the 1930s. Maybe she had some old letters, papers, some early hymns or sermons, but when we went in she was lying down, and her face was turned to the wall. There was no electricity and when she turned to us, she had no mask on—it was a face tormented by some grief. I still remember recoiling from the agony in her eyes. I do not think it was the lack of a fan, or her asthma. It was a corrosive and terrible grief that made me stop in my tracks.

I was twenty-five, and not very good at handling grief. My patriarchal and repressive father who had caused me various existential crises was after all a *normal* patriarch. It was unlike the female-centred house Arundhati writes about. So, since Mary Roy was in no position on that hot afternoon to discuss her family's role in the Mar Thoma movement, with the anthropologist's *élan* at hiding professional interests, I pretended that it was just a social visit.

I could not fit her into my data. The 'Mary Roy case' came into its own in 1984, but it was the other two women who fought the case (single and helpless) who fitted into my frame. Mary Roy was too much like the Delhi-ites I knew and *didn't* then study: modern, feminist and, in some odd way, individualist.

When I read Arundhati Roy's book, a lot of things fell into place. The younger Roy defined pathology as the normalcy of her life, and etched these in a language both friendly, well crafted and yet excessive. She had the qualities of a good mimic, and so brought to life the nuances and cadences of what it meant to be on the margins. One Malayali critic said 'I wept reading what a sad and bitter life these children had led'.

Somewhere fiction and fact merged so that nobody knew any more what the actual position of Christian women in Kerala was. Even today, nobody admits to falling in love with their servants. For a woman to feel so intensely for a lower-caste man (*adima*) is unthinkable. A philosopher teaching in Delhi has said that he has stopped telling people that he is originally from Ayamennam because of the excitement generated by Roy's book! Malayalis have, however, generally been pleased that Roy wrote this book because, as one theologian Mathai Zachariah told me, 'She has done a service to humanity in general and to the Syrian Christian community in particular'. What is this service? It is to unveil the hypocrisy by which people have lived their lives. It is to state that so-called pathologies are 'normal'—that one can love someone who is not of one's own class or caste. Love him because he is so beautiful, so noble, so true, so proud, so unreal.

The problem of class certainly distinguishes the interpretation of Christianity by the women of Kerala. If the plantation owners of Kottayam represents the life that Roy's book depicts accurately, we see that the absence of the father is substituted by the strong patriarchal presence of the son, the inheritor of property. The sister Ammu is problematic because Syrian Christians have no place for the daughter once she is married off. Mary Roy's class contention that daughters must inherit an equal share of the father's property was immediately countered by the writing of wills by a Syrian Christian patriarch. Even the priests of many of the Syrian

Christian churches come out against the Supreme Court judgement of 1984 saying that it would affect the patriarchal bases of Christianity.

The Christian women of Kerala who belong to the St Thomas tradition are generally articulate and strong-willed. Matriarchy persists in the institution of motherhood and mother-in-lawhood because, while men define the aspects of the external world and the relationship to it, it is women who control the inner spheres of the house.

It is this tension between assertive patriarchy and the implicit matriarchal compulsions which are bound to exist when sons are close to their mothers and avoid their fathers that I wish to delineate. Certainly while the father is alive, he makes the decisions about how income is spent, or whom his offspring will marry, or who may expect to inherit what. Yet, there is no doubt that women's sexual and emotional bonds with their husbands do allow them to have some say in the nature of proceedings. It is true that this is offered only as an 'opinion', not even as 'advice', but men do listen even if seemingly absent-mindedly or impatiently. The final decision on any important event is taken by the patriarch seemingly alone, or in the shared and cooperative wisdom of other lineage members. But, as much as my data have shown, Syrian Christian ethos, however patrilineal, is very subtly loving and protective of daughters.

Dowry, which is the greatest scourge of this high-status community, expresses the deep sense of obligation that fathers feel for their daughters. It is love, terror, misery—to give away a daughter, to hope that she falls in the right hands, to consider mortgaging one's property, borrow from relatives, give away a daughter-in-law's *stridhanam* so that one may be assured that she marries well, lives well. This anguish is shared by mother and daughter in equal terms. Women certainly do not have the courage to refuse the terms of marriage—the payment of *stridhanam*. This is why I have termed it as groom-price (Visvanathan, 1993). In a logical process called 'the redistribution of father's wealth', women also tend to see stridhan as their *avakasham* or right, their 'pre-mortem inheritance'.

What I wish to affirm is that mothers, sisters, daughters and wives play very significant roles in men's lives. The oppression lies in that whatever they say or think or feel is deemed to be insignificant. Yet, this does not mean that they do not have influence or cannot affect men's dispositions.

The relationship of mother-in-law to daughter-in-law has perhaps the greatest immediacy of all. After all, daughters and sisters must be married out. Wives influence husbands in the subterranean mode. Mothers and sons have a teasing light-hearted affectionate relationship which can be utilized to good effect as sons grow older and take over from the deceased patriarch. Mothers, as widowed mothers, wield the greater influence over their sons who are by title and responsibility the heads of the household. Yet, the power of women and the authority of their sons are qualitatively different, as Michelle Rosaldo has so vividly argued.

Women do have authority over daughers-in-law. This they express through every symbolic form of encounter—language interaction and silence. If the woman submits to the will of her mother-in-law, peace reigns in the household. Friendship, amity and cooperation revolve around the sharing of that scarce variable—the figure of the son-husband. It is in this dual and hyphenated sense that men live their lives. Veena Das has shown how men resolve this tension in the case of Punjabi kinship. Amongst the Syrian Christians, the relationship of love, contempt and desire mingle in the attitude of a man to his wife—frequently he refers to her in direct conversation as 'mollae' or daughter.

Emotional relationships are ambiguous. People say one thing, yet often experience something quite different. What interests me are the intricacies of intimacy in patriarchy. What is it that allows women to consent to patriarchy? Why do Syrian Christian women (across denominational schisms) accept the superiority of male wisdom, power and authority as if these can never be questioned? How do they create their own enclaves where their destiny as 'dependents' can be played out?

It is the daughter-in-law who traverses this path with so much tact and care. In this respect, it is important to go back to the ceremony of marriage to know what is expected of a bride. To a great extent, the Syrian Christians have remained self-consciously endogamous, except for a few rule-breakers. Sons see from their parents' marriage how supportive women are to their husbands' aims and ambitions, how, given the greatest cleavages by opinion or circumstance, women still stand by their husbands in an attitude of complete devotion and trust. Divorce is still almost unheard of even in the '90s except amongst those who have married out of the community. Christian patience, love and fortitude are invariably built in the contract of marriage. The men, in return, provide shelter, dignity and identity to women in society where single status is seen to be a state of virginal frustration and personal deprivation.

Marriage is thus seen to be a sacramental and permanent bond, and is entered into only after much discussion over the merits, demerits and compatibility of the partners-to-be, by members of the extended family. It is believed that if the families are compatible, then the individuals concerned are bound to have a happy marriage. While not admitting to a belief in destiny, the Syrian Christians definitely believe in God's will and, within that framework, all negotiations are always possible.

Once the betrothal takes place, the stridhanam is exchanged, the date is fixed and the wedding guests invited—the excitement of a traditional marriage is the most palpable thing in the household. Gifts are usually unilateral forms of presentation, as Vatuk has described it for north India where the hierarchies of wife-givers and wife-takers are clearly established. The pleasure of giving a daughter and gifts of gold to the groom's family is enacted, even though in reality the bride's parent may feel the pinch of both in very real terms.

THE MARRIAGE SERVICE

The Syrian Christians, specifically the Yakoba, have rites which use Syrian liturgical and ritual paraphernalia, and the marriage ceremony consists of two interlinked events. The 'blessing of the rings' is the first. It is actually a ceremonial betrothal. The 'blessing of the crowns' is the ceremonial act of uniting man and woman, and symbolizes the inherent homology between Christ the King and the groom, and between the Church and the bride. This establishes the dominantly male symbolism of Pauline Christianity, which privileges spiritual love rather than erotic love. Because of this homology, marriage is a mystery, carrying within it implicitly the nature of grace.

Recently I attended a Syrian Christian wedding. The young couple were mediated by the presence of six priests and one bishop, by their parents and father's sisters on either side. An anthropologist colleague said at the end of the ceremony: 'They (the bride and groom) are still standing so far apart!' Of course, the young people, modern and cosmopolitan though they were, felt embarrassed by the pageantry, the spectacle of it all. Custom demanded that they keep up a stance of reserve in front of their elders. In the modern contexts of the nuclear family, this reserve would perhaps immediately disappear insomuch as the husband allows it. In the extended family, the demeanour of detachment and controlled affection would be steadfastly maintained. In fact, Syrian Christians feel very threatened when husbands and wives express affection in public. Tender glances, leave alone any demonstration of passion, such as being enclosed with the spouse for long periods of time would put a great deal of strain on the emotions of parents, siblings and offspring. Sexuality is controlled by the expectation that time, space and other social relationships will mediate the expression of desire.

In an odd rendering of passivity as power, the woman is seen to be constantly searching for the groom. Christ represents the completeness of virtue in a man, who is seen to be the sun, while the woman is the day.

This passivity, this dependence of the Christian institution of marriage is based upon the desire of a woman in a patriarchal society to bear legitimate children, preferably sons, and to share the privileges of her husband's property which she may not necessarily own in tandem.

After the 'blessing of the crowns' (a ritual circling a gold chain and cross over the heads of bride and groom), the tying of the *tali*, or marriage locket, and the placing of the *mantrakodi* (cloth bought by the groom) over her head takes place. At this juncture, the girl's attendant who is usually her father's sister is substituted by the groom's sister. She now 'belongs' to them.

The next ritual is the joining of hands of bride and groom. The verses that follow articulate that the woman must leave her family for her husband. He must love her and have kindness. Even if he is naked, he must clothe her. As she loves her own life, she must love him. Even if he goes thirsty, he must give her a drink. Keeping the commandments, she must live with him in love and tenderness. The bride and groom must say the creed *visvasa pramanam* together, articulating their faith in Christian precepts.

The service concludes with the formal signing of the contract of marriage. The bride changes into the new sari the groom had placed over her head during the marriage ceremony. This is the first material gift that he makes to her, bonding her through the intimacy of clothing.

Just as the case of the Syrian Christian cannot be self-explanatory of Christian community and culture everywhere in India, so also the ethnographic uniqueness of the Syrian Christian expresses its cultural alienation from other Christian communities in Kerala itself.

A picture of direct contrast would be the lives of the women of the fishing community in Kerala, specifically those who belong to the Latin Christian community. The argument here is that men's occupations affect the lives of women.

The Scenario Today

Syrian Christian women are generally prosperous—wives of merchants, bankers, white-collar professionals, capitalists and trawler-owners, farmers and landowners. Whatever the class oscillations among them, they see themselves as an aristocracy. They might not be an elite, but they have the self perceptions of being one. They might do all the housework themselves, or hire maidservants to do their chores (which is practically non-existent now), but they are always cushioned by the memory of their community identity. Hard work is not seen to be demeaning. In fact,

Syrian Christian women have been the backbone of the hospital system in many parts of the world by providing nursing and paramedical care. They are seen to be efficient, educated, clean, wellmannered, from good families and ready to work long hours for little pay either out of poverty and helplessness, or Christian virtue. Once married, they may give up their professions as teachers, nurses, secretaries or lab assistants and settle down to keeping house with equal vivaciousness. For those who require a salary to maintain the home in the style they are used to, the double burden of career and domestic chores is systematically handled. The leisured among them, who have servants and do not need to go out to work, nevertheless take pride in cooking and serving, and in nurturing their children. A certain boredom sets in during late middle age when the children are grown, married, and settled professionally in distant cities. Husbands never tend to 'retire' and remain active in their offices, the Church associations, their clubs. The silence of a leisured middle age is one of the most painful and deafening of all life's circumstances. It is spent waiting for the post, for telephone calls, for the possibility of a journey to America or to Allahabad to visit children, for the husband's return from office or club, for the evangelical workers' visit, for friends from the local 'prayer meeting' group. The earlier stamping and scuffling of growing children, the groans and demands of ageing parents-in-law, the shared responsibilities of parenting was a busy and noisy affair. The nostalgia for years gone by is captured by the incessant phrase *pillar valiyuda ayegi poyi* (the children are grown). Old age has its own attendant pleasures—the spiritualism, the delicacy of dependence and helplessness between two partners who have never dreamed of breaking their bond or living apart (unthinkable among the Syrian Christians even now) and the exquisite and subtle curiosity of 'waiting for the bridegroom' (death/ Christ). The final answer to that question 'What is it like?' is a time of mediation, prayer, and even longing.

I will contrast this briefly with the wives of the fishermen. The data were collected in the summer of 1998 in Alleppey district. Of course, women's position cannot be understood segmentally in such traditional societies—their lives are conjoined with those of the men.

The fishermen of Ponappra are an active educated set—Christian and Marxist—comfortable with the vocation associated with the friends of Jesus. In the same breath, they are *malysia thozhilaligal*—fish workers.

The women of the fishing community are used to hunger, deprivation and to the thought of death. They are often in debt in terms of sums which are staggering to the average middle-class Syrian Christian peasant, banker or merchant. When the catch is good, the men bring home money to pay debts, gold ornaments for their wives, a new pet for the children or an expensive tape deck and, of course, alcohol. But, there are many days when the sea delivers nothing. It is truly empty.

Every time fishermen take out a boat to sea with forty men on board, it costs them up to a lakh of rupees. There is the cost of hiring the boat from the *modulali* (lord or capitalist overlord) as well as the cost of buying or hiring an outboard motor, the cost of diesel for running the boat out to sea for 6–12 hours, and the costs of feeding the *thozhiyalali* (workers) for this time. Tea alone comes to Rs 40 per person. The fishermen often suffer from vomiting and are unable to eat anything while out at sea. One of them said 'Love the sea? Are you joking? We are not on a beach. This is our work. It has its dangers. Some of us don't return.' In case they come back empty-handed, each fisherman is thousands in debt for that one day. They say they can come back empty-handed for ten days at a time before their luck takes a turn. They have known what it is to go without food for three days at a time. Yet, they assert to the generosity of their community. If a men gets ten baskets of fish, he gives two to the poor as alms, and two to the agent. The value of the remaining six he keeps.

But the ideal situation of catching ten baskets does not often happen. Because of sustained trawler overfishing, the sea is now emptying species by species. The fishermen live in decent dwellings in Ponappra—neat two- or three-room homes which they have put up with the aid of loans from the Church or the government. They remain unfinished, however, because of lack of funds.

The women among this specific local community do not often or necessarily participate in the catching or merchandising of fish. Some do wait at the beach, particularly if they are fishermen's widows, and buy fish as it comes fresh off the nets, which they then sell. Most fishermen deal with an agent (commission agent) who takes over immediately from them when they come in with the haul. These men are from upper-class Latin Christian households, profiteers who live in comfortable and stable houses some distance from the beach. There is some tension between the fishermen and the agents. The fishermen feel themselves unable to handle the constraints of the market; they do not really feel that, in practical matters, they have a union. The fishermen see themselves as innocent victims of the market and of the state. 'We have no union: anybody can join and anybody can leave.' This would come as a surprise to Tom Kocherry and others who lead the fishermen's struggle, who keep records of the union networking at a global level. The fishermen of Ponappra look to the skies, and pray to different Gods that govern their particular religion.

I will not go into the relationship between poverty, literacy, health and political awareness. Clearly this community feels the pulverizing quality of financial oscillation in a way that other people cannot imagine. If the haul is good, there is a great deal of money which can be shared between forty men, and goes into paying costs and debts. If it is bad, then there is only hunger. But as they say, someone will always give an empty-handed fisherman a few fish for his family to fry.

The anthropology of subsistence societies or the culture of poverty has to handle the emotional mechanisms by which people orient themselves to wealth and degradation in equal measure. One thing they do realize is that the very basis of their life as communities, as families, as conjugal units is threatened by an ecological disaster such as overkill.

It is now difficult to imagine the status of the Latin Christian women who have to share the burden of their husbands' tribulations—the dangerousness of the sea, the poverty of their work, their illiteracy, their indebtedness to the moneylender landlords. Many women weave coir ropes to supplement their income. This is a laborious process of shaping the coir into rope by using their hands, and then plaiting it into strands. It is monotonous back-breaking labour. They sit upright with their legs stretched out, a pile of raw material at their side. Their hands are calloused. For four to six hours of work, they are paid approximately seven rupees. In spite of their degradation, they are somehow hopeful. The Church represents a very positive element in their life. It provides them with loans, helps them save money in a Church-sponsored credit thrift society. The priest who is most supportive to their cause and has helped organize the fishermen's movement in Ponappra tells a story that is woman-centred.

> My father and grandfather were away for long periods—they were in the Navy. So I grew up with my mother. We were very poor. And because of our poverty, our wealthier relatives were ungenerous and unkind. I grew up with the fishermen's sons. It was they who gave me my sense of being, my sense of place. I was really one of them. But then, as I grew older, my hatred for those who had been so contemptuous of our poverty became the blinding force in my life. I became part of a group of young men who were so wild, so terrible that one day my mother said that she cursed the day she had become mother to one such as I. That hurt me very much. It was the turning point of my life. And priesthood was the other side of the coin.

So this man, highly educated, theologically motivated, with a story somewhat like that of Frances of Assissi, trains bands of committed young people who work for the fishermen. Such priests are many. And many wives of fishermen wish their sons to go for a theological training. They will be released from their poverty, they will work for their people.

Ponappra cannot be understood without looking at the story of coir, and the place of the Church. Both the coir and the Church are central about women's location in the fishermen's community. The Church is substantially trying to organize the labour of women by providing them with wooden frames for weaving coir, where their earnings per day can go up from Rs 7 to Rs 25. There is also an understanding that with the ecological degradation of the sea, the community of fishers may be doomed to extinction. Problems of health and literacy are very high. One solution the highly motivated priests feel is to diversify coir and handicrafts production. They also feel that there is a movement, but not a union. Whether it is wages, ecological concerns or conjugal solidarity, women are centrally concerned. The axes of their lives centre around their husbands, the poverty they share and the daily terror of existence.

I use the fishermen's case as a very preliminary statement of the problem of women in Christianity in India. Class, language and region play a significant part in the interpretation of Christianity. The myths of conversion provide completely different bases to Christian ideology and life. Thus, the analyses of women in Christianity must seek to articulate the subject position of women in a very patriarchal system. Whatever transformations are to occur in their status can only be provided by the impetus that the Church and the power-holders in a community set forward. The very ideology of Pauline Christianity subjugates women, whether of upper status or poor. If Christianity is seen to be a radical transformative movement affecting the lives of the poor, then women impoverished by patriarchal Christianity must see in themselves the voice of power that the oppressed always signified for Jesus.

Bibliography

Ardener, Edwin, 1986, The Problem of Power in Leela Dube, et. al., *Visibility and Power*, Oxford University Press, Delhi.

Arendt, Hannah, 1958, *The Human Condition*, University of Chicago Press, Chicago.

Das, Veena, 1976, *Masks and Faces* in *Contributions to Indian Sociology*, n.w. vol. 10, no. 1.

Dernet, J.D.M., 1970, *Law in the New Testament*, Darton, Longman and Todd, London.

Illich, Ivan, 1981, *Shadow Work*, Marion Boyars, London.

—— 1982, *Gender*, Pantheon, New York.

Mies, Maria, 1986, *Patriarchy and Accumulation on a World Scale*, Zed, London.

Mies, Maria, Veronika Benrhold-Thomsen and Claudia von Werlhoff, 1988, *Women: The Last Colony*, Zed Books, London.
Roy, Arundhati, 1997, *The God of Small Things*, Flamingo, London.
Rosaldo, Michelle and Louise Lamphere (eds), 1974, 'Woman', *Culture and Society*, Stanford University Press, California.
Showalter, Elaine (ed.), 1989, *Speaking of Gender*, RKP, New York.
Visvanathan, Susan, 1993, *The Christians of Kerala*, Oxford University Press, Madras.
—— 1994, The Fishing Struggle in Kerala, *Seminar*, November.
Warner, Lloyd W., 1975, *Family of God*, Greenwood Press, Connecticut.

Feminine Presence: The Case of Santal Tribe

Madhu Khanna

Tribal Setting and Terms of Discourse

About 80 million people in India (roughly 8 per cent of the population) belong to primal communities, variously designated as 'tribes', 'scheduled tribes' (*anusuchit janjati*), *inhabitants of the forest* (*vanavāsī*), castes of the forest (*vanyajati*), hill dwellers (*pahari*), and aborigines. The most common and widely known term is *ādivāsī,* the first settlers or the primal communities that inhabit India. It is widely accepted that the tribal communities are the earliest known inhabitants of India and 'the history of India is not complete without a thorough knowledge of the history of tribes'.[1] The great epics mention several non-Aryan tribes inhabiting the wildest forest regions. The tribals do not form a homogenous group. There is considerable biological, linguistic and cultural diversity among them. The tribes of peninsular India (Mundas, Santals, Kols, Hos and Bondas) come from the proto-Astraloid stock, while tribes of the north-east (Nagas and Bodos) trace their origin from the Mongoloid stock. On the other hand, the Dravidians are represented by the Oraons, Gonds and Khonds. The tribal communities exist at two different levels. Historian Kosambi in the early fifties had drawn our attention to the fragmentary 'tribal' survival in an urban non-tribal setting.

Kosambi states:

Nearest to me in location are a tent dwelling nomadic group of *Ras Phase Pardhis* whose basic costume (for the man)is a simple loin cloth, who never take a bath, but who retain the natural cleanliness, mobility, superior senses of wild animals. They have six exogamous clans or septs whose names have become surnames of feudal Maratha families: Bhonsale, Pawar, Cavahan, Jadhav, Sinde, Kale. The last is actually a Citpavan brahman surname; the penultimate once denoted 'son of a slave girl' (without acknowledged father) till it was ennobled by the rising to the kingdom of Gwalior .... Besides begging and petty stealing, these *Pardhis* are expert bird snarers ... . There never was any question of racial purity, for strangers used to be adopted into a clan on payment of a fee. The real basic reason for their new willingness to abandon tribal life is its impossibility: game has almost vanished, while none of them can afford a hunting licence.[2]

Set apart from these fragmented groups, there is a running tribal belt in north, central and north-east India of tribals living in the secure refuge of nature or far-flung regions untouched by pre-modern or modern conquests. In India, there is an uninterrupted tribal concentration in the hilly and forest belt starting from Gujarat, Thane district in Maharashtra in western India, stretching right through Mayurbhanj in Orissa, and cutting across Surat in Gujarat, Mandla and Sahdol in Madhya Pradesh, and Santal Parganas, Ranchi and Singhbhum districts of Bihar. Other belts of tribal population are found in north-east India and in Bastar district of Madhya Pradesh and Agency tracts or Orissa and Andhra Pradesh. Tribal population is also found in south-western hills and *ghats*, and in the Andaman and Nicobar islands.[3]

There are about 360 tribal groups which have been recognized by the Indian government and are distributed unevenly over different regions of the country, composed of different races and cultures. The internal movements of the tribal groups are so wide and extensive that none of their habitats can be considered to occupy their original homeland. The tribes of middle India and the adjacent western part of India, for example, constitute nearly 50 per cent of the tribal population but, owing to their successive migrations, it is not possible to locate their original habitat. Their economic occupations are equally diverse, largely shaped by the ecology of the area. Some live solely on hunting and food-gathering, like Birhors in Bihar or Chenchus in Andhra Pradesh. Others like the Todas in the Nilgiris, Tamil Nadu and Rabaris in Gujarat are dependant on pastoralism. The tribes of the north-east subsist on shifting cultivation. Nearly 54 per cent of tribals are settled cultivators and have become skilled agriculturists. On account of their bewildering diversity of location, culture, language and biology, a generic presentation on tribal women would be too diffused and will only partially do justice to the macro-scale culture in a short essay. Hence, this discussion centres on the representation of feminine presence in the Santal tribe at various levels of their participation. What follows is a 'micro' exploration into one of India's largest tribal groups, the Santals. The purpose is to use a micro-level analysis to gain insight into the feminine presence in a pre-modern tribal society and its assimilation in the post-industrial urban setting.

The word *tribe* or *tribal* has come to denote a significant category of discourse for the anthropologist. In a generic sense, it is a metaphor for the most barbaric and victimized group of our society. As 'tribal' generally represents an early pre-industrial or pre-modern form of human organization, it is looked upon with derision as a fossilized remnant of pre-modernity—backward, stunted or retarded. The upholders of this view regard pre-modern cultures as essentially an archaic stratum. This perception subverts the reading of our human past. Current scholars are beginning to redefine the paradigm of studying cultures.[4] It is increasingly recognized that in terms of the historical evolution of societies, one may 'speak of development of technology and not of culture'.[5] In terms of our discourse, the tribal society is made to appear primitive only when paradigm and parameters of the 'urban' technological and the so-called civilized society are applied to it. The tribal society is culturally literate, and is rooted in its own value system, social dynamics and perennial virtues. It is well grounded in a communally structured, ecologically sound model of growth, so much so that contemporary ills of the so-called 'civilized' urban world, such as crass materialism, consumerism, violence and greed, are absent. In all these respects, a tribal community is far more balanced and developed. Our discourse uses the word 'tribe' in a positive sense.

Introduction

The Santals are numerically one of the major tribes of India next to the Bhils and the Gonds. Biologically, they come from the proto-Australoid stock and, linguistically, the Santali language is traced to Austro-Asiatic group. Although the Santals have a language of their own but, because of their physical distribution, they write in different scripts—Oriya, Bengali and Devanagari. The Santals are a homogenous group both biologically and linguistically, and to a great extent even culturally, and in their pursuit of economic activity. The mainstay of the Santals is settled cultivation or plough agriculture. They are widely spread out in three states of India. They live in the Santal Parganas, Dhanbad, Hazaribag and

Singhbhum districts of Bihar. Their settlements are found in Birbhum, Purulia, Bankura and Midnapur districts in West Bengal. Another Santal concentration is found in the Mayurbhanj district in Orissa. The Santal Parganas is not the original home of the Santals. It is an area that was divided and demarcated by the British. It was formed after the Santal revolution in 1857. The Santals are a very vibrant and proud group. Although for nearly 3000 years they have been part of this country, in many parts of the country they have been in constant encounter with the Hindu and non-tribal groups. Legends of their past often record encounter and migration to different regions in the country. The Santal tribe is traced to the generic Munda family and their traditions, whose ancestors come from north-east India following the line of the sacred river Damodar to the Chhotanagpur plateau. There are also several references in the primal narrative to the tribe's migration from the land of Hihiri Pipri through Khoj Kaman, and further east into Bihar, West Bengal and Orissa. On account of the early impact of the British and the German Evangelical Lutheran Church, many of them living in the Santal Parganas have adopted Christianity. Two important events have shaped their history. First, the establishment of the Santal colony in Damin-i-koh on the hill tract of Rajmahal, north of Dumka in Bihar. About 500 square miles on the foot-hills were given to the Santals. The second was the Santal insurrection of 1855.[6] By virtue of the toil of the Santals, the land of Damin-i-koh flourished with rich crops. But their prosperity was short-lived. Traders and moneylenders of that area took advantage of their innocent ways and cheated them mercilessly in every transaction. The result was that large sections of the Santals were dispossessed of their land. Distressed, they could not tolerate such exploitation any more and, out of sheer desperation, took to violence to free themselves. They organized a rebellion under the leadership of Sido and Kanhu in 1855, looting and killing non-tribals. The British government retaliated but the Santals, with their traditional weapons, fought for two years. The rebellion was subdued in 1857 and brought their plight to the attention of the government and led to certain administrative reforms. A separate district called Santal Parganas was established and has survived since as the core of Santal tradition and activities. Santals of the district enjoy special legislative protection.

By 1883, almost every part of Santal Parganas was reached by the Christian missionaries whose main aim was to propagate Christianity under the guise of philanthropy. Inspite of their efforts, only 5 to 6 per cent of the Santal population in the district of the Santal Parganas have adopted the Christian faith, possibly owing to the obsessively puritanical approach of the Church. Running alongside this, the Santals have been subjugated to many social movements which have greatly affected their solidarity and cohesiveness. Some, as the Kharwar movement, essentially reformist in nature, played an important role. Led by Bhagirath, the goal of this movement was to absorb certain Hindu devotional practices dedicated to Lord Ram into the Santal fold. This movement also did not gain much popularity and split into several religious groups, such as Babaji, Safai and the Janeodhari Santals. These movements have introduced a certain amount of stratification in their society, unknown to them in the earlier period. Some have begun to follow diffused forms of Hindu rituals. However, despite their wide distribution and history of migration, the Santals living in the borderland of Bihar, Orissa and West Bengal have continued to preserve their culture. The Santal society today is striving to preserve its bonds of solidarity. It is widely held that the material prosperity enjoyed in the past is eroded by the *diku*, the hostile outsider responsible for the decay that has beset their society today. Some Santals find themselves caught in what anthropologists describe as 'solidarity-emulation conflict'. They have a superior image of their own tribe in relation to others. This superiority is undercut by their desire to emulate the 'high' tradition and is invariably counter-productive, as it impels them to overemphasize the uniqueness of their own culture.

The subject of the study is to trace the visibility of women in the Santal tribe. It explores the feminine presence in the Santal tribe at various levels of their participation in the community, and the cosmology and worldview that has given shape to their value-system and Santal identity. It also explores the social roles that women play in the Santal community. The most current discourse on feminism (largely centred on the urban women) assumes that women are better understood if the humanity of women is looked upon as a separate entity, set apart from other social groups. This presupposition goes against the very grain of tribal ethos where women are a part of an integral community. The Santals, like most tribal communities, maintain very intense intercommunity and inter-family ties. A Santal village functions as an integral unit with a very sound internally structured community bond, akin to a live organism in nature where perfectly matched parts form a complete 'whole'. There is no concept of individual voice or individual eccentricity. The entire community responds together in unison with one voice, as it were. In sharing joys or sorrows, births or deaths, mournings, celebrations and festivals, they are one integral unit. These bonds extend beyond the self and the person. The Santals share a deep attachment to the land they inhabit, the streams, the hills, the rolling valleys, open fields, trees and sacred groves that surround their settlements and protect their well-being and land. The bond shared with each other and a sense of belonging is part of ancient memories. As stated by Mahapatra:

The acceptance of the natural order constitutes an integral element in Santal view of life. The Santal working on the land does not set himself in opposition to it. He works with the elements and not against them. There is no attempt whatsoever to conquer the elements. He depends for his livelihood on rain, sunshine and the soil. Nature is not exploited. It is enjoyed in the spirit of humility and love. And the enjoyment is mutual.[7]

This is the broad setting of the Santal woman, within which she grows and lives. The setting alone commands a very different parameter of analysis. For our analytical tools, the terms of reference run counter to the reference categories by which the tribe defines its identity. The dichotomy or the distance we share in our modern industrial society with the tribal people has a bearing on the very notion of empowerment of women, or what empowerment means to a woman in an indigenous 'tribal' setting. In this case, we shall explore the world of the Santal women as a feminine presence in relation to their own mindset. How visible is she in her own community? What are the roles assigned to her as a woman? How free or constrained is she in playing those roles? Are there any specific areas of her participation which empower her? The focus is thus on an alternative worldview of societies very different from our own in urban areas.

We essay the first, through two significant categories of Santal consciousness, the *Binti*, the creation narrative, and the *Jaher-than*. Binti reiterates the overwhelming concern of the feminine and charts the map of the roles women are meant to play in society. Central to Santal consciousness is the notion of Jaher-than, the sacred grove and is presiding deity, *Jaher-era*, the goddess of the sacred grove which reflects the woman/nature complex in Santal worldview and worship. Both these need considerable elaboration for a full appreciation of the feminine in Santal society. They provide the key cognitive structures that have contributed to ethos and identity of Santal women.

Introduction to the Binti

Binti describes the Santal concept of creation. The Santal narrative defines the individual's social, psychological, cultural and gender position in a community. Thus the myth is a mechanism of self-representation and also includes the cosmic and trans-cosmic world of the gods, spirits, super-sensible beings, cosmic spaces and their total worldview. Binti is recited and sung on many occasions. The *Jom Sing Binti* is recited after five, twelve or thirteen years of birth in the rite of *Coco Chattier* when a young man or a pubescent girl is admitted as a member of the society. *Janam Chattier* is recited in the name-giving ceremony of the child. *Bapla Binti* is recited during marriage ceremonies and *Bhanan Binti* at death ceremonies. *Baha Binti* is sung in the spring festival by men and women in the form of a dialogue. There is no audience; every one participates in the celebration. *Karam Binti* is recited during the Karam-tree festival and during the plantation of a karam sapling symbolized as a female deity to mark a new Santal settlement. An important occasion is in times of crisis when the community recovers its collective memory to reaffirm clan solidarity. The event usually takes place for the whole night. It is also recited to restore a state of order when the web of social fabric is disrupted by an uncalled for event or an ill omen.

Binti unfolds the story of creation and the history of their earlier migrations and unsettled life. Several versions of the narrative have been recorded[8] (see Appendix I for comparisons). The readings of the myth do not reflect theological variations but are limited to descriptions and episodes of the myth. Santals living under Hindu influence often identify the supreme deity, formless and invisible, with the Upanishadic concept of the supreme being. Christian Santals relate the episode with biblical ideas.[9]

Binti: The Santal Creation Narrative

High above in the heavens lives Thakur, the supreme god who is not seen by the human eye but who sees all.[10] He lives with Thakuran, his consort, the supreme goddess with two other deities, Devalo and Lita (Maran Buru). The gods have a meeting place where all of them meet from time to time. One day, Thakur expressed his boredom and asked Lita, the messenger god to search for a suitable new abode. Lita informed him that there was a beautiful place called the earth (*monchopuri*) but the place was dry and arid. Thakur insisted on going there with all the members of heaven. They descended on earth with the help of a gossamer thread (*toresutem*) and began to live there. But life over there became unlivable owing to the lack of water. Lita brought a divine stick (*parchihapa*) that belonged to Thakur and pierced a half dug well. When the celestial elephant pressed the stick hard it went deep into the bowels of the earth. Water spurted out, overflowed and flooded the earth. Then Lita created creatures that had no face or limbs (*nigaria-mimuria*). After them, the aquatic creatures and plants were born. Thakuran, on her part, created a pair of male and female geese/swans from her collarbone and named them

Has and Hasail. They were imbued with life and were sent to the flooded earth, where they lived for a long time. One day they laid two eggs. In Campbell's version, the eggs were eaten by a boar. Then, Thakur sent Jaher-era to guard the eggs. Jaher-era is the national goddess of fertility, her task is to preserve and protect life from the stage of foetus to a full grown baby in a mother's womb.[11] The male child was named Pilchuharam and the female child, Pilchuburhi. The geese carried them away and were crying for shelter. Thakur was informed about this. He instructed Lita to create the earth with the help of other animals. The earth, called Pipiri, became the new house of Pilchuharam and Pilchuburhi. When they grew up, Lita desired them to procreate, but they were innocent. Lita went far and wide in search of an intoxicant herb. They reached Tatiyhari, a picturesque place under a hill, where they found intoxicated monkeys. Lita collected a herb root called *ranuran*, and prepared a rice-beer of grass seed (*erierba*). The rice-beer (*handi*) was properly brewed and given to Pilchuharam and Pilchuburhi to drink. Under the spell of its intoxication, the primal man and primal woman of the Santal community cohabited and had five sons and six daughters. According to Campbell's version, Pilchuharam was instructed to make a plough, sow grains and grow the first fruits, and Pilchuburhi was taught to reap and thresh the grain, husk rice and cook food. Then they were instructed to identify the intoxicant herb *Ranu*, and given the recipe to prepare rice-beer (handi). Hembram's version of the story records that they had seven sons and seven daughters who lived in two separate localities under the care of Pilchuharam and Pilchuburhi. On a hunting trip, the men met the women and bonded with them. The Santal population multiplied. As their numbers increased, they moved from place to place and wandered far and wide for food and shelter. They visited Khaman, Khoj, Ereatna, Peterbare and Sasangbede. At each place, they stayed for twelve years. During their wanderings at Harata, they became victims of fire rain (*sangal-jari*). At Khoj Khamen, it rained fire for seven days and seven nights. The fire rain was brought about by sinful living and was a curse by Thakur to punish them. It destroyed their jungles, trees and animals. This was the 'rain fire of destroying sins' where the 'earth becomes hot and the sky red'. After the great destruction, they entered the seven-river valley called Champa where the soil was fertile and the plants and seeds thrived and the birds sang. They made this place their abode for twelve years[12] and named this blessed and prosperous region *Cea-Champa*. It was the land of light and happiness where a seed could be sown. Whenever the Santals identify a settlement, they must locate the presence of a tree (*sorjom*), a bird (*sim*) and grass seed (*erierbe*) in a forest as an auspicious sign.

Feminine Presence in the Binti

The narrative provides a 'remote sensing device' on the ethnic history and ideas of feminine identity in their society. The feminine presence is central in the creation myth. Man and woman existed at the pre-creative stage of creation, in their formless aspect as Thakur and Thakuran. Their invisible presence acquired visibility in the creation of the first man, Pilchuharam, and the first woman, Pilchuburhi. The primal pair are coeval and share equality throughout the epic. The feminine presence reasserts itself in the first social group of the Santals which consists of five sons and six daughters of Pilchuharam and Pilchuburhi. The twelve septs of the Santals trace their lineage to this first group of heavenly ancestors. Binti describes at great length the migration pattern where men and women are co-partners in the journey and women endure pain and suffering along with the men. The primal couple, Thakur and Thakuran, are the archetypal male and female, and share a continuity with the human male and female on earth. At various points of the myth, the following male and female couples are introduced and they play complementary roles:

Male	*Female*
Thakur	Thakuran
Pilchuharam	Pilchuburhi
Maran Buru (=Life)	Jahar-era
Hansa (male goose)	Hasial (female goose)
Man on earth	Woman on earth

It can be inferred that values of partnership and complementarity of the sexes hold dear to the Santals. A popular Santal saying is 'left hand (*legeti*, standing for woman) is equally useful and powerful as the right one (representing men)'.[13]

Some passages of Binti describe the specific roles assigned to men and women in Santal society. Even here, superiority of one sex over the other is not proclaimed. Boys are taught the art of agricultural activities and are instructed to make the plough. Girls are taught household chores such as to keep the house clean, to separate, thresh and winnow the grain. Campbell's version of the narrative records the recipe for making rice-beer (handi) which till today is the preserve of women.

T. Hembram (1996: p. 126) has drawn attention to the 'aetiological motif' of the narrative. In simple language related to the matter of the heart, it takes into account the natural attraction between genders and the need for pairing together to foster a harmonious relationship. The Santal narrative gives a gender-inclusive model of the origin myth (ante) that is open to women. The divine feminine is both legitimate and normative, and provides a role model for the women. By giving a significant place to the feminine principle in the Binti from the very abstract (Thakuran), to the concrete, the first woman (Pilchuburhi) of the human race, women members of society participate in the collective power of the 'feminine' that far transcends their position and their culturally constructed identity in society.

Feminine Presence in the Jaher, the Sacred Grove

The Santal religion is a living example of one of the most primal forms of worship. The Santals do not worship idols or a built temple; nor do they invoke the deity in the form of an image. They have an unassailable faith in a creator god who has many epithets, called *bongas*, eternal supernatural beings, whose spirits are accessible everywhere. They worship in an open-air sanctuary called *jaher* or *jaher than*, a sacred grove of sal trees, established outside the village. Whenever a village is established a jaher or an open-air shrine is located. According to anthropologist, nature as an object of worship appears in the religious consciousness of the world in eight or nine thousand BC—a form of nature worship which appeared between the close of the food-gathering and early agricultural period of human civilization. The jaher reflects the primacy of faith preserved in ancient times. A Santal settlement is usually established in a picturesque setting surrounded by rolling hills, water courses and cluster of trees that are inseparable from Santal life, such as a cluster of sal (*Shorea robusta*), mahua (*Madhuca indica*), karam (*Adina cordifolia*), pipal (*Ficus religiosus*), palas (*Buta frondosa*), lac-bearing kusum (*Schleichera triuga*). The most predominant tree is the sal, called *sarjom*, a tree yielding timber, straight and tall with lush broad leaves.

I visited a jaher outside Karandih village. Before 1965, the jaher was very large and full of cluster of trees. With the spread and flow of industrialization, the area of the grove has been reduced considerably. The Santals living in the area have built a primary school about 100 yards away from the shrine. They have covered the open-air shrine with a roof and cemented the floor. At the base of the tree lie three stones representing their three gods: Jaher-era, Marang Buru and Moreiko. In contrast to the modern urban jaher, in Talsa village, the jaher is located outside the village. It has ancient trees belonging to the primal forest. It is essential that a jaher must have a cluster of sal trees standing in a row of two, three or five. This jaher had three sal trees in a row; the fourth is an ashan tree with a stone at it base representing Pargana Bonga; the fifth and last was a mahua tree under which the goddess Gosain-era is established.

The relationship of the great goddess to nature is perennial and can be traced in many ancient cultures of the world. In the case of the Santals, this relationship is expressed as the adoration of the feminine principle in the form of a grove, with Jaher-era, the lady of the grove as its presiding deity. The jaher is the residence of four other deities. Apart from Jaher-era, there is Marang Buru (literally the highest mountain), who is regarded as the creator god, a source of knowledge, water and human acts. The next god is Moreiko, which means five[14] primal males who established the Santal village. Turuiko (meaning six) refers to the six females who are responsible for the succeeding generations of Santals, and Gosain-era, the spirit of motherhood. Thus, there are three Santal female figures who play a significant role in the jaher.

Here the sacred manifests itself as the most primal of forms of the deity, the mother principle in its raw, natural aspect as nature itself. The feminine presence in the jaher manifests as Jaher-era, the mother goddess, whose latent and potential power of germination, fertility, growth and abundance is celebrated during different periods of the year: in the five-day festival of *Sihore* in the harvest season (November-December); in springtime during the *Baha-Parab* (February and March); in *Erok-puja* at the time of sowing (June-July); in *Hariar Sim* when the first shoots of the rice paddy burst in to bloom (July-August); and in *Janthar-puja* during the first gathering of husked rice (November-December).

Jaher-era, the presiding mother goddess is consistently invoked throughout the year for protection, abundance and for good fortune of the community, animal kingdom, forests, plants, rivers, mountains and the whole of nature. The whole of nature is holy and sacred. This perception of wholeness is echoed in the invocations and prayers to the mother goddess:

> We pray that (May the goddess) keep the animals away
> But do not harm them,
> Keep them harnessed,
> Keep them covered,
> Tie them if they are too many,
> Drive them away, so that they should not be harmed
> and,
> We should not be harmed.
> May you take this offering and also feed
> those whose name I do not know.
> Accept this offering,
> And accept it with joy.[15]

In the nature-woman complex of the Santals, women are excluded from performing any significant rituals at the jaher. However, during the spring festival, Naika-era, the priest's wife, who is looked upon as 'an earthly representative of Jaher-era'[16] is the first one to be informed about the forthcoming festival as a mark of reverence. The message is communicated through a song which is meant to alert her about the forthcoming festival.

The intimate connection of the feminine spirit to vegetation in Santal society is possibly responsible for women being repositories as well as custodians of traditional plant lore of the area. On investigation, it was found that women of the villages visited were aware of the following different herbs and their medicinal properties that were used as home remedies: (1) *kari-buhu* (used for blood cleansing), (2) *neem* (used for making oil and for purification in smallpox), (3) *sal* (bark used as medicine), (4) *mahua* (flowers used in food and fruit used for compressing oil), (5) *rannu* (an intoxicant herb used in making rice-beer), (6) *bansa* (bamboo shoots used for cooking), (7) *sarso* (mustard seed used for oil), (8) *rali* root (used for colds and coughs), (9) turmeric (used in cooking and birth ceremonies), (10) *japa* (flowers for oil), (11) mango seed (used for dysentery), (12) *lowa* (fruit for women's ailments), (13) *bija* bark (for the stomach), (14) *nilakantha* (root for male ailments) and (15) *gai-gotor* (creeper for heatstroke).

The inseparable connection between women's fertility and vegetative fertility is vividly expressed in the karam tree (*Adina cordefolia*) festival in which the worship of the tree goddess is performed by women alone. The ceremony takes place in the *manjhithan*, a sacred platform located in the village square. A branch of the karam tree is placed on the raised platform. Unmarried girls sow a variety of seeds of the supporting crops of the area in earthen pots and sprinkle water on it for seven days during the harvest season. The seed of crops that are propitiated provide food for six months. One may draw a parallel between the fertility of the soil and the power of the fertility of women. The Santal terminology and poetic expressions draw out these metaphors rather successfully. During pregnancy a woman is described as 'one who has collected a bundle of seeds', and during birth as 'bursting of a paddy bale'.[17] These equations link women's fertility and soil regeneration. The associations of women with vegetation is perhaps the basis of the statement made by C.R. Manjhi who deeply regards that the 'Jaher is in the memory of women'.

Feminine Presence in Socio-economic and Cultural Spheres

The Santal woman, like in most tribal communities, share the responsibilities of daily existence on equal terms with the menfolk. The division of labour between men and women is not only equitably distributed, women play a significant role in almost all spheres—economic, social or cultural—and work side by side with men. Throughout the year during the high seasons, the Santal husband and wife jointly engage themselves in agricultural activities. Throughout the day, women are engaged in weeding, winnowing of paddy, sowing and collection of crops from the field for harvesting. Domestic chores like fetching water, firewood, cooking, housekeeping, marketing, caring for the children, making rice-beer (handi), decorating and painting the facades of their village huts are the exclusive preserve of women. Today, market forces have inspired the women to take up other jobs as construction workers, or run small grocery shops, or make a living by selling leaf-plates, mats and brooms. Santal women who have had some access to modern education are taking up office jobs as well. Women are responsible for household cash and finance in the home, and in all domestic management, male and female hold equal power.

It is interesting to observe that, theoretically, women appear subordinate (as Santali folk tales often reflect a lower status for women)[18] but, on the practical level, they are very far from being subservient or a drudge. A Santal woman has a very strong position in the domestic sphere. The social relations between men and women are free, open and natural. The women have a clearly defined role in the home and share an honourable position. With the growth of urban centres round their village, Santal women also work in the town and are equal breadwinners. Santal informants in Karandih recalled the complementarity between the sexes and said 'We advise our men, if you understand women (= wife), you will be able to keep a balance between nature and power in your march of life'.[19]

The most significant feature of the Santal is that there is no stigma attached to being born a girl. The course of life for a young girl is shaped by the ethos of the community in which she lives. In tribal Santal families, all members of a family contribute to the day-to-day activities and share responsibilities. A girl is mostly found helping her parents in agricultural activities. However, to be a girl child in the deep sylvan environment of a Santal village means to share domestic affairs and economic activities of the family. As a child of three or four years, she begins her work for the family as a sister. She plays with her younger brother or sister, either carrying or cajoling the child in a piece of cloth slung from her neck. As the young girl grows up, her work as a babysitter decreases; she follows her mother to the waterfront to fetch water and joins her in household work. As she grows older, she may accompany her mother to the fields to pick fruits, herbs, mahua flowers, and to collect edible roots and leaves. A little older, she gets involved in seasonal activity. She husks paddy during harvest time and plasters the doors and verandas, and keeps the kitchen clean. Till the age of ten to eleven years, she is her mother's trail. After that begins the age of freedom when she gets a respite from daily household chores. From then on, she may enjoy her freedom and join the other girls of her age. She, with her peer group of boys and girls, goes to the marketplace and festivals. As she grows older, she gets more freedom. When she grows to full womanhood, she is usually her mother's replica in miniature and is able to control and act as a young mistress in the house. She normally has the ability to cook, clean and serve food three times a day and take care of the family and domestic chores. Children are gently treated and are seldom whipped. The girl child enjoys the same freedom and privilege as the boys.[20] The most important stages of growth are marked by ritual in which the whole community participates—for instance, when the girl child is usually named the third day after her birth. The girl child is named on the basis of traditionally established rules. The eldest daughter is given the name of her paternal grandmother, the second that of the maternal grandmother, the third that of the paternal grandfather's sister, and the fourth that of the maternal grandfather's sister. Most Santal women have two names. One is the 'real name' (*mul*) and the other is the nominal second name (*balina*). The first corresponds to the relative after whom she is named. After the naming ceremony, another rite of significance is *caco chattier*, an initiation rite which admits the child as a full member of the Santal society. Both boys and girls must undergo the ritual in order to be full members of the community.

As the girl grows to womanhood, she is expected to marry. In Santal communities, age is no criterion for marriage. The bride may be younger, older or of the same age as the groom. There are seven types of marriage.[21] The Santal term for marriage is *bapla*. In case of the first, the most popular form, the marriage is arranged by a matchmaker, or may be arranged by the families themselves (*raebar-bapla*). A prominent role is played by the *jog-manjhi*, the superintendent of the morals of the youth. The parents of the bridegroom have to pay *pan* or bride price. In return, the parents of the girl have to give certain auspicious items to the groom such as a cock, a brass cup, and a brass utensil. When a similar form of marriage is arranged by very poor people, there is no payment of any kind. The simplest form of marriage is known as *tunki bapla*, deriving its name from *tunki*, a small bamboo basket in which the bride-to-be carries her things to the groom's house. The ritual is simple. When the bride comes to the groom's house with her tunki, he smears her head with vermilion powder. If a widower of a divorced man marries a widow or a divorced woman, the *pan* is half of what is given for an unmarried girl. This is known as *sang-bapla*. Other forms of marriages outside the normal rung are also acceptable. In *chardi-jawac-bapla*, the bridegroom comes to live with the family of the bride; in the *kirin-jawac-bapla*, a husband is arranged for a girl who has been made pregnant by a man who cannot marry her. Although marriage by force is rare, marriage can be forced on a young maiden by smearing her forehead with vermilion or red ochre (*itut-bapla*). On the hand, if a young man has had physical relations with a girl and refuse to marry her, she is allowed to force herself in his house (*nir-bolok-bapla*) in a 'run-in' kind of marriage. The girl sits quietly in the boy's house and the mother-in-law tries to burn chilli, pepper and tobacco leaves inside the room where the girl has taken shelter and shower abuses on her. If the girl can withstand the trial, the mother-in-law yields and accepts her. She calls the girl to come out of the room. If the young man agrees, the couple is married and both of them pay a small fine. No bride price is paid for this form of marriage.

In another form, the marriage is arranged by the couples themselves, i.e. it is a love marriage, where the choice of the partner rests on the individuals. This has been called *appangir-bapla* or marriage by free choice. The Santal youth, male and female, mix freely and meet during the fairs and seasonal festivals. They may even strike a friendship in the fields where they work. These free and open meetings often assume permanent bonding in marriage. The courtship ritual of love has its own dynamics and mode of communication. The lovelorn man often approaches his paramour with a flower as a token of his love. If she accepts the flower, it indicates her willingness that she has accepted his offer.

The courtship is socially acceptable and there is no gossip about their relationship. When the couple is noticed, they are summoned by the panchayat in the presence of the parents of both the parties, along with the village headmen. The boy and girl disclose their courtship before the panchayat. It is customary that the village headmen condemn their secret meetings and advise them to marry. If they agree to the advice, all the people present in the assembly agree to go ahead with the arrangements for their marriage. A love marriage is less elaborate and is usually performed in the presence of the village headman and the panchayat. After the wedding, the groom is required to pay *suffi* money as fine for a feast for the whole village.

There is no term in Santali language for husband and wife. Both the genders are called by the common word *begait*, which echoes an equality between the sexes. The relationship between the Santal husband and wife is based on mutual respect and caring, and is often romantic. Inasmuch as the roles of the couple are divided in the home, they are shared in equal measure outside the home.

The Santal norms are fairly free and pro-women as far as divorce[22] and widow-remarriage is concerned. Divorce may be granted in three circumstances: (1) a wife may divorce an adulterous husband; (2) a husband who is unwilling to cohabit with her may seek divorce; and (3) in some rare cases where a woman is denounced as a witch by consensus of the community, the husband may divorce his wife. In case of a divorce, a woman returns to her parents' home and is given a maintenance. The logic behind this custom is explained by the Santals—'we gave her in marriage not to die but to live; therefore, a woman has to be supported and maintained'. The divorce usually entails certain payments and a formal ceremony that socially terminates the matrimonial relations.

The Santals have their own institution of widow-remarriage with widowers, or in some cases, with bachelors. In this form of remarriage, the formal consent of the widow is necessary. The widows can remarry with the consent of the village council. If a woman with sons becomes a widow and has possessions, the male members of the house are obliged to see that their wealth and rights are protected and they have no right to interfere with her.

One of the most liberal institutions of remarriage is found among one of the earliest of Santal institutions of hunting. Although, Santal women were given bows and arrows to protect themselves from the Muslims and allowed to participate in archery competitions with men, they were not allowed to accompany the men for their traditional hunting escapades. However, they were set free to remarry if their husbands were killed during the hunt. This progressive pro-woman custom still prevails among the Santals who go for a hunt of a predatory animal into the deep jungles. The men 'release' the women by performing a simple ceremony. An iron bangle worn by women as a sign of marriage is offered to the mother earth (*dharti ayo*), then daubs of vermilion are applied to the joint of the bangle, and the forehead of the woman is marked with the same vermilion. Women repeat this daily ritual. The bangle is taken out and given to the husband who goes for a hunt. If the husband returns unharmed, the bangle is returned to the wife. If the husband dies in the hunt, the woman is free to marry again. There is a women's lore connected with good and bad omens which proclaim the husband's condition at the hunt.[23]

The male attitude towards women tends to be sympathetic. Santals take collective pride in their womenfolk, and their protection from aliens

is considered to be the duty of every male member. There are known instances where collective social action has been taken by men to save the honour of women. Often the case of man born of a Santal woman and a Birhor, a tribal from another community, is quoted widely. The man named Madhu Singh from a Birhor tribe was regarded as an alien, and the Santals did not consent a woman from their community to marry an alien. Threatened by his presence, the tribe left Cea Champa area and settled elsewhere. A similar provocation, by the king of Saont motivated the Santals to migrate to another place.[24]

On the whole, outside marriage as well as in marriage, the relationship between men and women is open, free, caring and congenial. Raghunath Tudu, an artist of repute, writer and a person responsible for bringing Santal women into modern theatre, explained:

> There is no eve-teasing, no rape, no social tension about dowry or *dahej*, no dowry deaths, or suicide in our tribal society, as it is in our urban society today. Men relate to women in a subtle and pure way. We consider woman to be our mother. A woman is a part of *purusha* (a man); without her there is no *samaj*, no society.

The Santals have a well-organized socio-political structure which is responsible for the discipline of the community. It is widely known that the British administration was highly impressed by the well-knit social organization of the Santals.

The smallest social organization[25] of the Santal village responsible for regulating day-to-day life in the village consists of five persons, each with a distinct function. The headman of the village is known as *manjhi*. He is assisted by *paramanik*. Then comes the village priest known as *naeke*, who is the ritual specialist responsible for conducting the yearly rituals and other celebrations; the next is *jog manjhi*, who guards the conduct and morals of the tribe; the last is *godet*, the messenger whose job is to inform the villagers of the place and time of the meetings.

The next level of administration is known as *pargana*, consisting of ten to twenty villages, with the *pralgnit* at its head and several *manjhis* below him. The third, or the highest, level of administrative unit is the *shikar parishad* or *lo bir*, which is the seat of the traditional form of supreme court of the Santals that mainly deals with cases of breakdown of morals. The agency has the authority of *bitlaha*, or pronouncing a Santal from their community as an outcaste—a punishment usually granted to an over-indulgent man or woman who has entered into an adulterous relationship with an alien.

This well-established, long-standing system of authority has undergone changes under the police administration of the Indian Constitution. The Santals as citizens of the nation state have had to adhere to government rules with the local panchayats having judicial power. The traditional structure of the village councils is sometimes undercut or even rendered ineffective. Disputes are discussed at the village council first. Usually, cases related to women are restricted to the village council as it is against their prestige to 'go public'. While, women are not part of the village council, it is a custom among the Santals that, during interrogation, a woman's word is taken as truth and is never doubted.[26] It is obligatory on the part of the council to ask her to convey her grievances. The system of '*lo bir*' has almost gone underground as criminal cases are dealt by the court. Women are more bound to the traditional system and often fall prey to the 'double-structured' administrative system of modern society. Yet, all informants were of the view that the continuity of modern Santal identity is largely contributed to by the parallel existence of the traditional unit of social organization. Experience bears witness to the fact that the traditional village council can, in a matter of a mere week, bring together thousands of Santals to fight for a common cause (as they did to raise awareness of a rape case) or to share moments of joy in their seasonal celebrations. Most Santals I met feel that the alien interference must be checked by revision of traditional values.

Even a cursory glance at a Santal hamlet will show the significant role women play in creative pursuits of the community.[27] Women's participation in the cultural life is visible throughout. Women play an important role in building and decorating a Santal house. The lower portion of the habitat is built by women and the upper portion by men. The outer walls of the house are neatly smeared with cowdung and decorated with taut geometrical linear motifs and lyrical floral patterns. The primal designs, with the perfection of line with minimalistic symbols, bear ample proof of their innate aesthetic sense. The floors of the house are spotlessly clean. A unique feature of Santal life is their love for songs and dances. There are special songs, musical compositions accompanied by dances for each and every occasion. Women with their male partners are the main participants in such event. There is a dance for every occasion: for marriage ceremonies, seasonal agricultural activities such as sowing, transplanting and harvesting, for stimulating friendship, inviting rain, and there are any number of devotional dances performed at the jaher, the sacred grove celebrating the bounties of the mother goddess and the rhythm of the seasons. In all these performances, women are co-partners in the cultural events of the community.

Taboos for Women

Despite these roles, there are certain taboos for women. Women are excluded from direct participation in religious worship and from sitting in a village council. While they construct and decorate their mud huts, they are debarred from putting the roof of a house. A more pervasive taboo is linked to the plough. The touch of a plough is inauspicious for women; they cannot hold, touch or use it. If the necessity arises, they should seek help of male members. A recent local daily *Johar Sakam*[28] reported the case of one Sanjoni Kisku whose alcoholic husband refused to help. Through sheer desperation, she picked up the plough to till the soil. Her efforts were met with a mixed response. The plough broke into two and she left it in the field. When the men of the village heard about it, all hell broke loose and they beat her up, dragged her and tied her at the place where animals are kept. Sanjoni Kisku reported the behaviour of the menfolk to the Adivasi Mahila Samiti of the area. Opinion is divided on this issue. All informants in Karandih agreed that the old custom should be revised in cases where men do not give helping hand to women.

Feminine Presence in Forbidden Realms: Empowered Healers and Enemies of Society?

While we survey the roles women play in Santal society, it is important to draw attention to the Santal response to the presence of the mysterious power of women. Power lies hidden in the personalities of mothers, wives, sisters, and daughters. While domestic roles of women are readily accepted, the power linked to women who assume religious, or often defiant, roles is looked upon with great suspicion. In mainstream Hinduism wherever the notion of power is applied or linked to women, it invariably acquires an evil, degraded form. It has been pointed out that only those constructions of the feminine role receive privilege 'which accord with the prevailing (or emerging) patriarchal ideology'.[29] On the other hand, it is generally in the tribal or folk context that the evil role of the feminine gets accommodated alongside the benign. The tradition of the empowered women that scholars have labelled as 'witches' is an inseparable part of the Santal social life.

Field studies on the Santals and the age-old retellings in the *Horkoren Mare Hapramko Reak Katha*, as retold by the Santal patriarchs, state that there is a long-standing tradition of women who have access to special magical powers. These powers, mostly negative, are acquired under special training, by women, who are in touch with the forbidden mystically complex world of the Bongas. These women are sometimes designated as *dains*, the demonic females (*bisayanis*), and poisonous females (*phukrins*) who are skilled in spells. Critical scholarship has applied the broad label 'witches' to describe such women. In current modern feminist discourse,[30] the term 'witches' is taken to mean 'the wise women'. However, the usage is not free from their negative associations to describe the women of evil or malevolent intent.

It is difficult to state why or how the tradition came to occupy an important place in Santal society. We know that women are excluded to participate in rituals in the Santal tribe. Legend holds that Marang Buru, the presiding deity, wanted to impart a secret teaching to men so that they could subjugate the women. But the reverse happened. The story of the origin of witchcraft,[31] essentially a woman-centred myth, is an instance of the ritualized rebellion designed by women to empower themselves and to find their feet in the world of men. The story goes that one day an assembly of men went to Marang Buru and entreated him to give them power to exercise control over women as their commands were ignored and flouted. Marang Buru complied, and asked them to mark out some sal leaves with their blood. The men decided to come the next day. The wives, on their part, had secretly followed the husbands and learnt about their plan of action. On their return home, the women questioned the justice of men and reflected: 'before they marry us, they flatter us and follow us like dogs; now when we become wives, they deem us bad and want to get rid of us'. Having thought so, they returned home and fed their husbands a sumptuous meal with liberal draughts of rice-beer. Satiated with the drink, the men fell asleep. Then in secret, the women worked out a strategy of action with their sister network and assumed the guise of men. They donned themselves with male loin-cloths, wore turbans and fixed beards and moustaches with goats' hair. They went to Marang Buru for an antidote, prayed and told him that they were disgusted with their wives. Marang Buru readily asked them to make the special sign on the sal leaf with their blood, taught them the secret technique (*jharani*) and the incantation (*mantra*) relating to witchcraft, which qualified them to paralyse or devour anyone with a spell. Their mission accomplished, the women returned home empowered.[32]

The next day, the men set out to meet Marang Buru to find that a bunch of men (actually their wives) impersonating them had already taken the secret formula from him. Marang Buru realized the trickery of the women, and so he taught the men the craft of witch-doctors (*ojha* and *jan-guru*). Since then the female witches and male ojhas/jan-gurus are enemies.

While the former have the power to manifest, the latter are agents who neutralize their power. Some observations on this story may be summerized. Firstly, the story centres around a power struggle between the sexes; secondly the women's initiative to acquire power challenges the accepted norms in Santal society. Thirdly, women build an innovative strategy based on trick and delusion to acquire power. Fourthly, they negotiate a place for themselves in a ritualized context, an area denied to them in the social sphere. The only power divested to women is negative power which ultimately gives licence to men as ojhas to exercise control over them. The legend is a striking example of heresy, of crossing boundaries of the accepted Santal norms that pose a challenge to male authority. In the likeness of heresy, the legend mirrors the protagonist as a trickster who offers a corrective to imbalanced social behaviour. In the story, the women delude the Bonga by their male garb to create a position of authority for themselves. Being a heresy, the phenomenon of hostility and violence has created an institution based on suspicion. Thus, one can infer that while the Santal imagination is relatively open to accommodating radical personifications of the feminine presence, they are generally intolerant of the expression of power on the social plane.

The witches have been a part of Santal subculture and have survived. The history of the witch in Santali land is the history of the power of the demonic feminine who causes grief, sickness and disease. Rarely does one find instance of the positive power of the feminine. Witches carry a power to be dreaded, feared and ultimately banished or surpressed. It is held that witches induce sickness, spread the 'seed of disease', create enmities between people and family members, break relationships, create quarrels; they can cause a cattle epidemic or a blight of crops.[33] They also act as agents of murder and death by exercising their power over a victim. The witches use intractable and invisible means to achieve their ends. On account of their ubiquitous nature and invisibility, they are dreaded and despised. Hence, they have been described as 'thorns of the Santal social fabric' (Mukherjea 1962: p. 293), 'an enemy of society, ruthless as a murderer, as criminal, the worst foe' (Archer 1946: p. 23). A great majority of witches, whenever identified by a *jan-guru* (witch finder), were excluded, ostracized, prosecuted, tortured and even ruthlessly killed by the community.

The belief in witchcraft and the power of the evil woman has worked havoc in Santal communities.[34] Although both men and women can be declared a witch, invariably it is women who are victims of the accusers. In the course of time, witchcraft has become an established institution built on suspicion. Time and again, it is the vulnerable and supportless woman who is victimized by close relatives. Jealousy or family feuds are the hidden reasons for proclaiming women as witches. Very often, it is the handiwork of scheming relatives who want to settle scores. Most often property disputes and land rights motivate people to pronounce a woman as a witch. Widows who have life interest in land and legitimate claims over property are the most vulnerable victims. Once denounced as a witch, it would imply dire consequences for a woman; but for the male agnates of the family, it would be a *cause célèbre*. According to the Santal custom, the portion of land would be immediately passed over to the husband's male agnates. Govind Kelkar and Dev Nathan have observed that witch-hunting in the Santal community is not due to the lower status ascribed to women but due to the strong position they have in terms of rights in land. According to the two authors, the phenomenon of witch-hunting is an attempt to 'reduce their status' and to 'establish in its place a patriarchy'.[35]

A closer look at the ideology of women's power as supported by the legend (ante) would have us believe that there are two ways of looking at the witch phenomenon in the Santal tribe. If we look at it in the light that it was a heresy instigated by women to free themselves from the authoritarian rule of men, we may come to regard the witch as an enemy of society. However, it is interesting to observe that there is no indigenous term in the Santali language for witch or witchcraft. The closest parallel is *phukrin*, from the term *phuka*, which means one accomplished in the art of healing by means of blowing wind *(phunka)* from the mouth or incantations. A term widely used by Santals in Orissa is probably taken from the Bengali word *jharphuk*, which refers to a process whereby the person removes physical maladies by blowing wind from the mouth. Although the term occurs in the Santali vocabulary, it is of uncommon occurrence. It is replaced by the widely used word *fuskin*,[36] a corruption from the word *phukrin*. Other words in Santali to describe evil women are *dain*, a demonic female, widely used in Orissa, or *bisayani*, the poisonous women (from the Bengali, *bisa* poison, popular in Singhbhum District) and *jharani*, which is popularly applied in the process of exorcism, the technique of casting a spell by means of *jadu*, malefic spell; *nazar*, casting an evil eye; or through *baanamara*, shooting an arrow, symbolically on a human figure drawn embodying the person one wishes evil. All these terms are known in Karandih village. Further, we see that scholars have continued to use an alien term (witch) to describe an indigenous experience. The terms associated with the notion of the power of women have been understood through an occidental perspective and give an outsider's view of Santal society. It is widely accepted there that the term *phukrin* was originally associated with power of healing but, over a period of time through several mutilations and colonial subversions, it has acquired derogatory meaning. If any conclusions are to be drawn through mere usages of these words to describe the phenomenon of the 'witch', we may see that the terms themselves can be interpreted in positive or negative way. However, only the negative associations have survived. If we look at the tradition of the witch from the perspective that these women were/are in fact custodians of a mysterious power which can be used for benign purposes, the 'witch' would appear as an 'empowered healer'. Although the studies on Santals have mainly highlighted the negative powers of the witch,[37] there is a certain strain of ambiguity that runs through the interpretations that have been offered. Mukherjea, citing an old legend contends: 'Witches can be useful devils and can be of immense service to men. This we see in the story of Ranjit Bonga, where a witch, on her secret being out, pronounced to be a tribal *ojha* and cured the diseases of the Santals'.[38]

Although, instances of women diviners and healers are rare, I quote a case of Smt Namita Pramanik a Santali woman recorded by Choudhuri, who was denounced as a witch but later found to be an empowered healer:[39]

> Even before my marriage I used to see 'Visions'. The realisation of some sort of power came to me one day when my eldest son was running very high temperature: my husband had forsaken me and I had nobody to look upon for help. I was penniless. I was frantically seeking the divine grace of Goddess Tara throughout the night and fell asleep early at dawn. While I was coming out of my hut I found a twenty rupee note lying on the road. I picked it up and spent the money to get medicine for my son. He recovered. This incident convinced me of the divine grace of Goddesses. On several occasions I dreamt of herbal medicines and later on those herbs were used very effectively by me on various occasions. My co-villagers dubbed me initially as a fuskin (= phukrin) but later on, my success on various applications of those herbs convinced them of the good service that I have been offering them. Presently they are very helpful and obliging. They have restored the landed property of my maternal grandmother to me.
>
> I perform worship of Goddess Tara and Goddess Shyama Kali on Thursdays and Saturdays. During these worships I pass into a state of trance. People normally ask me questions when I am in such condition. To divine the real cause, I clean a spot in front of the altar and sprinkle vermilion thereon, light up incense; betel-nut with pan leaves, sugar and sugar candy are offered to the Goddesses. After a short spell of meditation, I recite incantations and at the same time draw vertical lines on the spot cleaned. If the recitation is completed by the time I draw ten lines, then it would be proclaimed that the suffering was due to some

omissions on the part of the sufferer—like he/she might have omitted to offer some promised sacrifice to some God/Bonga. If the recitation ends at fifteen lines, the suffering is due to bad actions of the sufferer; if incantations end at twenty, there would be the machinations of the witch, and if the incantation exceeds twenty lines, there would not be anything to be done by me. In such cases, I politely advise the querents to try elsewhere. In other cases, I normally suggest medicines or expiation to be done.

According to my informant, Dalpati Murmu, the Santali words to designate the 'witch' themselves unfold a double-structured world of the Bongas, the gods of the Santals—the evil Bongas who work through the dains and the bisayanis, and the luck-bringing benign Bongas who empower the phukrin and the jharani or the ojha, a witch-doctor to remove the evil spells, in sickness and in grief that attack individuals. We are inclined to believe that it is plausible that these are two separate traditions among the Santals. Unfortunately, only the instances of negative power of women has been spoken of and recorded. The positive healing powers of women have gone largely undocumented, unrecognized or willfully suppressed under the influence of a thoroughly narrow patriarchal interpretation.

Concluding Remarks

This brief overview brings to light that the criteria that are applied to assess the empowered status of women in urban areas cannot be applied to women living in pre-modern tribal societies. For many of us living at the hard cutting edge of modernity, empowerment is defined in relation to the worldview and value system of industrial societies. It is paradigm that expresses itself as an aspiration for autonomy, free choice, opportunity and freedom that an individual enjoys in a social community. The contemporary paradigm of empowerment runs counter to the tribal ethos. All pre-modern societies have had to cope with the intrusion of industrial urban values. The encounter between the pre-modern and post-industrial value system has worked havoc. Tribal cultures today are barely struggling to survive. Some are totally dislocated and decentred from their cultural roots. In others, there is a revival to assimilate and transform to keep pace with the socio-economic changes. However, one cannot deny the difference between the two cultural sensibilities. So vastly separated is the pre-modern sensibility from the post-industrial perception that parameters that define and validate the worldview and value system of technological societies of today contradict and disrupt the cultural sensibility of pre-modern societies. The deep concern for the fragility of the earth's ecology and its multifarious implications for human survival has inspired a different and more serious kind of attention to the worldview of pre-modern cultures. This is primarily because their life patterns were governed and inextricably bound by nature. We have seen earlier that nature has a strong presence in Santal life—the role of the jaher, the sacred grove, and the ethos that pronounced a prudent and sustainable use of resources. Based on a harmonious partnership of man and nature, the Santal tradition represents a survival of 'the golden age of ecological balance' which is fast disappearing under the impact of rapid industrialization. As the British took over the forest resources and introduced the concept of money economy, alien interventions slowly and systematically transformed the common vital resources into commodities for trading and generating profit. It is no longer possible to relegate the nature-bound lifestyle of the Santal as a mere target of objective study. On the contrary, it is an example of an alternative knowledge system from which we can learn something about the reorganization of society and a reorientation to thought and life.

Empowerment in the Santal tribal context would be defined by the paradigms set out in ideologies of collective memory and an integral view of human beings and nature. While the modern paradigm values individualism, the Santals believe in the shared partnership and participation of men and women in all the spheres of life, be it economic, social, cultural, or even psychological. The idea of complementarity between male and female forming one entity, perhaps the smallest integral unit of social organization, is intrinsic to their faith and identity. This complementarity features in their myths, rituals, songs and dances, and is echoed in their social and economic roles. This idea gets translated in daily life through the social institution of marriage and continues as a singular guiding feature in defining their role and identity. The parameters of an indigenous notion of empowerment impel us to pose the women's question in the collective setting in a different way. Are the Santal norms and practices flexible enough for women to negotiate their respective choices?

If we apply this perspective, we can say that, on the whole, the Santals have an abiding sensitivity towards the feminine. This sensibility is reflected in the conceptual model of their universe in the Binti, in the notion of the sacred grove, as well as their patterns of worship. Man and woman form an unassailable unit. Their relationship is one of complementarity. This relationship gets extended into the social world and creates a system of positive dependency between men and women. We have seen that the Santal system of social relations, as expounded in the institution of marriage, divorce, and widowhood are unbelievably flexible, and lend themselves to considerable number of options and choices. In this respect, a Santal woman appears to be relatively freer than her urban sisters. The hieararchical divisions that are the basis of the caste system do not exist among the Santals. The Santals are given to natural sense of order and go about their respective job, mutually sharing responsibilities. Clearly, the women seem to have a sense of themselves. The contemporary paradigm of empowerment, which holds true in an urban setting, thus runs counter to the tribal ethos. The search for a model to make an assessment has to come from the roots of the tradition which is being explored.

In more ways than one, the Santals are separate from us, so how will their voices be heard? It is interesting to observe that in time of need, Santal women have shown a remarkable resilience and have risen to the occasion. The Santal women have been part of the reform movement. It has been recorded that in the Santal rebellion of 1856, nearly 50 per cent were women and children. Many of them fought the British; some of them also acted as informers. In the tribal tradition of *jansikar*, there is a custom where women in men's guise go for hunting, or to fight enemies. It was reported in a local daily *Sambad Bhaskar Patrika* that one Santal leader who fought with great courage was found to be a female in a male dress.[40] Women were part of the Birsa movement and have continued to participate in tribal cultural movements linked to the preservation and adoption of the Santal language and script, and have played an active role in social development causes. There has been a growing consensus among Santal women about the recent Jharkhand movement. The formation of the Jharkhand Mahila Simiti and its recent meeting in 1987[41] was a landmark in the history of tribals in Bihar. The meeting was attended by a large number of Santal women to discuss their indigenous issues in the light of women's liberation. This goes to show that the Santal women are visible and their voices are being heard.

If we situate the Santal woman in relation to the value system of our urban post-modern categories, we not only distort our interpretations of them but do a disservice to the community under observation. We have only to question the legitimacy of our own approach to the understanding of those cultures. There is an urgent need among feminists to recognize cultural plurality and diversity among women. While the notion of sisterhood is now looked upon as global and embraces all women across the world, we can no longer undermine and marginalize other theoretical positions and lifestyles. Nor should we venture to subsume ethnic cultures into a mainstream universal model of feminism. In this respect, we have much to learn from the Santals.

ACKNOWLEDGMENTS

I wish to record my deep gratitude to all those who made my research project on the Santals a reality. I would like to express my deep sense of gratitude to Dr Kapila Vatsyayan whose support enabled me to carry out fieldwork in Karandih village near Jamshedpur. My special thanks to Shri M.C. Joshi who offered his invaluable help and support. I am indebted to Shri Girija Dutt, the then Director of Bihar Institute of Rural Development, Ranchi, for his kind hospitality and for the excellent arrangements he made for my field trip. I visited four Santal villages near Jamshedpur, namely, Karandih, Talsa, Marcha and Sarjamda. My visit to these places was greatly facilitated by my four informants, all Santals, who either belong to or are well acquainted with the areas I visited. P.C. Hembram, New Delhi, guided me to Karandih; Dalpati Murmu, Archeological Survey of India, Ranchi, D. Hansda, Principal, Lal Bahadur Shastri College, Karandih, and C.R. Manjhi, headman of Karandih, relentlessly answered all my questions and guided me throughout my field trip. I am also indebted to Raghunath Tudu, writer and theatre director, Karandih, for his help and support.

APPENDIX 1

The Binti: The Origin Narrative of the Santals

Campbell's version	*P.C. Hembram's version*	*In popular memory (C.R. Manjhi's version, Karandih)*
1. Thakur Jiv, the heavenly being and the waters pre-existed creation	1. Early life on the earth (*monchopuri*) was flooded.	1. In the beginning, all was water.
2. Malin Budhi made an attempt to make a pair of human beings with froth or still clay. The first attempt was foiled by Sin Sadom. She again tried to fashion them and then animated them with life of birds. They appeared as a pair of geese.	2. Then came the creation of aquatic plants and animals.	2. Maran Buru made the earth, Hiri Pipri.
3. Thakur Jiv raised the earth from beneath the waters with help of fish, crab, earthworm and tortoise.	3. Thakuran in heaven created two birds, Hansa and Hasial, male and female goose from her collar grime. Thakur gave them life and they flew to monchopuri, the earth.	3. The earth with a karam tree was surrounded on three sides by water.

	Campbell's version		*P.C. Hembram's version*		*In popular memory (C.R. Manjhi's version, Karandih)*
4.	Thakur Jiv caused to grow plants like karam tree and sirom, dhubi, and ghas.	4.	They laid two eggs on a lotus leaf and the primal male and female Pilchuharam and Pilchuburhi were born from there. The leaf sank and the two were carried by the geese until they found a place on the earth.	4.	The place was full of green. There were trees, grass, creepers and animals on the land, and fish, snake and tortoise in water.
5.	The female laid a pair of eggs, the boar ate them. Thakur sent Jaher Era, the goddess, to protect the eggs. She hatched the eggs and the primal male and female Pilchuharam and Pilchuburhi were born.	5.	When they grew up, Lita/Maran Buru planned to increase their progeny and set to find a stimulant	5.	Maran Buru created two birds, who laid two eggs.
6.	Thakur-Jiv created Kapil-cow, who had two bull-calves.	6.	Rice-beer was brewed and, under its spell, they cohabited.	6.	The eggs were on the karam tree near water.
7.	Maran Buru taught (i) how to make a plough, (ii) sow the grains, and (iii) to offer first fruits.	7.	They had five sons and six daughters.	7.	Out of the two eggs, the first man and woman were born.

	Campbell's version		*P.C. Hembram's version*		*In popular memory (C.R. Manjhi's version, Karandih)*
8.	Maran Buru taught how to reap and thresh the grain, and instructed the girl to husk rice and cook it.	8.	The sons and daughters adopted professions, intermingled, and multiplied.	8.	They came to Hiri Pipri where, over a period of time, seven sons and seven daughters were born.
9.	Maran Buru taught them to collect ranu, herb and to prepare handi, rice-beer or an intoxicant drink.	9.	They migrated from place to place for a permanent source of livelihood. They travelled many regions for twelve years.	9.	They lived on the banks of the seven rivers.
10.	Maran Buru poured out the drink for the couple who were stupified by the intoxicant.	10.	On one occasion, they faced a great natural calamity. A rain of fire (lo-bichar) engulfed them for seven days at a stretch.		
11.	They cohabited and made coverings, from banyan leaves. In time to come, they got seven sons and seven daughters.	11.	Finally they reached Champa, the fertile seven-river country, the land of light and happiness, lush with sal plants and trees.		

References: Campbell's version is recast by Hembrom, T. (1996), pp. 88-98; Hembram, P.C. (1984), pp. 6-11, and my informant, C.R. Manjhi, at Karandih (Oct. 1998).

BIBLIOGRAPHY

Archar, W.G., 'The Santal Treatment of Witchcraft', *Man in India*, June, 1947, pp. 103–21.

Biswas, P.C., *Santals of the Santal Parganas*, Bharatiya Adamjati Sevak Sangh, Kingsway, Delhi, 1956.

Boas, Franz, 'Anthropology', *Encyclopedia of Social Sciences*, vols. I–II, Macmillan.

Bodding, Paul Olaf, 'Some Remarks on the Position of Women among the Santals', *Troisi*, vol. I.

Bodding, Paul Olaf, et al., *Traditions and Institutions of the Santals*, Oslo Etnografiske Museum Bulletin, Oslo, 1942.

Bompas, C.H. *Folklore of the Santal Parganas*, London, 1909.

Campbell, Rev., 'Santal Tradition', *India Evangelical Review*, vol. XIX, no. 73, 1892, pp. 1–13.

Culshaw, W.J., *Tribal Heritage: A Study of the Santals*, Butterworth Press, London, 1949.

Choudhuri, A.B., *The Santals Religion and Rituals*, Ashis Publishing House, New Delhi, 1987.

Chawla, Janet, A., 'A Blessing in Disguise', *The Sunday Time of India*, New Delhi, 22 October 1995, p. 16.

—— 'A Woman Activist Theologizes', *Vidyajyoti, Journal of Theological Reflection*, August, 1995, pp. 528–38.

Datta, Kali Kinkar, *The Santal Insurrection of 1855–57*. University of Calcutta, 1988.

Das, A.K. & S.K. Basu, 'An Overview of Santals — Their Past, Present and Future'. Ray, Ujjival Kanti, Basu, S.K. and Das, Amal Kumar, *To Be with the Santals*, Cultural Research Institute, Special series no. 28, Calcutta, 1982.

Hansda, D., *Dr. Doman Sahu 'Samir' (A language and literary profile)*, Santal Sahitya Academy, Karandih, Jamshedpur, 1998.

Hembram, P.C., *Sari-Sarna (Santal Religion)*, Mittal Publications, Delhi, 1988.

Hembrom, T., *The Santals Anthropological—Theological Reflections on Santals and Biblical Creation Traditions*, Punthi Pustak, Calcutta, 1996.

Hunter, *The Annals of Rural Bengal*, vol. I, London, 1868.

Indian Anthropological Society, *Tribal Women in India*, Anthropological Society, Calcutta, 1978.

Johar Sakam (Newsletter on Santals in Hindi) Anka 10, October 98, p. 5.

Kelkar, Govind and Dev Nathan, 'Women's Land Rights and Witches', Mrinal Miri (ed.), *Continuity and Change in Tribal Society*, Shimla, 1993, pp. 109–18.

Kochar, Vijay Kumar, 'Ghosts and Witches among the Santals', *Troisi*, vol. 1.

Kosambi, D.D., *Introduction to the Study of Indian History*, Pilgrim Publishers, Bombay, 1956.

Law, Bimla Churn, *Tribes and Ancient India*. Bhandarkar Oriental Series No. 4, Poona, 1973.

Man. E.G., *Sonthalia and the Santals*, Mittal Publications, Delhi, 1983. (First Indian Edition).

Mahapatra, Sitakanta, *Modernization and Ritual: Identity and Change in Santal Society*, Oxford University Press, New Delhi, 1986.

Mukherjea, Charulal, *The Santal*, A. Mukherjee & Co., Calcutta, 1962.

Murmu Dalpati, 'Kalka: A Ritual Trial for Hunting Disputes in Santal Community', *Journal Indian Anthropological Society*, 18: 129–36, 1983, pp. 129–39.

Narayan, Sachindra, *Play and Games in Tribal India*, Commonwealth Publishers, New Delhi, 1995.

National Commission for Women, *Report on Development of Female Education Among Tribal communities*, National Commission for Women, New Delhi, November 1994.

O'Malley, L.S.S., *Bengal District Gazetteers, Santal Parganas*, The Bengal Secretariat Book Depot, rpt., Logos Press, New Delhi, 1984.

Orans, Martin, *The Santal: A Tribe in Search of Great Traditions*, Wayne State University Press, Detroit, 1965.

Prasad, Narmadeshwar, *Land and People of Tribal Bihar*, Bihar Tribal Research Institute, Ranchi, 1961.

Ray, T. (comp), *Santal Rebellion*: Documents, Subernrekha, Calcutta, 1983.

Ray, Ujjwal Kanti, Basu, S.K. and Das, Amal Kumar, *To Be with Santals*, Cultural Research Institute, Special Series no. 28, Calcutta, 1982.

Raut, Siba Prasad, 'Witchcraft among Santals of Mayurbhanj, *Troisi* vol. 6.

Roy Chaudhury, P.C., 'The Creation of the Santal Parganas', *Bengal Past and Present*, Calcutta, 1962.

Shashi, S.S., *The Tribal Women of India*, Sandeep Prakashan, Delhi, 1978.

—— (ed.), *Encyclopedia of Indian Tribes*, Anmol Publications, Delhi, 1994.

Saha, Chaturbhuj, *The Santal Women. A Social Profile*, Sarup & Sons, New Delhi, 1996.

Singh, J.P., N.N. Vyas and R.S. Mann, *Tribal Women and Development*, Rawat Publications, Jaipur, 1988.

Singh, K.S. *The Scheduled Tribes*, Oxford University Press, Delhi, 1997.

Sinha, R.P., *Santal Hul* (Insurrection of Santal 1955–56) The Bihar Tribal Research Institute, Ranchi, 1991.

Troisi, J. (ed.), *The Santals: Readings in Tribal Life*, Indian Social Institute, 1979, vols. I–X (mimeo).

Tudu, Kanahilal, *Jom Sim Binti* (In Santali Language), Ashaparej Parsalet, Jhargrm, Midnapur, 1993.

NOTES

1. Law, Bimla Churn, *Tribes in Ancient India*. Bhandarkar Oriental Series No. 4, Poona, (1973), III.
2. Kosambi, D.D., *Introduction to the Study of Indian History*, Pilgrim Publishers, Bombay (1956), p. 25.
3. Singh, K.S., *The Scheduled Tribes*, Oxford University Press, Delhi (1997).

4. Mahapatra, Sitakanta, *Modernization and Ritual: Identity and Change in Santal Society*. OUP, Delhi, 1986, Chapter 1, pp. 1–8, 42–4 and 108–15.

5. Ibid., p. 42. For discussion see, Boas, Franz, 'Anthropology', *Encyclopedia of Social Sciences*, vols. I–II, Macmillan, p. 103.

6. For a detailed account of Santal insurrection, see, Datta, Kali Kinkar, *The Santal Insurrection of 1855–57*. University of Calcutta, Calcutta (1988).

7. Mahapatra, Sitakanta, (1986), op. cit., p. 43.

8. There are two main versions of the creation myth. The first is given in the *Horkoren Mare Hapr Amko Katha*: The traditions and institutions of the Santals, Benagaria, Santal Mission of Northern Churches. The collection is taken down by Rev. L.O. Skrefsurd in 1870–71 from an old guru named Kolean, the elder. The first edition of this was published in 1887. In our discussion, we have used P.C. Hembram and Campbell's version recasted serially by Hembrom, T. (1996), pp. 88–98; Hembram, P.C., (1988), pp. 10–11; Mahapatra (1986), pp. 146–9 & 190–2; Bodding (1942) p. 132ff.

9. 'The missionaries made use of the Santal creation narrative, not in order to compare the biblical creator God *elohim* or *Yahweh elohim* with the Santal creator God Thakur Jiv, but to compare the Thakur Jiv's emissary (angel) to the first parents to be their guardian with the Satan to the Christian faith, who in their faith introduced the sin of sexual intercourse between husband and wife, the first parents. For the Santals, successful sexual intercourse between husband and wife is a gift of God, without which the creator God could not have achieved the continuity of humanity upon this earth. The identification of Maran Buru, the emissary (i.e. an angel) of the creator God to mankind who taught them the basic principles of human life with the biblical Satan (though it is now being abandoned and regretted), was one of the greatest theological errors of the Christian missionaries, and it was this identification that arrayed the Santals to take a defensive posture against Christianity.' Cited in Hembrom T. (1996), p. 75.

10. Bodding, P.O. (1942), p. 132.

11. Hembrom T. (1996), p. 112.

12. The number twelve is of special significance to the Santals. The Santals have twelve exogamous totemic septs (*Paris*), divided on the basis of their vocation. Each of them is assigned a geographical location: (1) Kishu, who enjoyed the status of a king located in Champanagar; (2) Hembrum, the noble man given the region of Pouwagulin; (3) Mandi, a wealthy person whose shelter is Ajodya; (4) Siphahi warriors who are not allotted any particular region; (5) Tudu, whose shelter is Duisanagar; (6) Hansala, the agriculturists, who have their abode as Tatijhari; (7) Besra, famous for performing dances, are given Bethl Nagar; (8) Basky and (9) Murmur are known as Thakur. The Murmur are blessed with the power to read and predict human destiny. They are assigned Saragpuri as their abode. The last three groups, Chore, Dodka and Pouria, adopted forbidden practices in family life. They inhabit Gagichowri, Diyan Buru and Setapuripara Pachit areas. It is well recognized that these groups enjoy equal status and

few restrictions exist for establishing matrimonial alliances between them, with the exception of Kisku and Mandi, Tudu and Bisra.

13. Hembram, P.C. (1981), p. 81.

14. According to my informant, C.R. Manjhi, the five here refer to the five elements or energies; earth, water, fire, air, and space.

15. Translated by C.R. Manjhi, Karandih, Bihar.

16. Hembram, P.C. (1989), p. 84.

17. Narrated at the conference on 'Santal Worldview' organized by the Indira Gandhi National Centre for the Arts, September, 1997.

18. See, for instance, the folk tales collected by P.O. Bodding and translated by Bompas, C.H., *Folklore of the Santal Parganas*, London, 1909.

19. According to my informant, C.R. Manjhi, Karandih, Bihar.

20. Narayan, Sachindra, *Play and Games in Tribal India* (1995), pp. 95–6 cite some games meant for Santal girls.

21. For Santal tradition of marriage, see Mukherjea, Charulal (1962), pp. 195–220; Bodding, P.O. (1942), pp. 29–82; Datta Majumdar, Nabendu (1956), pp. 42–45, 83.

22. See Bodding, P.O. (1942), pp. 82–3; Datta Majumdar (1956), p. 45.

23. According to my informant, Dalpati Murmu at Karandih, Bihar. See also, Murmu, Dalpati, Kalka: A Ritual for Hunting Disputes in Santal Community, *Journal Indian Anthropological Society*, pp. 129–88.

24. Cited by Choudhuri (1987), p. 149.

25. Mukherjea, Charulal (1962), pp. 151–85.

26. According to my informants, D. Hansda and C.R. Manjhi in Karandih, Bihar.

27. For a description of Santal dances, see Mukherjea, Charulal (1962), pp. 365–75; and of Santal poetry, see Mahapatra, *Tribal Studies of India, Series T. 145*, Inter India Publications, Delhi, 1992, pp. 157–88.

28. See *Johar Sakam* October 1998, p. 5.

29. Chawla, Janet, 'A Women Activist Theologizes', *Vidyajyoti, Journal of Theological Reflection*, August 1995: p. 531.

30. For some modern interpretations on witches and witchcraft, see Walker, Barbara G., *The Woman's Encyclopedia of Myths and Secrets*, Harper & Row, San Francisco, 1983, pp. 1076–90.

31. For the origin of witchcraft, see Bodding (1942) p. 60; Mukherjea (1962) pp. 94–300; Archer (1947), pp. 103, 121; Raut in *Troisi*, pp. 396–7.

32. On training of witchcraft, see Bodding, P.O. (1942), p. 163; Mukherjea (1962), pp. 300–2.

33. For the power of the witch, see Choudhuri, A.B. (1987), p. 68.

34. For instances of witchcraft, see Raut in *Troisi* (1979) pp. 409–10; Das, Nitayanda, in *Troisi* (1979), pp. 98–9; Choudhuri, A.B. (1987), pp. 1–14; 104–7; 111–13; 115–45; 155; 158–60.

35. Kelkar, Govind and Dev Nathan (1996), p. 118.

36. From Phukrin, a word taken from Khortha dialect. See Choudhuri, A.B.

(1987), p. 95; Cambell, *A Santali-English and English–Santali Dictionary*, Santal Mission Press, Pokhoria, 1933. (2nd Edn.).

37. See references to note 34.
38. Mukherjea (1962), p. 342.
39. Choudhuri (1996), pp. 215–17.
40. Cited by Saha, Chaturbhuj (1996), pp. 105–6.
41. Ibid. Saha lists the main agenda of the movement. See, pp. 121–2.

Women within the Baha'i Community

Susan S. Maneck

The Baha'i faith is the youngest of the world's religions. Baha'u'l-lah , the prophet-founder of the Baha'i faith, was born in Iran in 1817. He claimed to be the latest messenger sent by God, an assertion that irremediably separated the Baha'is from their Islamic background. Baha'is believe that while all religions have been ordained by God, the social teachings of religions have varied according to the needs of the age in which a prophet appears. The central theme of the Baha'i message is the establishment of the unity of humankind in a single global society. This necessitates the establishment of a world government, the achievement of universal education, the elimination of all forms of prejudice and the attainment of full equality of men and women.

No other world religion has been quite as explicit as the Baha'i faith in its support of the principle of the equality of men and women. Baha'is themselves proudly assert it as one of the distinguishing features of the new revelation. This equality does not refer solely to the spiritual plane, for Baha'i scriptures explicitly state that there should be 'no difference in the education of male and female in order that womankind may develop equal capacity and importance with man in the social and economic equation'.[1] They further assert that 'women will enter confidently and capably the great arena of law and politics'.[2]

Yet the understanding of this principle varies considerably among

Baha'is. Many support a higher evaluation of women's traditional roles, particularly in family life, but foresee little change in the roles themselves. Others call for a fundamental transformation of the very structure of relations in community life, which would incorporate values from Baha'i scriptures. Regarding family life, the secretary of the Guardian of the Baha'i faith wrote on his behalf: 'The task of bringing up a Baha'i child, as emphasized time and again in Baha'i writings, is the chief responsibility of the mother.'[3] The Universal House of Justice, the supreme governing body for the Baha'i world, asserts that the corollary to this is that the financial responsibility for supporting the family rests with the husband. The exclusion of women from the Universal House of Justice (which will be discussed later) has tended to perpetuate arguments for 'separate but equal spheres' in other realms as well.

At the same time, Baha'i ideals for a new world order cannot be attained without a change in societal structures, with women playing a leading role:

> The world in the past has been ruled by force, and man has dominated over woman by reason of his more forceful and aggressive qualities both of body and mind. But the balance is already shifting—force is losing its weight and mental alertness, intuition, and the spiritual qualities of love and service, in which woman is strong, are gaining ascendancy. Hence the new age will be an age less masculine, and more permeated with the feminine ideals—or, to speak more exactly, will be an age in which the masculine and feminine elements of civilization will be more evenly balanced.[4]

Many Baha'i women today have tried to hold together all of these statements in the writings by exhibiting the 'supermom' syndrome: fulfilling their roles as wives and mothers while attempting to excel in their chosen careers. Needless to say, this doubling of duties creates tremendous stress for these women. Baha'i are often unaware of the historical contexts in which various pronouncements are made regarding their proper understanding. This issue is confounded by the fact that the development of the Baha'i faith in its early formative period took place in two radically disparate cultures and continents, and its largest expansion has been in yet a third culture. Originating in Iran in the middle of the nineteenth century, the religion spread to North America in the 1890s. By the early 1970s, however, India had the largest population of Baha'is in the world. In the course of this chapter I will trace the role of women within the Baha'i faith from the time of its inception as the Babi movement, through its introduction to the West, and discuss the present challenges it faces within the Indian context.

Tahirih: A Baha'i Paradigm of Womanhood

Nearly every religion has its paradigm of the 'ideal' woman. In Hinduism this has been Sita, the perfect wife who remains faithful to her husband at all costs. In Christianity the most eminent woman is the Virigin Mary, the symbol of motherhood. Islam has Fatimih, daughter of Muhammad, who models the roles of mother, wife and daughter together. Tahirih, the most well-known woman in Babi-Baha'i history, presents a startling contrast to the former models.[5] This gifted poet of nineteenth-century Iran, far from being a dutiful daughter, continually opposed the theological positions of her father, Mulla Salih, a prominent Muslim cleric of Qazvin. Neither is she admired for her success as a wife and mother, since her estrangement from her husband resulted in her forced separation from her children as well.

In 1844 ACE(1260 AH) Siyyid Ali Muhammad al-Bab secretly revealed himself to be the Qa'im, the messianic figure expected by the Shi'ite Muslims. He selected eighteen followers as his chief disciples and entitled them, along with himself, the Nineteen Letters of the Living.[6] At the time, Tahirih was a leading figure within the Shaykhi[7] sect. Although she had never met the Bab, she immediately embraced his religion and was appointed a 'Letter'.

Tahirih, whose given name was Fatimih Bigum Baraghani, was the daughter of the leading clerical family of Qazvin. She had received an excellent education in all the traditional Islamic sciences and was able to translate many of the Bab's writings from Arabic into Persian. Despite her background, Tahirih's writings were fiercely anticlerical. Basing her authority on her claim to an inner awareness of God's purpose, she instituted a number of innovations within the Babi community. Claiming that much of Islamic law was no longer binding upon the Babis, she refused to perform the daily ritual prayers. But her most audacious act was occasionally to appear unveiled in gatherings of believers.

According to Abbas Amanat, this was probably the first time an Iranian woman had considered unveiling at her own initiative. The circle of women who gathered around Tahirih in Karbala, and later Qazvin, Hamadan, Baghdad and Teheran, were perhaps the first group of women in those regions to have attained an awareness of their deprivations as women.[8] Yet Tahirih's activities did not represent a woman's liberation movement in the modern sense. For Tahirih, removing the veil was primarily an act of religious innovation. Neither the writings of Tahirih nor the Bab concern themselves with the issue of women's rights as such.[9]

Apparently Tahirih experienced the Bab's revelation as liberating, whether or not it addressed itself to the status of women per se.

Tahirih's activities created much controversy within the Babi community itself. Many Babis did not view the Bab's revelation as requiring a total break with the past or with Islamic law. They regarded Tahirih's behaviour as scandalous and unchaste. For this reason, the Bab gave her the title by which she is now known, Tahirih, meaning the 'pure'. The opposition of the non-Babi ulama (Islamic clergymen) went much deeper. During the month of Muharram, 1847, Tahirih deliberately excited their reaction by dressing in gay colours and appearing unveiled instead of donning the customary mourning clothes to commemorate the martyrdom of Imam Husayn. She urged the Babis, instead, to celebrate the birthday of the Bab, which fell on the first day of that month. The enraged clergy incited a mob to attack the house where she was staying. Finally, the governor intervened and had Tahirih placed under house arrest before having her sent to Baghdad.

Tahirih's father dispatched a relative to Iraq who induced the governor to order her return to Iran. On the arrival in Qazvin, her husband, Mulla Muhammad, from whom she had been long estranged, urged her to return to his household. She told him:

> If your desire had really been to be a faithful mate and companion to me, you would have hastened to meet me in Karbila and would on foot have guided my howdah all the way to Qazvin. I would, while journeying with you, have aroused you from your sleep of heedlessness and would have shown you the way of truth. But this was not to be. Three years have lapsed since our separation. Neither in this world nor in the next can I ever be associated with you. I have cast you out of my life forever.[10]

Tahirih's uncle and father-in-law, Muhammad Taqi, had a reputation for being virulently opposed to both the Babis and the Shaykhis. On numerous occasions he had incited mob violence against them. After one of these incidents, Mulla Abdu'llah, a Shaykhi and a Babi sympathizer, decided to retaliate. When Mulla Taqi appeared in the local mosque to offer his dawn prayers, Mulla Abdu'llah fatally stabbed him and fled.[11] This led to the arrest and torture of many of the Babis in Qazvin. Tahirih was implicated as well. In order to stop this orgy of violence, Mulla Abdu'llah turned himself in. Despite this the other Babis were not released and many were executed. Tahirih escaped with the assistance of Baha'u'llah, who hid her in his home in Teheran.[12]

Later, following a general call to the Babis to gather in Khurasan, Tahirih and Baha'u'llah travelled to a place called Badasht, where some eighty-one Babi leaders met to consider how they might effect the release of the Bab, who was then imprisoned, and to discuss the future direction of the Babi community in the face of growing persecution. At the meeting tension developed between Tahirih, who headed the more radical Babis advocating a complete break with Islam as well as militant defence of their community, and the more conservative Quddus, who initially advocated policies aimed at the rejuvenation of Islam and prudent accommodation with religious and secular power.

The Babis generally accepted Quddus as the chief of the Bab's disciples, but Tahirih reportedly said with regard to him: 'I deem him a pupil whom the Bab has sent me to edify and instruct. I regard him in no other light.' Quddus denounced Tahirih as 'the author of heresy'.[13] At one time when Quddus was rapt in his devotions, Tahirih rushed out of her tent brandishing a sword. 'Now is not the time for prayers and prostrations' she declared, 'rather on to the battlefield of love and sacrifice.'[14]

Her most startling act was to appear before the assembled believers unveiled. Shoghi Effendi vividly describes that scene:

> Tahirih, regarded as the fair and spotless emblem of chastity and the incarnation of the holy Fatimih, appeared suddenly, adorned yet unveiled, before the assembled companions, seated herself on the right hand of the affrighted and infuriated Quddus, and, tearing through her fiery words the veils guarding the sanctity of the ordinances of Islam, sounded the clarion call and proclaimed the inauguration of a new Dispensation. The effect was instantaneous. She, of such stainless purity, so reverenced that even to gaze at her shadow was deemed an improper act, appeared for a moment in the eyes of her scandalized beholders, to have defamed herself, shamed the Faith she espoused, and sullied the immortal Countenance she symbolized. Fear, anger, bewilderment swept their inmost souls, and stunned their faculties. Abu'l Khaliq-I-Isfahani, aghast and deranged at the sight, cut his throat with his own hands. Spattered with blood, and frantic with excitement, he fled away from her face.[15]

Unperturbed, Tahirih declared, 'I am the Word which the Qa'im is to utter, the Word which shall put to flight the chiefs and nobles of the earth!'[16]

Eventually Quddus conceded to Tahirih that Islamic law had been abrogated.[17] So complete was their reconciliation that the two departed from Badasht riding in the same *howdah*. When they neared the village of Niyale, the local *mulla*, outraged at seeing an unveiled woman sitting next to a man and chanting poems aloud, led a mob against them. Several people died in the resulting clash and the Babis dispersed in different directions. Pitched battles raged between the Babis and the government forces between 1848 and 1850 in the Iranian province of Mazandaran and in the cities of Zanjan and Nayriz. Tahirih remained in hiding, moving from village to village for about a year. Around 1849, authorities arrested her on charges of complicity in the assassination of her uncle. On 9 July 1850, the Bab was executed in Tabriz by order of the Shah. Two years later a small group of Babis sought to take revenge by assassinating the Shah. The attempt failed and general massacre of the Babis ensued. The government decided to execute Tahirih as well. She was taken to a garden and strangled to death.[18] Her body was thrown down a well. Her last words (perhaps apocryphal) are reported to be. 'You can kill me as soon as you like, but you cannot stop the emancipation of women.'[19]

Baha'i Women in Iran 1868–1892

I have dwelt at length on the figure of Tahirih, for she had become the most widespread model of the ideal woman within the Baha'i community. As such she represents a marked departure from the typical norm found in other world religions. Yet, except for her, in the years preceding the introduction of the Baha'i faith in the West, women are most notable by their absence. During the Babi upheaval a few women donned male clothing in order to participate in armed conflicts, earning the admiration of men. Others, not surprisingly, were Tahirih's protégés. More commonly Persian Baha'i hagiographies mention women as the wives and mothers of martyrs, spurring on their men to sacrifice.

Peter Smith, in his otherwise admirable overview of Babi-Baha'i history, suggests that both religions tended to have been originally male preserves and that generally women learned of the faith from their menfolk. The significance of women, he holds, increased during the Baha'i period, but men were the primary carriers of religion, women were important in ensuring the religious socialization of their children.[20] This assessment appears premature and largely based on an uncritical reliance on written source. Baha'i historians, particularly in Iran, have been overwhelmingly male. Where women have found their way into the biographical literature, they do so mainly because they managed to make their mark within the male sphere of activity, which in nineteenth-century Iran was virtually any function outside the home. Such women functioned essentially as 'honorary men'. Given the very separate spheres imposed by Iranian society, that any woman would have been able to function publicly is, in itself, extraordinary. But the few biographies of Iranian Baha'i women that do exist indicate that women had their own networks, self-sustaining and self-led, within which religious ideas could be disseminated and promulgated, apart from the observation of men. These networks were never recognized as important factors in the historical works written by men.

Recent but unpublished research[21] suggests that women played a significant role in the dissemination of the Baha'i faith, at least among the Jewish community. Women's networks must be painstakingly reconstructed on the basis of oral histories. Literary sources will not, by themselves, enable us to obtain a full picture of the role of women in early Babi-Baha'i history. However, even given that women may have played a larger role in promulgating the new religion than they have usually been given credit for, it still must be admitted that with the notable exception of Tahirih, women played virtually no public role in the development of the initial administrative organization of the Baha'i community within Iran.

WOMEN IN THE WRITING OF BAHA'U'LLAH

The writings of Baha'u'llah unequivocally proclaim the equality of men and women, asserting that 'in this day the Hand of Divine Grace hath removed all distinction. The Servants of God and His Handmaidens are regarded on the same plane.'[22] Elsewhere he suggests that differences between the sexes are the result of 'vain imaginings' and 'idle fancies', which by the power of his might had been destroyed.[23] He further insists on the education of girls.[24] Yet Baha'u'llah's writings do present some problems from a feminist standpoint.

The *Kitab-I-Aqdas*, the book that contains Baha'i sacred law, was written in Arabic, a language that by its nature requires the male gender to be used for collectives. Most of its admonitions and laws are addressed to men. A literal reading of its text would suggest that divorce was solely the male's prerogative.[25] Bigamy appears to be permissible, although monogamy is preferred.[26] Should a marriage be contracted on the basis of a woman's virginity, and the man subsequently discover she was not a virgin, the marriage could be repudiated and the dowry forfeited, although Baha'u'llah states that it would be preferable to conceal the matter and forgive.[27]

In certain contexts, women are given special treatment. They are exempt from the obligation to perform pilgrimage.[28] They are also exempt from the daily ritual prayers and fasting during their menses.[29] Other exemptions exist for pregnancy and nursing.[30] Most problematic is Baha'u'llah reference to 'the men of the House of Justice' which has been interpreted as excluding women from the highest administrative body in the faith.

This androcentric view, which a cursory reading of the text gives, is not, it should be recognized, the manner in which Baha'is have typically understood the Aqdas. Baha'u'llah's son, Abdu'l Baha, whom Baha'is recognize as the authorized interpreter[31] of the sacred writings, stated that since bigamy was conditioned upon equal treatment of both wives, which is impossible, monogamy alone is permissible.[32] Shoghi Effendi states that women have the same right as men to use for divorce and that the requirement for virginity can certainly be applied to either sex. Only in the case of membership in the Universal House of Justice has the male-oriented language been taken literally. As the Universal House of Justice states:

> It is apparent from the Guardian's writings that where Baha'u'llah has given us a law as between a man and a woman it applies *mutatis mutandis* between a woman and a man unless the context should make this impossible. For example, the text of the *Kitab-i-Aqdas* forbids a man to marry his father's wife (i.e. his stepmother), and the Guardian has indicated that likewise a woman is forbidden to marry her stepfather. It should also be borne in mind that Baha'u'llah envisages the possibility for specific conditions to be laid down and agreed upon by the parties prior to their marriage. This means that in addition to the spiritual covenant the parties become committed to, they are permitted by the Author of our Faith to enter into a form of contract, if they choose, with defined conditions and provisions binding on both parties. In one of these cases you cite, for example, that of a wife who is found by her husband not to have been a virgin, the dissolution of the marriage can be demanded only 'if the marriage has been conditioned on virginity'; presumably, therefore, if the wife wishes to exercise such a right in respect to the husband, she would have to include a condition as to his virginity in the marriage contract.*

When read within the context of nineteenth-century Iran, the Kitab-i Aqdas presents some startling contrasts to the norms of male-female relations. While the Aqdas make it optional for women to perform the obligatory prayers or fast during their menses, within Islam they are not permitted to do so at all, since they are regarded as ritually unclean at such times. The Baha'i faith does not recognize any ritual uncleanliness. Many of the laws contained in the Aqdas were addressed to specific concerns raised by individuals, usually male, within the community. For instance, Baha'u'llah made parental consent a prerequisite to marriage. The question immediately arose as to whether this was binding on men as well as women, and if it was binding on women who had been previously married. Baha'u'llah refused to make any distinction between

* Letter written on behalf of the Universal House of Justice, February 1982.

male and female in this regard, insisting that this regulation existed solely for the unity of the family and had nothing to do with the status of women.[33]

Most startling is Baha'u'llah's treatment of sexual issues. The sexuality of women, in both Judaism and Islam, has been seen as a potentially dangerous force that threatens the honour of the family and, indeed, the whole social fabric. The duty of male relatives to defend that honour historically had led to the strict seclusion of women. Women who violated sexual mores were commonly killed whereas men received the death penalty only if they had intercourse with a married woman, thus violating another man's rights. But according to the Aqdas, adulterers are subject to a fine, not the death penalty.[34] Baha'is are even discouraged from divorcing on the grounds of adultery. Control of sexuality in the Aqdas is a matter of great spiritual significance, with important social implications, but it is not treated as the glue of community life.

Baha'u'llah's treatment of certain economic issues with regard to women is somewhat more problematic. The inheritance laws presume a situation where the male is the primary breadwinner of the family. These laws are quite complex, but generally speaking, in the case of intestacy, female heirs are awarded somewhat less than what their male counterparts are.[35]

Another issue that might be raised with regard to Baha'u'llah's writings is the use of gender in connection with the deity. It has been argued, with good reason, that the exclusive use of male gender in referring to God leads to a perpetuation of male dominance. Baha'u'llah's legal writings were composed in Arabic, a language which necessitated the use of the male gender when referring to God. In order to preserve the integrity of the text, Shoghi Effendi has stated that it is impermissible to change the gender of the writings even in the use of prayers. Baha'u'llah's more mystical writings, however, are in Persian, which has no gender. Nevertheless, these writings have, without exception, been translated into English using the male gender. The mystical-erotic language employed in many of these texts, which refer to God as the beloved, might suggest that the female gender would be more appropriate. Sufi mysticism often depicts God as a beautiful woman and Baha'u'llah's Persian writings utilize much Sufi imagery. But perhaps the most interesting treatment of gender in Baha'u'llah's writings can be seen in connection with the symbol of the Heavenly Maiden or the *Huri*. In the Qur'anic vision of paradise black-eyed damsels or huris are thought to serve its inmates. Within the Baha'i context of fulfilled eschatology, the huri comes to symbolize the Holy Spirit, the personification of Baha'u'llah's revelation and the vehicle through which he receives it. His initial revelation in the dungeon of the *Siyal-Chal* consisted of a vision of this Maiden who informed him of his divine mission. She appears in the later mystical works by Baha'u'llah. The feminine theophany has a symbolic relationship with Baha'u'llah and is ultimately inseparable from him.[36]

FROM EAST TO WEST

In 1893 the Baha'i faith was introduced to the West. As was the case in nearly all religious groups in nineteenth-century America, women played a prominent role. Female converts generally outnumbered men by two to one. The 20 August 1910 issue of Baha'i News noted that women comprised 'nine-tenths of the active workers'. Not all Baha'i men were delighted with this state of affairs. That same issue contained a letter from Charles Mason Remey complaining of the situation.

The belief existed among many American Baha'i men that women ought to confine their activities to the teaching work, leaving the administrative activities to men. This opinion was apparently reinforced by many of the Iranian Baha'i teachers sent to America by Abdu'l-Baha. In March 1900 Thornton Chase reported that Chicago had formed a 'Board of Counsel' consisting of ten men. Later that year Abdu'l-Karim Tihrani reorganized the board, expanding its membership to nineteen and including women. The following year Mirza Assadu'llah Isfahani again reorganized the governing body, insisting only men could be elected. At that time the board began calling itself the House of Justice. Corinne True appealed to Abdu'l-Baha to rescind the directive confining membership of the House of Justice to men. Abdu'l-Baha replied that the House of Justice, 'according to the explicit text of the Law of God, is confined to men, this for a wisdom of the Lord God's which will ere long be made manifest as clearly as the sun at high noon.'[37] Seven years later Abdu'l-Baha ruled that this exclusion applied only to the as yet unformed Universal House of Justice and allowed women in America to serve on local bodies.[38]

FROM WEST TO EAST

The introduction of the Baha'i faith to America had a profound effect on the position of Baha'i women in Iran. Western Baha'is began travelling to Iran, where they spoke to Baha'i gatherings. In the opening years of the twentieth century, Iranian Baha'i women were still excluded from participation in Baha'i administrative institutions, had little access to education and, in most cases, still wore the veil. In 1909 Dr Susan Moody arrived from Chicago to join a small group of Iranian Baha'i doctors in establishing a hospital in Teheran. Over the next few years, Elizabeth Stewart, a nurse, Dr Sarah Clock, and Lillian Kappes, teacher, joined her. At this time a number of girls' schools were operated on an informal basis by Baha'i women. Since, with assistance of American Baha'is, the community had maintained a highly reputed boys' school, Dr Moody persuaded the executive committee of that school to adopt one of these girls' schools as a separate department. Eventually this school became one of the finest girls' college preparatory schools in Iran. In 1911 God-seah Ashraf became the first Iranian Baha'i woman to travel to America for the purpose of pursuing graduate work in educational psychology.[39] She then returned to Iran and taught in Baha'i schools.

During Abdu'l-Baha's travels to the West in 1911–12, he made Baha'i teachings with regard to women's rights more explicit, stressing especially the need for women's education, the lack of which he viewed as the sole reason for the perceived inferiority of women. He deemed the education of mothers so essential to the proper upbringing of children that he held that the education of daughters should take precedence over that of sons. But Abdu'l-Baha did not restrict women's function in society to the home. He urged women to excel in all the arts and sciences and, further, expected their participation on an equal footing in the political sphere as well. He stated that women's political participation would be a prerequisite for peace. The only field (aside from membership on the Universal House of Justice) where Abdu'l-Baha did not extend full and equal participation was in military endeavours, since he regarded the taking of human life incompatible with women's role as mothers.

Copies of Abdu'l-Baha's talks were distributed throughout Iran, and these, along with the influence of American Baha'is residing in Iran, awakened Iranian Baha'i women to possibilities unthought of in previous generations. Apparently, they began to advocate the immediate abolishment of the veil, as well as agitating for women's full participation in administrative affairs. Abdu'l-Baha was not entirely pleased with these developments, for, besides the stress and disunity these issues were creating within the Baha'i community itself, he felt that actions such as discarding the veil would bring on needless persecution in an already volatile situation. Abdu'l-Baha pleaded with the Iranian women not to do anything 'contrary to wisdom'.[40] Women's assemblages at this time should be confined to educational matters so that 'differences will, day by day, be entirely wiped out, not that, God forbid, it will end in argumentation between men and women.' Their efforts should be in the spiritual, not the political realm. Abdu'l-Baha stated that he himself would in time insure that they achieved full equality with men in all areas. In the meantime, they ought not to agitate against the men for such changes. He chided the women for their impatience, saying 'this newly born babe is traversing in one night the path that needed a hundred years to tread.'[41]

While women were allowed to vote within the Iranian Baha'i community, it was not until 1954 that they were permitted to serve on Baha'i institutions. As late as the 1970s one observer could only count two women delegates out of the more than one hundred attending the national Baha'i convention in Teheran.[42] Yet when the members of the National Spiritual Assembly of the Baha'is of Iran were arrested and executed in 1981, the chairperson was a woman, Zhinus Mahmudi.[43]

Baha'i Women in India

Currently the largest Baha'i community in the world is found, not in Iran or the United States, but in India. The Baha'i faith was introduced to India virtually from the time of its inception, for even some of the early Babis were from India. Initially those attracted were primarily of urban Muslim or Irani Zoroastrian background. This situation dramatically changed in the sixties and early seventies as the Baha'i community experienced a mass movement of enrolments on the part of those of rural Hindu background, raising the population of the Baha'is in India to more than two million. The mass movement itself began largely as an effort on the part of one Baha'i woman, Mrs Shirin Boman Meherabani, who was informed by her brother of the interest expressed in the Baha'i faith in Bhilala village in Madhya Pradesh. During the next few weeks Mrs Meherabani made several excursions to Kweitiopani and then invited those who believed in Baha'u'llah to declare themselves as Baha'is. As a result nearly 75 per cent of the village's largely illiterate population of around two hundred put their thumb prints on enrolment cards. Kweitiopani became the first rural community in India to experience mass conversion.[44] Mrs Meherabani, accompanied by her son-in-law, Mr K.H. Vajdi, continued to travel extensively by jeep in the rural areas of Malwa. Over the next two year period more than 85,000 declarations were received, majority from the scheduled castes in Malwa and the rural regions surrounding the city of Gwalior. In 1964, Shoghi Effendi's widow and Hand of the Cause, Ruhiyyih Khanum, toured the mass teaching areas and encouraged the Baha'is to maintain the momentum.

While Baha'i women, primarily Iranis born in India, played a significant role in the teaching and propagation work, the enrolments themselves were overwhelmingly male. Recognizing that such a gender disparity within the Baha'i community would not augur well for the future, the National Spiritual Assembly, under the guidance of the Universal House of Justice began to make a concerted effort to reach women and to insure their advancement.

This emphasis on women, combined with increasing interest within the Baha'i community in social and economic development projects led to the establishment of Baha'i Vocational Institute for Rural Women in 1985. The aim of the institute was to empower the women to become agents for social change in their families and communities, with such programmes as small business development, basic hygiene and health, literacy training and advanced gardening. The institute serves women, both Baha'i and non-Baha'i, within a radius of 200 kilometres around Indore in the districts of Dhar, Jhabua, Khargone, Ujjain, Dewas and Indore.[45] Women are brought to the institute, free of cost, for periods ranging from ten days to three months. By 1996 a total 769 rural tribal women from 119 villages had been trained at the institute. Follow-up studies of these women indicate that 45 per cent had established small business of sewing clothes, earning an average of Rs 20 per day, while 62 per cent had become functionally literate or semi-literate. In addition, the health, sanitation and nutrition of these women and their families had improved significantly. It is unlikely, however, given the limited numbers of women participating in this project as compared to the size of the Baha'i community as a whole, that it has had any impact on the gender gap as yet.

Conclusion

Perhaps no other religion offers a stronger scriptural basis for women's rights or a richer history for women to draw on than does the Baha'i faith. Yet while all Baha'is in theory believe in the equality of men and women, there is no unanimity as to what that equality means. In many instances Baha'i conceptions of equality have distanced them from more radical forms of Western feminism. Whether Baha'i women will fully utilize the potentialities of Baha'i scriptures and history, or whether they will be relegated to 'separate but equal spheres' that perpetuate structures of male dominance, remains to be seen. There exists no single theory of Baha'i feminism, but Baha'is, men and women alike, are agreed on one principle: hierarchical system that place men above women in a divinely ordained order have no sanction within the Baha'i scriptures. In this respect the Baha'i faith is unique among revealed religions.

NOTES

1. Abdu'l-Baha, *The Promulgation of Universal Peace* (Baha'i Publishing Trust, 1982), p.. 108.

2. Abdu'l-Baha cited in *Women* (Oakham: Baha'i Publishing Trust, 1986), p. 33.

3. Ibid., 29.

4. Ibid., Shoghi Effendi, entitled the Guardian, served as head of the Baha'i community from 1921 to 1957.

5. Tahirih is not, in the theological sense, the most important woman in Babi-Baha'i history; that distinction belongs to Navvab, the wife of Baha'u'llah, and Bahiyyih Khanum, his eldest daughter. Of the first figure, however, very little has been written in English or, to my knowledge, in Persian. Bahiyyih Khanum is much better known, since she served as the de facto head of the Baha'i community several times. She has usually been depicted as playing a supportive role in relation to Abdu'l-Baha and Shoghi Effendi, although in the opinion of this writer she was much more of an independent actor. She has not attracted as much attention as Tahirih, about whom numerous (partly fictionalized) biographies exist. Tahirih is, in a word, a legend, and as such plays a much more important role among Baha'is as the paradigm of womanhood. Both in Iran and America, her name is probably the most popular Baha'i name given to girls.

6. Nineteen letters make up the Arabic phrase *Bismillh ul-Rahman ul-Rahim*, which introduces all but one of the *suras* of the Quran. Hence the number nineteen has been endowed with great spiritual significance.

7. The Shaykhi school, founded by Shaykh Ahmad Ahsai (d. 1826) is a small sect within Twelver Shiism, which differs from the majority in that it denies the appearance of the Qa'im. Most of the early Babis were drawn from this sect. Tahirih had left Qazvin around 1843 in order to meet Siyyid Kazim Rashti, the Shaykhi head. He died shortly before her arrival. Supported by the widow of Rashti, Tahirih moved into his household where she taught classes and apparently assumed control of the more radical elements of the community there.

8. Amanat, Abbas, *Resurrection and Renewal: The Making of the Babi Movement in Iran, 1844–1850* (Ithaca: Cornell University Press, 1989), pp. 306–7.

9. The Bab's teachings certainly aimed at improving the condition of women by abolishing the temporary marriage allowable in Shi'ite Islam as well as instant divorce, but their position could hardly be regarded as equal.

10. Nabil-I-A'zam, *The Dawnbreakers: Nabil's Narrative of the Early Days of the Baha'i Revelation* (Wilmette: Baha'i Publishing Trust, 1979), pp. 273–4.

11. After describing this incident, Abdu'l-Baha remarks: 'These things would take place before the reality of this Cause was revealed and all was made plain. For in those days no one knew that the Manifestation of the Bab would culminate in the Manifestation of the Blessed Beauty (Baha'u'llah) and that the law of retaliation would be done away with, and the foundation-principle of the Law

of God would be this, that "it is better for you to be killed that to kill", that discord and contention would cease, and the rule of war and butchery would fall away. In those days, that sort of thing would happen' (*Memorials of the Faithful*, Baha'i Publishing Trust, Wilmette, 1971, 198–9).

12. Tahirih's father remained convinced of her innocence as well as her chastity, but the accusations caused him untold grief. At one point, the prayer leader at the Friday mosque read a verse mocking Mulla Salih: 'No glory remains on that house/From which the hens crow like the cocks.' Mulla Salih was said to have remained silent, as tears ran down his cheeks to his beard (Amanat, Resurrection, 322).

13. *Dawnbreakers*, p. 297.

14. Nugaba'i, H., *Tahirih* (Teheran: 128 Badi/1972 ACE), p. 60.

15. Effendi, Shoghi, *God Passes By* (Wilmette: Baha'i Publishing Committee), p. 32.

16. Ibid.

17. Baha'u'llah apparently proved instrumental in bringing about the reconciliation, and Baha'i sources indicate that he even engineered the conflict to make a planned break with Islam more easily accepted. His subsequent actions indicate that he himself, while advocating a total break with Islam, believed in non-violent means for attaining the Babi aims.

18. Execution by strangulation was probably chosen to avoid the prohibition of shedding a woman's blood. Baha'i children were later executed in a similar manner.

19. *God Passes By*, p. 75.

20. Smith Peter, *The Babi and Baha'i Religions* (Cambridge, 1987), pp. 92–3.

21. This research has been conducted by Anthony Lee, but never written up in any formal form.

22. Research Department of the Universal House of Justice, *Women* (Oakham: Baha'i Publishing Trust, 1986), p. 2.

23. Ibid., p. 1.

24. Baha'u'llah, *The Kitab-I-Aqdas* (Hafia, 1992), p. 37.

25. Ibid., pp. 43–4.

26. Ibid., p. 41.

27. Ibid., p. 121.

28. Ibid., p. 30.

29. Ibid., p. 23.

30. Ibid., p. 25.

31. The independent investigation of truth is a paramount principle within the Baha'i faith and Baha'is are free and, indeed, enjoined to pursue their own understanding of the sacred text. Only Abdu'l-Baha (d. 1921) and after him, Shoghi Effendi (d. 1957) were authorized to make authoritative interpretations binding upon the body of believers. This is in direct contrast to the Shi'ite practice of having a select group of clerics (*mujtahids*, now commonly known as *ayatollahs*) who alone are deemed capable of interpreting scripture. The laity

must 'imitate' (*taqlid*) one of these leaders in all matters of divine law. Baha'u'l-lah has forbidden both this form of interpretation and 'blind imitation'. Shoghi Effendi is regarded as infallible in his interpretations of the sacred text, and the Universal House of Justice is considered infallible in matters of legislation.

32. Mazandarani, Fadil, *Amr va Khalaq*, vol. 4 (Tehran: 1974/5–131 BE), pp. 175–6.

33. *Aqdas*, pp. 110–11.

34. Ibid., p. 47.

35. 'We have divided inheritance into seven categories: to the children, we have allotted nine parts comprising five hundred and forty shares; to the wife, eight parts comprising four hundred and eighty shares; to the father, seven parts comprising four hundred and twenty shares; to the mother, six parts comprising three hundred and sixty shares; to the brothers, five parts or three hundred shares; to the sisters, four parts or two hundred and forty shares; and to the teachers, three parts or one hundred and eighty shares. Such was the ordinance of My Forerunner, He who extolleth My Name in the night season and at the break of day. When we heard the clamour of the children as yet unborn, we doubled their share and decreased those of the rest. He, of a truth, hath power to ordain whatsoever He desireth, and He doeth as He Pleased by virtue of His sovereign might.' Ibid., p. 26.

36. For a fuller discussion of Baha'u'llah's writings regarding the Heavenly Maiden, see Walbridge, John, *Sacred Acts, Sacred Space, Sacred Time* (Oxford: 1996), pp. 158–65.

37. Abdu'l-Baha, *Selections from the Writings of Abdu'l-Baha*, p. 80.

38. Cited in the 31 May 1988 letter of the Universal House of Justice to the National Spiritual Assembly of the Baha'is of New Zealand. It has been argued that this second letter as well referred to the Chicago House of Justice rather than the Universal House of Justice. Those arguing this position hold that the term (*'umma*) which has been translated as 'universal' meant simply 'general'. However, Abdu'l-Baha used that word in its present technical meaning as early as 1903 when writing his will and testament. Furthermore, it is clear that the recipient of this letter understood Addu'l-Baha to be referring to that body. Thorton Chase, who continued to oppose the participation of women on the Chicago body wrote: Several years ago, soon after the forming of the 'House of Justice' ... Mrs True wrote to Addu'l-Baha and asked if women should not be members of that House. He replied distinctly, that the House should be composed of men only, and told her that there was a wisdom in this. It was a difficult command for her to accept, and ever since (confidentially) there has been in that quarter and in those influenced by her a feeling of antagonism to the House of Spirituality, which has manifested itself in various forms ... Mrs True received a Tablet, in which it was stated (in reply to her solicitation) that it was right for women to be members of all 'Spiritual Gatherings' except the 'Universal House of Justice', and she at once construed this to mean, that women were to be members of the House of Spirituality and the Council Boards, because in some

of the Tablets for the House, it had been addressed as the 'Spiritual Assembly' or 'Spiritual Gathering'. But the House of Spirituality could not so interpret the Master's meaning. Chase to Scheffler, 5/10/10, Chase papers, National Baha'i Archives.

Further investigation on the part of the Chicago House of Spirituality showed that elsewhere in the United States Abdu'l-Baha had authorized the election of both men and women to local bodies. They therefore concluded that in organizing Spiritual Assemblies of Consultation now, it is deemed advisable by Abudl'l-Baha to have them composed of both men and women. The wisdom of this will become evident in due time, no doubt. Apparently the members of this body expected that when local and national bodies became official 'House of Justice' women would be removed from membership, but until then men would have to put up with the situation. The all-male administrative bodies finally were completely dissolved by Adu'l-Baha in his visit to America in 1912.

39. Armstrong-Ingram, R. Jackson, American Baha'i Women and the Education of Girls in Tehran, 1909–1934, in *Iran* (Los Angeles: Kalimat Press, 1986), pp. 181–210.

40. Besides carrying the general meaning 'wisdom' (hikmat) has a technical meaning in many of the Baha'i writings. To act according to wisdom generally infers behaving in such a way as not to attract opposition toward the Baha'i faith in a situation where persecution or misunderstanding might otherwise result even when it is necessary to compromise some Baha'i principle to do so. Acts of providence which might otherwise be seen as negative are also described as having a 'wisdom' if they benefit the progress of the religion in some unforeseen way. For a fuller discussion of this see, Susan Maneck, 'Wisdom and Dissimulation' in *Baha'i Studies Review* 6: pp. 11–23.

41. Portions of this letter are contained in *Women*, 5–6. Unfortunately no further information or even the date are provided regarding it, so I have been forced to be a little speculative regarding its context. The final line quoted is a well-known Persian proverb.

42. Caton, Peggy, *Equal Circles*, xvi, (Los Angeles: Kalimat Press, 1987).

43. Mrs Mahmudi had been a scientist of national prominence in Iran, where she served as President of the Iranian School of Meteorology. Unlike persecutions of the previous century, the Islamic Republic of Iran has shown no reticence about executing female Baha'is. On 8 June 1983, ten Baha'i women were hanged in Shiraz. Since then all Baha'i institutions in Iran have been disbanded.

44. Garlington, William, *The Baha'i Faith in Malwa: A Study of a Contemporary Religious Movement*, unpublished dissertation, Australian National University, 1976.

45. According to the website for the institute, the curriculum is designed to achieve the following objectives:

> To facilitate change in the traditional attitudes and practices which block or impede the efforts of men and women to live in equality with dignity and security.

To facilitate the initiation and execution of development activities in the communities.

To increase awareness and knowledge of the potential for improving the social and economic conditions in the communities.

To impart the skills and knowledge needed to initiate development activities, improve health and nutrition, raise household income, increase literacy, protect and improve the environment.

http://www.geocities.com/RainForest/2519/

Index